THE PYTHIA ON ELLIS ISLAND

Rethinking the Greco-Roman Legacy in America

Nancy Kassell

University Press of America,® Inc.
Lanham • New York • Oxford

Copyright © 1998 by
University Press of America,® Inc.
4720 Boston Way
Lanham, Maryland 20706

12 Hid's Copse Rd.
Cummor Hill, Oxford OX2 9JJ

All rights reserved
Printed in the United States of America
British Library Cataloging in Publication Information Available

Library of Congress Cataloging-in-Publication Data

Kassell, Nancy.
The Pythia on Ellis Island : rethinking the Greco-Roman legacy in
America / Nancy Kassell.
p. cm.
Includes bibliographical references and index.
1. United States—Civilization—Classical influences. 2. United States—Moral conditions. 3. Social values—United States. 4. Patriarchy. I. Title.
E169.1.K327 1997   973—DC21   97-35637 CIP

ISBN 0-7618-0942-2 (cloth: alk. ppr.)

FORDHAM
UNIVERSITY
LIBRARY
BRONX, NY
ROSE HILL

∞™ The paper used in this publication meets the minimum
requirements of American National Standard for information
Sciences—Permanence of Paper for Printed Library Materials,
ANSI Z39.48—1984

To the memory of Saul Moskowitz,

best ally

Prologue

It is a gray and foggy morning on Ellis Island. Waiting in the crowd is a refugee. Her face, lined with the wisdom of age, is partially concealed by a dark shawl. In appearance, she is indistinguishable from countless women who have arrived on America's shores. For generations she has been taught not to cause trouble, not to say or do anything to call attention to herself.

She is the Pythia, a priestess of the god Apollo at the oracle of Delphi in Greece. In the old country her job was to serve the god. His breath entered her body and she spoke his words. When not under his influence, there were many things she could have said about the foolishness of men's questions, the limits of their imaginations, their arrogance, and their misguided hopes of persuading the god to favor their grandiose quests and conquests. "There are other strivings," she would have told them had she been allowed to speak. Now, here in this land of the free, her thoughts, old and new, are about to be revealed.

Preface and Acknowledgments

The Pythia on Ellis Island explores the lasting influence of the Greco-Roman legacy on contemporary cultural attitudes and values and the contradictions between allegiance to Western European traditions and the quintessentially American drive for change. Understanding how the roots of Western culture developed can help us to see beyond the intellectual and moral fragmentation of postmodern times. Greco-Roman views of difference (immortals and mortals, male and female) became a kind of master template for subsequent interpretations of difference and its implicit fear of diversity. Feminist rereadings of literary and philosophical texts (Homer, Sophocles, lyric poetry, Stoic and Epicurean philosophy, New Comedy, Cicero, and Vergil) show how the classics shaped dualisms that inform Western thought.

Male culture in classical antiquity was created defensively and narcissistically against the power of the gods and the generative powers of nature and woman. Transcending death through heroism or other kinds of achievement (service to the *polis*, artistic and intellectual feats) became male-defined culture's raison d'etre, an attitude that informs American notions of work and worth. Drawing on the work of feminist ethicists and others, *The Pythia* seeks a morality that transcends traditional gender-derived values. What kinds of power and control should human beings aspire to? The Greco-Roman tradition defined the human condition in terms of a common destiny, that we all die. But it is also our common destiny that we all live, connected by universal human bonds and needs. Narcissism, self identity, feelings of powerlessness, and issues of separation and autonomy can neither define the human condition nor create an inclusive society. Transcending differences is an American ideal; recent challenges to patriarchy place the task of realizing that ideal in a new light.

I am indebted to Nadya Aisenberg, Marie Cantlon, and Mona Harrington, whose questions and suggestions helped me to clarify the focus of my work, and to the Humanities and Social Science Research Departments of the Boston Public Library. Thanks also to my colleagues at The Writers' Room of Boston, Inc.

Table of Contents

Prologue

Preface and Acknowledgments

Part I

    Chapter 1. This Ethical Juncture   1

Part II

    Chapter 2. Death Is the Difference   13

    Chapter 3. TranscendingMortality.
                  From the Heroic to the Achievement Ethic   47

    Chapter 4. Construction of the Other 1.
                  Flight from Nature, the Body, and Woman   75

    Chapter 5. Construction of the Other 2.
                  Connections and Beyond   103

    Chapter 6. Social Morality and Patriarchal Rule   133

    Chapter 7. Rome: Synthesis, Codification, Expansion   161

Part III

    Chapter 8. Other Voices, Other Values   193

    Chapter 9. Beyond This Ethical Juncture.
                  Values without Domination   237

    Select Bibliography   245

    Index   261

Chapter 1

This Ethical Juncture

Today, many Americans—caught up in materialistic mores, challenged by burgeoning technologies, beset by economic pressures, and not well served by public education—are deeply confused about values. Diverse and divisive moral points of view compete for our attention like so many strident special-interest groups. One constant in the present state of flux is a sense that, at the very least, American society does not measure up to its founding ideals and that at worst we are in a state of moral decline, destined to fall like the great empires of Athens and Rome. As a people, we are, of course, chronically dedicated to national self-examination and self-improvement. If we are sometimes excessive in our zeal, our capacity for self-criticism is neverthelesss one of our greatest strengths, and I hope my readers share in it.

People who immerse themselves in cultures that flourished over two thousand years ago tend to take the long view of things. I am one of them. I am going to present the Greco-Roman legacy as a collective source and vantage point from which to reassess some current moral issues in American society and to draw attention to some fault lines in our culture. I believe there is much we can still learn from studying Greece and Rome, but the lessons are not what most people think they are. I believe that late-twentieth-century North American society is at a critical ethical juncture because, though we cherish the ideal of an equality which transcends differences, most traditional models, such as those provided by Greek and Roman thinkers, are inherently flawed and at odds with that very ideal. I would argue further that far from being estranged from values inherent in the Greco-Roman tradition, we are at this very ethical juncture today in part because we have embraced certain of them too well.

"Ethics" (Greek *ethos*, habit, character) is a system of values, carrying the implication that those values to some extent define the character of a people. Unlike American, Greek and Roman societies were comparatively homogeneous in ethnic, linguistic, and cultural makeup. The very diversity of North American peoples, together with our commitment to democratic pluralism, raises questions about community and difference: Do we have *a* national character or identity? Do or can we have *an* ethics? Who in our society defines and names values? On what authority? Authority bestowed by whom or what? Questioning authority has been a recurrent phenomenon and social issue in America in the past few decades, during which we have experienced the civil rights, antiwar, and women's movements. The authority of the Greco-Roman legacy was undermined earlier in the century, when the classics began to be replaced by "more useful" and/or contemporary subjects in school curricula: Education should prepare young people to take their place in society as citizens and as workers.

We are, moreover, not just a diversity of peoples, but a conglomerate of individualists living under the protection of the First Amendment. The possibility of having a shared moral code (Latin *mores*, customs, habits, character), a set of socially agreed-upon values, seems problematic. One expectation we share is that "things," from VCRs to values, should "work." We Americans are a pragmatic, independent, and impatient people. We are open, optimistic, and forward looking. But because of our diversity of peoples and views, practical morality in our culture is very complex. We need and have developed strategies for negotiating consensus, strategies which, on the whole, much of the time, in many situations, do work. But does consensus produce anything we might call agreed-upon values? I suspect not. I think we judge matters on an ad hoc basis and leave the rest to individual conscience. In short, practical morality in America must be workable and consonant with our ideals, but it will not necessarily reflect values we all share.

I will argue that as long as patriarchal ideas and institutions were uncontested, essential connections among values, power, and difference implicated in the legacy of Greece and Rome—and still very much a part of mainstream Western culture today—remained unnoticed. Contesting them now helps us to understand why we have trouble accommodating difference in American society despite our desire to do so. Patriarchal values are not serving American society well.

Power and difference are at the center of my reading of the moral and intellectual tradition which begins in classical antiquity. The tradition was built by men speaking from within an established patriarchal context. Their authority to define and reflect values was predicated on social structure and was in some cases also derived from privileged social, economic, and political status. The values expressed in this tradition are inherent in the institutions and ideologies of power; the implications of conjoining values and power, as the Greeks did and as we do today, are still not fully recognized. Power was assumed by those who made those values, as it is assumed today by those who defend them.

Gender was the preeminent defining social and cultural difference, probably from very early historical times.[1] Definition of Otherness on the basis of gender and in binary terms ("a" and "not a"; either "a" or "not a") may be the paradigm for definition of all difference; the model, as seen in the Greco-Roman tradition, remains a blueprint for us even today. Values we regard as traditional assume and subsume social constructs of gender (as well as class and race). Others, the "not a's," are usually without power. The prevailing patterns of classical thought, hierarchic as well as antithetic,[2] tended to obscure or obliterate many aspects and kinds of difference by suppressing broader and more complex definitions. Great works of literature are supposed to be revelations of the complexities, ambiguities, contradictions, and inconsistencies of the human condition. Yet these revelations are circumscribed by the experiences, attitudes, beliefs, customs, and values of male-centered culture. The paradigms they provide implicitly deny the full human potential of Others—and their own.[3]

The Greco-Roman legacy is the main source in the West for the Great Dichotomies, to use Alice Jardine's phrase,[4] the dualisms and the hierarchies to which they gave rise, of our culture. In the ancient world, woman, perceived generically, was a force to be reckoned with, for, like nature, she possessed generative powers which men lacked. Dualisms were formulated in antithetical (frequently adversarial), bipolar, and mutually exclusive terms—society, culture/nature; public/private; mind/body; reason/passion, the irrational; good/evil; active/passive. In each pair, the first term was associated with men and assigned greater value than the second, which was associated with women. Understanding relationships among women, nature, society, and culture, as Jardine and other feminist thinkers have been pointing out, is fundamental to understanding how we think about values and difference. I share their hopes for bringing about ethical changes which will reflect the complexity and diversity of all human experience.

Let us review some of the ethical concerns that arise today in our everyday conversations and public debates. They are most acute when they touch on matters of life and death. In general, we tend to deny death or to regard it as an enemy, rather than as the natural end-point of the human life cycle. Because of dramatic advances in medical technology and genetics, medical decision making has become more complex than at any earlier time in human history. We have greater power to save the fragile at both extremes of the life cycle but lack the power to guarantee a good, sometimes even a minimally acceptable, quality of life. How far should we go in using heroic measures to prolong life? Under what circumstances is the use of the most experimental or expensive treatment justified? Does a fetus have a right to life? If so, do its rights take precedence over the rights of its mother? Is doctor-assisted suicide immoral?

The benefits of technology are also subject to economic considerations. Must we ration them, as we try to reform the health-care system in order to provide universal access to basic care? Will research and development suffer as we try to implement this goal? Most of us would agree in principle that it is undemocratic that access to care be tied to economic means, much less to privilege, though this is in fact the plight of million of Americans. Mankind has a history of devoting much more attention to dilemmas surrounding birth and death than to the plethora of ethical issues that arise between these two boundaries, those concerned with quality of life.

Attitudes to life and death depend in part on how we think about our place in nature. Like the Greeks and Romans, to whom myths and rituals of beginnings and endings were important, we have an ambivalent relationship to nature. We are—as they were—both masters and subjects. We hold dominion over her (and she is, by long tradition, female), yet we are (as some see it) imprisoned in our bodies, whose needs must be met, continuously, in order to sustain life itself; enslaved to her ruthless power, we are marched through time—a straight line; no turning back and no side trips—from the moment we are born until the moment we die. However civilized we become, we are confined within nature.

For us, as for the Greeks and Romans, values relating to life, death, and nature are implicated in issues of power and control: How much do human beings have? How much can we have? How much do we want? How much should we have?

From time to time, most recently in the countercultural sixties and seventies, some people turn their back on all the impedimenta of civilization and embrace life in nature (so that, for example, children may grow up knowing that food does not come from supermarkets). They seek a more holistic world view elsewhere, in the teachings of Eastern philosophies, for example. Today as we consider how to use the earth's resources intelligently, environmentalists and ecologists try to moderate our predatory attitudes, habits, and feelings of entitlement. Balancing conservation and development, protection and profit, nature and culture is not proving to be easy.

Once the twentieth century became the Nuclear Age, it seemed uncertain for a while whether the human race had a future. As we approach the end of the century, the specter of massive destruction has receded. What is left is violence as usual, war as a bad old habit, from ethnic, religious, political, and economic conflicts to tribal starvation and slaughter. We all say we abhor violence, but it is intrinsic to Western culture, a way of proving manhood today as it was in the culture which produced Homer's *Iliad*.[5] Violence is a means of gaining and keeping power. The costs of military preparedness are high. We are just beginning to get the idea that what we really need are peace-keeping forces and humanitarian aid at the readiness. The assumption that we must always be prepared to resolve conflict through force deflects our energy and resources away from the needs of life. Within our own borders, at a time when weapons pervade our neighborhoods, schools, streets, and homes, consider the irony that one of purposes of the Constitution was "to insure domestic tranquility."

The use of force is one means of mediating differences. There are primarily two traditional strategies for resolving conflicts in the West. Diplomacy is (supposed to be) the first; if negotiation fails, resolution by force is the second and final option. These strategies were expressed in the Greek antithesis between persuasion and force (*peitho-bia*). In both cases, those in power, an elite, the leaders of a nation or other political entity, make policy decisions and implement them hierarchically, from the top down. Neither is designed to accommodate difference or diversity—a multiplicity of viewpoints, needs, strategies, priorities— by, for example, allotting decision-making power to those at the bottom or in the middle of the hierarchy. The U.S. Constitution acknowledges that power should be distributed among all the people—through the electoral process and balance-of-powers principle, for example—but in practice that is not what happens.

Conflicts are often seen as a kind of contest, and contests involve competition. Competition is a driving force in North American society. We want to be number one in business, economic, and technological global marketplaces, and we want our ideology and institutions to prevail in the international political arena. The most often articulated aim of education is to "arm" tomorrow's workers with the skills (particularly in the sciences, mathematics, and technology) needed to make and keep America first. Language skills and cultural literacy are sometimes enlisted in the same cause. Competitiveness, the drive to primacy, is the byword of the contemporary work ethic, and it pervades the practices of the workplace, with special intensity in times of economic hardship. It aims to make profits and achieve success. The ethic of competition does not benefit everyone, however. Ross Poole calls attention to the expendability, dissatisfaction, and insecurity of the individual worker under late capitalism and the consequent attrition of a sense of community and alienation from work and the workplace.[6] The growth of corporations has greatly extended the scope of the competition ethic, which we, like the Greeks, regard as the opposite of a cooperative ethic.

We still look to a paradigm which appears in early Greek thought: Competition is associated with the broader categories of work and achievement. The alignment of competition, work, and achievement has restricted the scope of many people's lives, both men and women, but women have had special difficulty in gaining access to and acceptance in the arena of work and achievement. Birthing labor, "women's work" exclusively, does not count, and "women's work" performed at home in the service of their families has usually been regarded as ancillary and not "real" work. Women have always reproduced; reluctance to acknowledge that they also can and do produce—as members of the labor force, as leaders, thinkers, doers, and makers in all areas of endeavor—stems from our classical heritage, for the exclusion of women from competition is one aspect of the separation of women from the public (and their confinement to the private) sphere. According to the American myth, competition identifies excellence and allows access to achievement, success, or at least to employment; in practice, it does not and cannot serve as an effective means to overcoming differences in our postmodern economy or society.

Finally, current conversations about private and public often focus on what are commonly called family values. Those who defend family values usually assume the traditional division of labor between husband and wife: He earns a living; she takes care of their home and children. He works in the public sphere, she in the private and domestic.[7] This paradigm has not matched social and economic realities in America for a long time, but nostalgia often distorts the clarity of our vision. Out-of-wedlock childbearing, "alternative" life-styles (note that the phrase assumes there is a primary and correct model), divorce, single parenthood, the high costs of raising children, employment and other economic insecurities—these are the realities. In the eyes of many people, the family is supposed to be the primary location for nurturing children and the basic unit of society, the center of the private sphere. According to the classical model, articulated by Aristotle[8] but widely evident in literature before his time, a man is the head of his household, lord of his wife, children, and, in Greek and Roman societies, his slaves. As the competition and the achievement ethic raises questions about male dominion outside the family, the model of the traditional family raises questions about male dominion within it. Too often, this model fails to meet the needs of children, many of whom today do not receive adequate physical care, financial support, education, or emotional and psychological nurturance. Too often it also fails to meet the needs of parents, who bear heavy responsibilities without adequate support from society.

In recent years, the classics have been at the root, if not the center, of a fierce debate in academic and intellectual circles. The debate arises from common ground, zeal to reform American society, especially values and educational goals. On the one side, conservatives blame what they perceive as a decline in social morality on collective abandonment of traditional values. We have strayed from the principles that guided men for over two thousand years, a charge often fraught with quasi-religious overtones. Social order and national greatness will be ours again, once we get back to the moral, intellectual, and religious basics as taught by the Great Books of the classic and Judeo-Christian traditions.[9] Who are we to question, much less reject, Eternal Verities? To do so is hybris beyond anything the Greeks ever imagined. Universities, repositories of learning, have been taken over and destroyed by Others and their self-serving agendas.

At the other extreme, the position often described by the simplistic and pejorative term "political correctness" points to the exclusions of the Western tradition: women, people of color, third-world peoples, all who are not privileged in a hierarchically structured society, one in which values are made at the top and imposed from above upon Others. Since members of these groups were not the makers of traditional values, these values are not, and never were, universally valid. Why look for wisdom, why even read Greek and Roman texts, which are the *loci classici* for elitist, male-centered and male-defined values? Greek and Roman thinkers are "the oldest dead white European males," to use the current flip phrase which Bernard Knox good-naturedly took as the title for his lectures on the enduring contributions of the classics to civilization,[10] and they do not speak for everyone, much less for all time.[11]

"Well then," a conservative might retort (as Knox does), "let Others speak. Can they offer anything as splendid or wise as Greek poets and philosophers? Others will never be able to compete with the wisdom of the ages in the marketplace of ideas and values." Traditional values have been the cornerstones of intellectual and moral thought and education in the West. The American founding fathers, we recall, were great admirers of classical antiquity. They believed that democracy would extend the benefits of the best that had been thought and written to all citizens; knowledge and wisdom ought not to be the property of the select few.[12] This is the rationale of our system of universal public education.

"Give Others a chance to speak and be heard, and we'll find out," a PC partisan might reply. So goes yet another chapter in the contest between the Old and the New, tradition and change, not unlike that presented to fifth-century Athenian audiences by the comic poet Aristophanes in his *Clouds* and *Frogs*. In the former, a young man uses his training in the very latest techniques of argument to come to the conclusion that he is morally justified in beating his father. This is progress? Who paid for his instruction? (You guessed it.) In the latter, the poet contemplates changing Athenian values (with nostalgia) and the wisdom of entrusting political leadership to the young, charismatic, but mercurial Alcibiades (with trepidation). He concludes, as we must, that change is inevitable.

I have a theory about an overlooked origin of the key idea of difference, and in the next two chapters, I emphasize the following ideas. The first and foremost difference in early Greek thought is the separation of immortals and mortals, gods and men, the only dualism in which men are the secondary and less valued term. I explore how the social requirements of male rule were developed against, but in terms compatible with, the greater powers of the divine patriarchy. Men's cultural response to what they perceived as their own lack was obsession with power and control, the creation of a world in which men were primary and exercised power over weaker, less valued, and subordinated embodied and abstract Others. Male identity was forged defensively and narcissistically, against both the power of the gods and the generative powers of nature and woman. I argue further that feelings of powerlessness are at the root of men's desire to transcend death, to become like a god, through heroic actions or other kinds of achievements.

The values articulated in Greek and Roman works of literature and philosophy do inform our culture, but in ways we scarcely recognize. Neglect and ignorance rob us of the power to reevaluate the legacy of these works, thereby imposing self-defeating limits on our conversations about morality. In other words, some seemingly intractable contemporary moral issues are rooted in the classic tradition. Only better understanding of these roots will enable us to see our way more clearly to changes we all claim to want. Greek and Roman ethics were formulated in terms which failed to accommodate Otherness except as a power to be controlled: something imagined as negative and subversive which must be transformed so it would serve the needs of the "civilized," male community: family, society, State, empire.

Widespread public discussion about what an ideal American society would look like and how to prepare young people to take their place in it is a national pastime. The fact that we keep having this discussion is a tribute to the vitality of American idealism. The fact that we keep trying to translate our ideals into practice is a tribute to our pragmatism, optimism, and willingness to adapt to change.

As I have already suggested, I believe that far from being estranged from the values inherent in the Greco-Roman tradition, we are at this very ethical juncture because we have embraced certain traditional values too well. In reassessing them, we are, after all, only doing what Americans have been doing from our first beginnings as a nation, forging a New World from our old, European connections. This is the way we began; in a sense, we just never finished the job. America's ethical well-being concerns everyone. It is a basic tenet of our democracy that all of us are responsible for thinking about moral choices and that we are capable of doing so. Beyond our own individual orientations and concerns, moreoever, we should remember that received ideas and values have usually been redefined through processes of questioning, thinking and rethinking, formulating and reformulating. This is a quintessentially human task. Through entering into this process—yet again—we have the prospect of winning a better understanding of who we are and who we want to become.

Notes

[1] Gerda Lerner, *Women and History*, vol. 1, *The Creation of Patriarchy* (Oxford and New York: Oxford University Press, 1986). Azizah Al-Hibri, "Reproduction, Mothering, and the Origins of Patriarchy," in Joyce Treblicot, ed., *Mothering. Essays in Feminist Theory* (Totowa, NJ: Rowman and Allenheld, 1984), pp.81-93.

[2] G.E.R. Lloyd, *Polarity and Analogy. Two Types of Argumentation in Early Greek Thought* (Cambridge: Cambridge University Press, 1966), and Page du Bois, *Centaurs and Amazons. Women and the Pre-History of the Great Chain of Being* (Ann Arbor: University of Michigan Press, 1982).

[3] William J. Bennett, *The Book of Virtues. A Treasury of Great Moral Stories* (New York: Simon and Schuster, 1993), has collected stories drawn from the Greeks, the Bible, and later sources that illustrate moral virtues we are, apparently, in danger of forgetting. My point is not that we need to refamiliarize ourselves with the old models, but that we need to reconsider them from a critical, feminist standpoint.

In Greco-Roman societies, the main purpose of education—most especially literature—was to teach morals. Greek education was divided into *musike* and *gymnastike* [*paideia*], training for the mind and for the body. The *liberales artes* at Rome, especially as presented by Cicero [*De Oratore*, The Education of an Orator] were skills and all facets of knowledge befitting a free (*liber*) man. See Henri Marrou, *A History of Education in Antiquity* (London, 1956), and Stanley F. Bonner, *Education in Ancient Rome* (Berkeley and Los Angeles: University of California Press, 1977). (Additional references in Bonner, Bibliography, pp.380-392).

The intrinsic association of values and religion established in classical antiquity (and before) presented a difficulty for the American founding fathers. The quest for freedom of religion that brought many of its first citizens to this country led to the doctrine of separation of church and State; once religions were restricted to the private realm, where could universally recognized sources for public morality be located?

4 Alice Jardine, *Gynesis. Configurations of Women and Modernity* (Ithaca: Cornell University Press, 1988).

5 In *Achilles in Vietnam. Combat Trauma and the Undoing of Character* (Atheneum: Maxwell Macmillan, Canada, 1994), Jonathan Shay reflects on the unchanged nature of the war experience.

6 Ross Poole, *Morality and Modernity* (London and New York: Routledge, 1991).

7 For example, Jean Bethke Elshtain, *Public Man, Private Woman. Women in Social and Political Thought* (Princeton: Princeton University Press, 1981) and *The Family in Political Thought* (Amherst: University of Massachusetts Press, 1982); and Susan Moller Okin, *Women in Western Political Thought* (Princeton: Princeton University Press, 1979) and Okin, ed., *Justice, Gender, and the Family* (New York: Basic Books, 1989).

8 Aristotle, *Politics*, Book 1.

9 For the debate, see, e.g., *Partisan Review*, spring 1994, devoted to "The Politics of Political Correctness." Some proponents of the neoconservative position are William J. Bennett (above, note 3); Camille Paglia, *Sexual Personae. Art and Decadence from Nefertiti to Emily Dickenson* (New York: Vintage, 1991); and Alasdair MacIntyre, *After Virtue* (South Bend, IN: University of Notre Dame Press, 1981) and *Whose Justice? Which Rationality?* (South Bend,IN: University of Notre Dame Press, 1988). T.J.Jackson Lears, *No Place of Grace. Antimodernism and the Transformation of American Culture*, 1880-1920 (New York: Pantheon, 1981), explores the decline of moral consensus in modern society. See also Paul Johnson, *Modern Times: The World from the Twenties to the Nineties* (New York: Harper Collins, 1991 [1983]). As early as 1932, T.S. Eliot, in his essay "Modern Education and the Classics,"in *Selected Essays* (London: Faber and Faber, 1934), expressed discomfort over what he perceived as movement away from the traditions of Western morality and its intellectual foundations.

10 Bernard Knox, *The Oldest Dead White European Males and Other Reflections on the Classics* (New York: W.W. Norton & Company, 1993), and *Backing into the Future. The Classical Tradition and Its Renewal* (New York: W.W. Norton, 1994).

11 Women scholars in classics have sometimes discovered that they are anomalies; see Marilyn Skinner, "Classical Studies, Patriarchy and Feminism: The View from 1986," *Women's Studies International Forum* 10.2 (1987): 181-186; Page duBois, *Sowing the Body. Psychoanalysis and Women in Ancient Greece* (Chicago: University of Chicago Press, 1988), Part I, "The Woman as Classicist," pp.7-36; and Nancy Zumwalt [Kassell], "Exclusae Feminae," in Irene Thompson and Audrey Roberts, eds., *The Road Retaken. Women Reenter the Academy* (New York: Modern Language Association, 1985), pp.127-132.

12 For more traditional investigations of the classics in America, see Meyer

Reinhold, *Classical Americana* (Detroit: Wayne State University Press, 1984), and Reinhold, ed., *The Classick Pages. A Classical Reading of Eighteenth-Century America* (University Park, PA: American Philological Association, 1975), Introduction, "The Cult of Antiquity in America," pp.1-27; Paul A. Rahe, *Republics Ancient and Modern.* Vol. 1, *The Ancien Regime in Classical Greece*, Vol. 2, *New Modes and Orders in Early Modern Political Thought*; Vol. 3, *Inventions of Prudence: Constructing the American Regime* (Chapel Hill and London: University of North Carolina Press, 1994); and Susan Ford Wiltshire, *Greece, Rome, and the Bill of Rights*. Oklahoma Series in Classical Culture (Norman and London: University of Oklahoma Press, 1992).

[A]n immortal god is without qualities most men possess, being incapable of death and consequently deprived of the gallantry and understanding which men, short-witted though they are, acquire through the individual contemplation and social experience of death. As a sharpener of intelligence, a sundial to measure passing time, a heightener of present pleasure, and a fixed prospect of the future, death has values which the gods cannot touch but which are the common property of the "unluckier" race.
Emily Vermeule[1]

Death destroys a man; the idea of death saves him.
E. M. Forster[2]

Chapter 2

Death Is the Difference

The Greeks asked, as we do, how it is possible that we are born only to die. That despite our hopes and hard work, we can be cut down at any time and never learn how things turned out. That the reward for those who have lived full and good lives is still death. Although the Greeks cultivated grace under this absolutely unique but universal kind of pressure, as Emily Vermeule suggests, they regarded the uncertainties of human experience and the finality of death as both measures of human dignity and affronts to it.

In our view today, death is also un-American.[3] He is not a good sport because he doesn't fight fair; the contest is always rigged in his favor. He cannot be zapped out of existence by any trick of technology or bribed into taking his business elsewhere. He is never on the receiving end of the golden handshake. Dying is the ultimate injustice, and in America untimely, and sometimes even timely, death is occasion for a lawsuit. It is hard to believe that there is no recourse, anywhere.

The language of limit pervades Greek moral thought, and death is finitude, the final limit to a man's life. The Greeks believed that at death, the soul (*psyche*) left the body (*soma*) and traveled perhaps to a place below or at the ends of the earth,[4] although the spirit of a deceased family member also remained in the household and was an object of worship and prayer. *Gnothi seauton*, Know yourself, the famous motto inscribed on the wall of Apollo's temple at Delphi, meant "Know that you are a mortal." It was not a reminder to observe one's place in a given social order or—as it might strike modern, psychologically attuned ears—to seek self-knowledge through introspection. Death is the manifestation of the inexorable power of nature, confining men within nature and therefore within time. It obliterates all differences among men, for everyone, without exception, must die. It is our common destiny, the one thing we all have in common.

In this chapter, we explore the death-centeredness[5] that marked Greek culture from its early beginnings. The Greeks formulated their reflections on mortality in terms of difference, the separation of men from gods, which was defined and measured by degrees of power. Mortality determined men's place in the universe, subordinate and inferior to gods who were deathless and ageless, indestructible if not totally invulnerable, and endowed with far greater capacities.

Early Greeks often perceived their world in terms of either analogy or polarity: two things were either like one another or opposites.[6] The binary thinking which became prevalent in Western thought privileges one member of a pair of opposites over another. Life and death are binary terms. Life is the primary term, is it not? Yet both are assigned a subordinate place in relation to transcendence, a value forged against the condition of mortality, life as well as death. Transcendence releases a few men who have proven themselves worthy from death. In the Greek view, men who escaped the power of nature became like the immortal gods and, in rare cases, even joined their company. They were exceptions to nature's rule: exceptional men. Transcendence was a supreme value in classical thought and remains so in the dominant culture of the West. In this and the next chapters, we shall see how Greek thinkers understood the power of death and how they formulated the heroic ideal, man's quest for power over death, defensively, against it. Death and transcendence are both primary terms in a polar opposition; the secondary terms, the Others against which and whom these powers are differentiated, will be discussed in Chapters 3 and 4.

How much and which kinds of powers are proper to men—proper in the sense of belonging to human nature and to the human condition? We are going to see how some of the most respected Greek thinkers answered these questions, in order to reconsider them from the following perspective. Humankind has sought and gained many and diverse kinds of power since classical antiquity. Nevertheless, I believe we still define the human condition in terms of mortality and we still regard mortality as a fundamental limit to human power, a deficiency. The difference between men and gods, defined in terms of power, gave rise to other constructions of difference in classical thought: kinds and degrees of difference among men, the difference between men and women, both of whom were also defined in terms of power.

Greek perceptions of mortality and the limits of human powers—men's quest for godlike powers and for primacy among their peers, the degrees and kinds of ability and authority that distinguish men from one another—constitute the major themes of early and classical Greek literature. There are two kinds of beings, *thnetoi* and *athanatoi*, those who die and those who don't.

> The race of men, the race of gods
> are separate, though from one mother
> we both draw breath. From every defining aspect,
> it is power which divides us. The race of man
> is as nothing; the bronze heaven, secure and lasting home,
> endures. If we are a little like immortals
> in greatness of mind or our nature, we still
> do not know at the break of any day, through any night
> what given course fate has written for us to run. (Pindar, *Nemean* 6.1-7)

Although both men and gods are descended from Earth, the race of men is "nothing" in comparison with the race of gods, which is secure forever in its celestial home. There are moments when men may seem like gods, but even during their limited life span, the resemblance is extenuated by ignorance of the future—whatever the gods and fate have in store for them. The gods are superior because they are secure in domain and knowledge, and their power defines men's impotence.

From the hypothetical perspective of timelessness—not quite the same thing as eternity—even the longest life span is a mere moment. Men, like animals, are creatures of a/the day, *ephemeroi*, "short-witted creatures whose intelligence responds to or is shaped by each day's events and accidents." In an instant, men's lives may end or be changed irrevocably; no human powers—intelligence,[7] physical strength, technical skill, strategic planning—endow men with secure control over the future, or even the present. Such were the terms of the human condition as seen by Pindar, as well as by Homer, the tragedians, and many others. One way of regarding this view is to say that men, chagrined at their lack of control, conjured and drew consolation from an all-powerful, better-knowing, divine patriarchal order superimposed on its human counterpart. Only imagined beings such as these could have power great enough to set limits on their own.[8] Since differences between gods and men were defined by power and since gods were the more powerful, men saw themselves as Others in relation to them. Only in this relation were men subordinate and inferior; in all other contexts of difference—all other pairs of opposites—they construed themselves as the primary and dominant term. Death-centeredness, as we shall see, is also self-centeredness, and narcissism, too, incorporates polarities: feelings of power and grandiosity, feelings of powerlessness and worthlessness.[9]

The other suprahuman power to which men were subject was fate, and powers of fate were personified as female. In myth, the Fates (Clothes, Spinners) spun the thread of each human life. Women were the spinners and weavers in Greek and Roman societies;[10] the female fates performed women's work. The noun Homer commonly uses meaning "fate," *moira*, lot, destiny, was feminine, and the Moirai (pl.) oversaw human destinies. The root of this word also appears in the Homeric phrase *morsimon hemar*, fated day, day of death. A Latin counterpart, Parcae, also meaning Fates, is derived from *parere*, bear, from *parica, childbearing.[11] The power to give birth and the power to take away life are closely associated.[12] Birth and death, life processes, confine men to nature and both were assimilated to female power. The mortality of women, who were, as we shall see later, confined within nature by virtue of their natures, does not seem (in the eyes of male observers) to have presented the same problem as the mortality of men. Unlike the Fates, who were impervious to men's desires, members of the divine patriarchy were responsive to men's quests and requests, prayers and sacrifices. But the powers of the female fates were greater than those of the gods; no god could overrule them, and because they were inexorable, they were a greater threat to male autonomy. The greatest power in the *Iliad*, which Simone Weil called "the poem of force,"[13] is, as she pointed out, the force of destiny.

The heroic ethic, the predominant value in the *Iliad*, aspires to the optimum and maximum exercise of human power and control allowed to men by the gods and fate. The hero uses his powers to win honor (*time*) among his peers and fame (*kleos*) which will extend beyond his lifetime.[14] Heroism is forged against death and, concomitantly, against the difference between men and gods. Our understanding of heroism from Homer and beyond is so defined.

The essential conjunction of mortality and heroism in Homer's texts is often incorporated into critical interpretations of the *Iliad*, such as those of Seth Schein and James Redfield. Schein describes the *Iliad* as

> both a poem of death and a poem of life; in other words, it is a poem of mortality. With unwavering and unsentimental realism it presents the necessities and opportunities of human existence, tragic limitations that are at the same time inspiriting and uplifting to live with and contemplate. Its depiction of war and death is thoroughly traditional, but the tradition is transformed by Homer's characteristic artistry into a comprehensive exploration and expression of the beauty, the rewards, and the price of human heroism.[15]

The principal necessity is that a hero, like all men, must die; the principal opportunity, that he may die gloriously and be remembered. But by whose reckoning, we may ask, is that necessity "tragic"? Why is man's common destiny a perpetual collective tragedy, and why is the death of the hero, the embodiment of the best of humankind, more tragic than other deaths? The heroic ethic, by defining the end of human endeavors as transcendence of mortality, offers a severely limited view of the necessities and opportunities of "human" existence.

James Redfield presents the specialness of the hero in terms of an antithesis between nature and culture. Man mediates between nature, "a sphere of force, of things which may be exploited, enjoyed, or endured but which cannot be altered" and "an enduring order, a cosmos"[16], culture. The warrior-hero is a liminal figure, one who stands "on the frontier between" nature and culture.

> He is in a position to form a view of culture as a whole. Culture has created a human world within which men can live. The warrior knows that world to be insubstantial. Culture, which appears to us in our social lives so solid and enduring, reveals itself on the battlefield for what it is. The values conferred on life by culture are the only values we have, but they are a secondary product, sustained only by men's common assertion of them. For the warrior, culture appears as a translucent screen against the terror of nature. The heroic vision is of meaning uncertainly rescued from meaninglessness.[17]

In Redfield's view, only culture, which is a purification of nature, and art, which is a purification of culture,[18] can recover "for man a tragic meaning in the experience of meaninglessness."[19] For "meaning" I read "value": Redfield assumes that life in nature is without value, that culture is the creation of value, but value infused twice over with tragedy: first, because it is fragile and arbitrary, and secondly, because the hero acts with the knowledge of its fragility and arbitrariness. Although I do not find the polarity between nature and culture expressed by the heroes of the *Iliad* to be as broadly or clearly defined as Redfield does (see below), his definitions of value and culture suggest a number of questions. To what extent do we, still influenced by this interpretation of the early Greek heroic ideal, believe that life in nature is without value? Does culture not endure (something we are in a better position to know today than Homer's hero-warriors were), and is it indeed as fragile and arbitrary as Redfield suggests? Hasn't the heroic ideal survived for well over twenty-five hundred years? Have not a great plurality and diversity of cultures endured? Are there not values to be derived from nature as well as from culture? Why are the implications of mortality "tragic"? Is it only the death of the hero which is tragic, or man's common destiny?

Homeric warrior-heroes are not preoccupied with culture as an abstraction nor with its fragility. They fight in single-combat to survive and to win victory and glory. On the Greek side, this is a war to avenge the rape of Helen by Paris, prince of Troy; he violated the social order of the Greek world, a king's right to exclusive ownership of a prized woman and the institution of marriage itself. On the Trojan side, Hector, defender of the city, is the bulwark of his family's ruling dynasty and the hope of its survival. Chaos and meaninglessness in nature do not threaten Troy; Greek victory, which will entail the destruction of the city, the fall of Priam's dynasty, the murder of Trojan men and the enslavement of Trojan women and children, does.[20]

Homeric heroes are acutely aware of their mortality and ultimate powerlessness and voice that awareness regularly. As they face their critical moment, they acknowledge that success or failure is in the hands of the gods and that the "failure" which is (or results in) death is determined by fate. Their crowning valor is revealed not only in achieving victory (though that is greatly to be hoped for), but also by their initial willingness to risk their lives in battle: What greater loss can a mortal suffer? Achilles, (one of) the best and most godlike of the Achaeans, is destined to slay the best of the Trojans, Prince Hector. Hector's death will mark the beginning of the end of the war and lead to Achilles' own fated death at Troy. Three-quarters of the poem, the long battle narratives leading up to Book 16, give extended demonstrations of the best that male courage and daring, *arete*, can accomplish. From that point on, the story focuses on the successive deaths of major warriors. In each episode Homer repeats the same narrative pattern. Before dying, a warrior acknowledges that although it is an enemy's weapon which inflicts the mortal wound, the true agents of his death are fate and the gods. He also reminds his opponent that he, too, in his turn, will be overcome by the same powers.[21] Sarpedon, son of Zeus, is the first (16.491) to meet his fated day, *morsimon hemar*, and is killed by Patroclus, whom Zeus then lures into single combat with Hector. Patroclus breathes his last with:

> At this moment, Hector, you're talking big;
> Zeus, son of Kronos, and Apollo have given victory
> to you and defeat to me. Easy for them. It was they
> who took away my weapons. If twenty of you had come up
> against me, all would have perished by my spear.
> But dire destiny and Leto's son killed me,
> of men Euphorbus. You came third, only finished me off.
> I'll tell you something else. Store it up in your heart.
> You will not walk upon the earth for long. Already
> death and daunting fate have taken their stand by you,
> and you will be tamed by the hands of perfect Achilles,
> descendant of Aiacus.   (16.844-853)

The "I am meeting my fate now, soon you will meet yours" motif, a blend of self-comfort and taunt, will be repeated by Hector when he is slain by Achilles. But at this moment of his victory over Patroclus, he rejects the prophecy of his own death:

> Why do you prophesy my plunge into death, Patroclus?
> Who knows? Perhaps Achilles, son of Thetis with the lovely hair,
> will be struck by my spear and lose his spirit.   (16.859-861)

Although Hector now sees the outcome of his future encounter with Achilles as open, at the moment of death he, too, will recognize that his own destiny and the gods have overcome him.

When Achilles and Hector meet face to face in battle, Achilles promises to send Hector to the edge of doom, and he replies:

> Son of Peleus, don't hope to spook me with words,

> as if I were a child. I, too, know how to say insulting
> and evil things. I know, too, that you are a noble warrior,
> and I am much weaker than you. But these things rest
> on the knees of the gods. Though you are stronger,
> I might still hurl my spear and take your life,
> since in the past, its point was sharp. (20.431-437)

Hector hurls his spear, but Athena deflects it, and Apollo catches him up and hides him in a cloud. When Achilles tries in vain to spear the cloud, he recognizes that Apollo has intervened:

> You evaded death again, dog. Evil came close
> to you, but now once again you were rescued by Phoebus Apollo,
> to whom you pray, I suppose, when you enter the thunder
> of weapons. I vow to meet you later, and I will kill you—
> at least, I will if one of the gods stands with me as helper.
> For now, I'll go against other Trojans, anyone I can find. (20.449-454)

Enraged as he is, Achilles recognizes that he will kill Hector only if and when a god helps him. Later, even as he mocks the pleas of Lycaon, Hector's brother, to spare his life, he acknowledges that he, too, is promised to death:

> Patroclus died, too, and he was a better man than you.
> Don't you see how big and handsome I am:
> My father was noble and my mother a goddess.
> Even so, death and daunting fate will overpower
> both you and me. There will come a morning, or an evening,
> or noontime when someone will take my warrior spirit, either with his
> spear or with an arrow from his bowstring. (21.107-113)

At the opening of Book 22, fatal destiny compels Hector to stand outside the city gates, where he soon will meet Achilles for the last time. Zeus weighs the lots of each man's death in his golden scale, and Hector's *morsimon hemar* sinks down. Athena tells Achilles that he will now be victorious, and disguising herself as Hector's brother Deiphobus, she tricks Hector into taking a stand against Achilles. There is more verbal sparring. Hector, ignorant of his destiny, still thinks the outcome of the imminent fight is open: "Now my soul would have me stand and fight, / whether I kill you or am killed" (252f.). But suddenly

Deiphobus vanishes and Hector instantly knows the truth:

> Damn! The gods call me deathward. I thought
> heroic Deiphobus was standing by me, but he is
> inside the walls and Athena has deceived me.
> Now evil death is close, not far away, inescapable.
> Long ago this was dearer to Zeus and his son
> whose arrows hit their mark, though they used to rescue
> me with willing heart. Now destiny has overtaken me.
> Let me not die without a fight, ingloriously, but having done
> something big, to be known to generations to come.   (22.297-305)

In the last book of the *Iliad*, Achilles' achievement and those of other heroes are highlighted by remembrance of mortal destiny. After avenging the death of his friend Patroclus by killing Hector, Achilles, still raging over his loss, abuses the body of the Trojan prince by attaching it to his chariot and dragging it around the walls of Troy for eleven days. Aged King Priam, guided by the god Hermes, dares to enter the Greek camp and confront his son's killer in order to recover the body and give it proper burial. Achilles, too, will die before the war is over and knows it. The two men weep together—Priam for Hector and his many other sons killed in war, Achilles in anticipation of the grief of Peleus, his father, at his own death.[22] Achilles reflects on man's common lot in suffering and destiny and on the changeful fortunes of Priam's house and dynasty and those of his own family:

> There is no efficacy in icy grief.
> Thus have the gods ordained to hapless mortals,
> who suffer the pain of living. But they are without
> cares. Two jars stand at Zeus's threshold: from one
> he metes out evil gifts, from the other good.
> The man to whom Zeus who delights in thunder
> distributes both experiences now evil, now good. (24.524-530)

Such a man was Peleus, Achilles continues—prosperous, ruler of many, husband to an immortal wife, but father to only one child, himself, who now sits by the side of another old king, far from his home, and grieves with him. Such a man, too, was Priam—wealthy, blessed with many sons, whose dynasty now falls. Even the most fortunate are vulnerable to loss; indeed, the more favored and prosperous the man, the more he has to lose. Achilles invites Priam to share food and drink, reminding him that after bitter loss, survivors must repair body and spirit and reenter the cycle of life, until their own day of death comes. He recalls a mythical example: Even Queen Niobe remembered to eat after Apollo and Artemis had killed her twelve children as punishment for boasting that she had more children than their mother.[23] Mortal children die, as Priam knows too well and Peleus will soon learn. It is perhaps not by chance that a woman, mother of many, examplifies the necessity of life in nature; yet even heroic men must acknowledge that life goes on by remembering to eat. The death of children before their parents is unnatural, but the death of sons before their fathers has special significance in the male-centered context of the *Iliad*, for it disrupts not only the continuity of generations but also the legacy of patriarchy—a family tradition of *time*, *arete*, and *kleos* deserving of remembrance for all time. The heroic ethic determines men's status among men, both their own peers and the peers of their descendants.

The *Iliad* affirms that all men belong to the community of nature because they share a common, mortal destiny. Life in nature is uncertain, susceptible to loss, and, most important, finite; life in culture endures. Men strive to perform deeds that will win them fame, remembrance, and eternal glory, albeit at the price of suffering and death. Word of mouth and stories told in song are cultural vehicles that commemorate their greatness; rescued from oblivion and from their vulnerability and mortality, men are redeemed. Through its power to immortalize, song defeats death and bestows on men something like the power proper only to the gods. In the world of Homer, life in culture is already privileged over life in nature and seeds of opposition between nature and culture are taking root. The legacy of the *Iliad* is: Those spheres of actions that define culture belong to men, and extraordinary men deserve to be remembered not only because honor is due them but also so they may serve as examples for future generations. Culture is created by men for men, and the value of art lies in its power to memorialize men.

Confinement within nature is man's universal destiny. The warrior-hero aspires to escape mortality, to forge an identity that displaces the common life and life itself: All that he is and can be is set in opposition to death. This quest is the foundation of the heroic ideal and its legacy.[24]

* * * * *

For the classical age of Greece, which we know best from Athens,

Homer was Tradition—a primary source and reference point for moral, religious, social, and political values. His poems were the core of the educational curriculum designed to train the mind and spirit, *he musike techne*, complement of *gymnastike*, devoted to training of the body. In classical Greece, once written texts became available,[25] children learned how to read and write using the *Iliad* and the *Odyssey*, and many (not necessarily literate) people knew long passages of the Homeric poems by heart. According to Aristotle, the literary descendant of Homeric epic is tragic drama (*Poetics* 1448b30-1449a, 1449b4-5), one medium through which the values of Homeric palace warrior culture were transformed to meet the needs of the fifth-century *polis*.[26] The theater was one of the most important civic institutions at Athens; dramas were performed at religious festivals to honor the god Dionysus before audiences of 15-18,000 people.[27] Through retelling traditional myths in ways that addressed contemporary concerns, dramatic performances served as a form of public moral discourse.[28]

The god Dionysus represented the life force—fluid, indiscriminate energy. This force confounds differences within nature and is also perceived as a threat to difference in culture because it releases men—and women even more so—from the controls which society and culture impose. The domain of Dionysus

> is...the whole of the *hugra physis* [wetness of nature]—not only the liquid fire in the grape, but the sap thrusting in a young tree, the blood pounding in the veins of the young animal, all the mysterious and uncontrollable tides that ebb and flow in the life of nature."[29]

To exist within culture, the life force must be contained within boundaries.[30] In a sense, tragic drama asks, How may mortals use and control the force of nature, the indiscriminate generative and creative power which the god embodies, in a social context? Tragic drama wants to assume that nature, enclosed within the social, moral, and religious confines of the *polis*, has been civilized according to the requirements of patriarchy, and the themes of the plays reflect their location.[31]

Accordingly, tragic drama enacted the theory and practice of patriarchy in the civic and social context of the *polis*. How much power does man have to create his own world? What kind of world provides him with the control he seeks? How can he both challenge and abide within limits imposed both by nature and by the almost limitless powers of the gods? How can he create and preserve the cultural beliefs, customs, ideas, and institutions that constitute his own unique powers?[32]

As the requirements of patriarchy in a civic context are defined, connections between private and public, the family and society emerge. Though separate spheres, they are interdependent. The stories of Greek tragedies are family dramas that are inevitably also public dramas with social and political implications. The central relationship in both spheres is that of father and son, which must be protected by control of sexuality and generation within legitimate marriage. Protection of family bonds as defined by the fathers is critical to the well-being of society as a whole. Relationships among leading men in the public sphere and that of ruler and his subjects, paternal and fraternal models prefigured in Homeric epic, were also fundamental to tragic definitions of patriarchal power.

Death and the problem of mortality cast a fainter shadow over mortal lives in tragedy than they do in epic. What looms larger in Sophocles' plays, on which our discussions will focus, is powerlessness—man's ignorance of the future, of the full implications of his present acts and circumstances, and of forces within himself that may lead to self-sabotage. Fifth-century Athenians articulated a new and more complex perception of uniquely human powers—intelligence, speech and reason (*logos*), and human inventions and discoveries. In early Greece knowledge was seen as a prerogative of the gods, who imparted it to a few select men such as poets and kings. Now it came to be understood as a form of power more available to men, and power, in turn, as a kind of knowledge. The so-called fifth-century Enlightenment[33] coincided with the flowering of Athens's economic power, political influence, and intellectual and cultural productivity. Just as memories of heroes and their accomplishments were handed down from one generation to the next, first through the oral transmission of Homeric epic and later through written texts, other and different kinds of knowledge and expertise, too, came to be seen as forming an inheritable tradition. Language and argumentation (rhetoric) played a prominent role in Athenian public life. Greek tragic drama also assumes that language is a powerful means of control and influence, since moral claims and viewpoints differ and often come into conflict.

These powers became especially problematic when protagonists expressed different moral values. Clytemnestra's arguments in support of her usurpation of the throne and murder of her husband, King Agamemnon, in Aeschylus's Oresteia trilogy— menacing but compelling examples of the power of speech—conflict with those of her husband and her son, who defend male power within the family and State, and only divine intervention brings about a resolution.[34] Medea and Jason's clashes in Euripides' *Medea* also reflect conflicting male-female viewpoints. Jason's arguments in favor of consolidating his social and political status by divorcing his wife and marrying the Corinthian princess are flagrantly self-serving even within the context of traditional male privilege, while Medea, though a foreigner and sorceress, defends her marriage in rational and conventional Greek terms. Which of them speaks for traditional values? Awareness of the potentially insidious powers of language reflects a new influence in Athens, the appearance of rhetoricians who called themselves "sophists" (wise men) and claimed that for a fee they could teach men to argue any side of a question, a posture their opponents characterized as "making the worse appear the better cause." Since sophists also claimed to be able to teach virtue, their approach appeared to subvert established values and to raise the specter of moral relativism.[35] Fifth-century Athenians faced a conflict similar to the one we are experiencing today: how to make moral judgments and choices once traditional values have been challenged.

Tragedians filled a time-honored and authoritative role, that of poet as educator; poets loved by the gods and privileged to receive divine wisdom through inborn talent and god-sent inspiration, imparted that *sophia* to other men. Although theater audiences at Athens may have included women and slaves,[36] it was primarily male citizens, and especially those who had status within the patriarchy whom tragedians addressed. Tragic protagonists, drawn from heroic-age myth, were larger-than-life paradigms. Because their situations, though extreme-case scenarios, were thought to represent recurrent human dilemmas, their moral choices were supposed to be intrinsically similar to those experienced by the fifth-century audience. Many who speak on behalf of tradition today also assume a moral continuity in human experience, while others, citing the particularity, diversity, and complexity of individual moral experience, as well as the different moral experiences of men and women, challenge this assumption. The fact remains, however, as Oliver Taplin put it, "*We* are now the audience of Greek tragedy."[37] But who is "we"? How applicable to us, a collective plural, in our collective diversity, are Greek tragic definitions of what it means to be human, how applicable the terms in which ancient tragedians cast moral choice and decision making?[38] Most tragic dramas focus on a critical moment in the life of a hero, a man who has enjoyed high privilege, a moment which is leading, before our very eyes, to a reversal of his fortune (*peripateia*, Aristotle, *Poetics* 1452a-b6): His power, his ability to control his own fate are catastrophically challenged. The Sophoclean hero, Bernard Knox has argued,[39] is a moral absolutist; he is vulnerable because he is a mortal, because he is at the pinnacle of human power, and because he holds an extreme view of human affairs. How did Sophoclean heroes differentiate their own powers from those of the gods? Unlike the Homeric warrior-hero, who chooses to risk death for the sake of honor and glory, the tragic hero-protagonist does not seek death. He is an "established king . . . preserver of stability,"[40] caught up in the midst of civic life by events which threaten him with loss of status and prestige, his preeminent place within the patriarchy. The dramatic setting is sometimes the battlefield (*Ajax*), but more often the palace in the city where he rules as king (*Women of Trachis, Oedipus the King, Antigone*). Occasionally, a hero experiences a positive reversal. Orestes (*Electra*) recovers the throne of Mycenae, usurped by his mother and her lover. The exiled Philoctetes, in the play named for him, returns to Troy and victory. Oedipus in Sophocles' last play (*Oedipus at Colonus*) is awarded semidivine powers after his death.[41]

Although writing from within the dominant culture, tragedians are not simply spokesmen for it. As political philosopher Arlene Saxonhouse has suggested, fifth-century tragic dramatists insisted on a complex vision of human experience, which they set against a monolithic view of culture and the unitary ideology of the emerging *polis*.[42] Others must be incorporated within the *polis*,[43] but interestingly, although women often threaten the social order in ways which are already almost stereotypically subversive, Sophocles also recognizes men who undermine or overturn patriarchal power from within as threats to patriarchal rule. A man's inner conflicts undermine stability and continuity. Because the tragic protagonist is a man of high position, an outstanding man, his downfall—whatever the circumstances that cause it—is catastrophic for both his family and his community. The society of the *polis*, to which the tragic context anachronistically refers, is especially vulnerable at the point where family and society intersect.[44]

Women of Trachis translates the Homeric theme of mortality to the tragic genre in order to show that even the most exemplary of all heroes in Greek myth, Heracles, son of Zeus himself, must die. The play also reveals dangers inherent in patriarchal marriage. Destined from birth to be tormented by Hera, wife of Zeus, because of her anger at Zeus's infidelity,[45] Heracles was famous neither as a warrior on the Homeric model nor as a ruler. Known as Euergetes, Benefactor, he roamed the Greek world performing fabulous labors, *ponoi*. He defended threatened communities, vanquished menacing beasts, and, over and over again, proved his extraordinary strength by performing superhuman feats. Nevertheless, even *he* had to die. The destiny which overtakes him is closely associated with his immortal father, king of the Olympian gods. According to a prophecy recalled several times in the play, the hero's current labor is to be his last, for until now, some god, presumed to be Zeus, has always saved him.[46] His wife, Deianira, is the unwitting agent of his death. After learning that Heracles has destroyed the town Oechalia in order to win Princess Iole as a spear bride, she is determined to defend her marriage and win back her husband's affection with a love charm.[47] She smears an ointment given her many years earlier by the bestial centaur Nessus[48] onto a robe which she sends her husband as a gift; he must wear the robe when he makes thanksgiving sacrifices to Zeus. The charm is a poison and when it touches Heracles' flesh, he begins to die a slow, agonizing death. The greatest exemplar of human labors howls that he is now weak as a woman, vanquished by a mere woman (1070-75). When she learns what has happened, Deianira kills herself with a sword, choosing a man's weapon and a man's death, ironic symbols of her heroic "victory."[49] As Page duBois puts it, a woman unwittingly colluded with a beast to subvert heroic action and the order of civilized space which Heracles' famed labors upheld.[50] In trying to protect her marriage from an outside threat, a new wife, Deianira upholds the integrity of her family and the institution of marriage itself.

Heracles' agony ends only when his son, Hyllus, at his father's request, places him alive on a burning funeral pyre on Mt. Oeta. Hyllus also promises to take Iole as his bride, thus insuring the continuity of his family and its rule. Hyllus is angry but pious: "There is nothing here that is not Zeus" is his final thought and the last line of the play. The gods, who are immune to change, have no empathy for human suffering, another difference between mortals and immortals. Though a woman and a beast are agents of Heracles' downfall, it is the power of death that is most subversive of all, and that power affirms the difference between men and gods. The humiliating end of Heracles, greatest paradigm of heroic action, demonstrates that even the son of the most powerful of all gods must die if born of woman. Further, woman, lacking wit, may become a destroyer. She is the stranger, the Other, within the palace and within the city. But the question of containing male sexuality within marriage is also raised. The heroic-age practice of bringing a captured spear-bride home and installing her in the palace is likely to disrupt domestic tranquillity; Clytemnestra in Aeschylus's *Agamemnon* is livid when Agamemnon arrives home with Trojan Cassandra. Sons born of such a union may become a threat to legitimate male succession; this is a custom which ought not be condoned within the *polis*. *Women of Trachis*, while updating Homer's treatment of heroism and mortality, also shows that unregulated heterosexuality, *eros*, that of both men and women, is a danger to the stability of civic life, which relies in turn on the stability of the family.

In *Oedipus the King*,[51] death, men's common destiny, is of little concern, for a very uncommon destiny presides over Oedipus's birth, one which causes havoc within his family and city. Although the story of Oedipus is one of the best-known of all ancient myths, modern readers may find it difficult to understand and even perverse. What did it mean in the context of Greek, rather than nineteenth-century Viennese (or twentieth-century American), culture? Why should fate compel a good, wise, intelligent man to commit heinous acts, especially when they have been foretold, and he has tried to avoid them? The Oedipus myth illustrates two important foundations of patriarchal social order by showing what happens if they are even involuntarily subverted. The birth of Oedipus condemns him to violate taboos against parricide and incest. Parricide strikes at the very foundation of patriarchal social order: patrilinear succession, continuity of the generations through the male line. Transference of power from one generation of males to the next is effected through the primary relationship, that of father and son.

Earlier I discussed the association of the female fates with nature and man's confinement within nature. In the case of Oedipus, fate undermines that very aspect of nature on which the social and cultural foundation of patriarchy depend, for Oedipus was doomed not just from birth but even before he was conceived. His parents, King Laius and Queen Jocasta, have learned from the oracle of Apollo at Delphi, the voice of fate, that if they have a child, he will be destined to kill his father and marry his mother. The royal couple is faced with an unnatural situation, to say the least, since fate contravenes not only the succession of male rule, but also heterosexual *eros*, which binds man and woman and perpetuates a family and the citizenry. The couple vows to remain childless, but in a fit of drunkenness, Laius rapes his wife.[52] The newborn Oedipus, though first-born son and heir to the throne, must be destroyed. But he survives to unwittingly enact his fate: kill his father, marry his mother, and taint the next generation by becoming brother-father to his own children, acts which disrupt the public sphere as well as the norms of patriarchal family relationships. Oedipus's fate presents a worst-case scenario for patriarchal social order.

Many critics have regarded Oedipus as a kind of everyman, embodiment of the best human traits and skills as defined by the fifth-century Enlightenment.[53] Oedipus's heroic pursuit is his quest for self-knowledge, knowledge of his true identity. Intelligent, resourceful, like a father to the citizens of Thebes, he is impatient to learn the cause of the plague and other disasters afflicting his city. Thebes, he learns through consulting the oracle, is threatened by *miasma*, religious pollution incurred by the shedding of kindred blood.[54] The city can be purified only by the expulsion of the source of the pollution, who is revealed, in the course of the action, to be King Oedipus himself. Although Oedipus is described through imagery of various *technai*— acquired skills in which fifth-century man prides himself (enumerated in the famous "Many are the wonders" choral ode; see below), his knowledge and skills are useless because he does not know the one thing he most needs to know. Since Homer, to know one's identity was to know one's father and birthplace.[55] Knowing his destiny but not his identity, Oedipus becomes an unwitting destroyer of patriarchy: a man who does not know whose son he is, a man who kills his father, a man who begets children with his mother. The generations are confused; father-son, parent-child, and parent-sibling relationships are confounded.

After Oedipus has wandered in exile for many years, cared for by his devoted sister-daughter Antigone,[56] the gods redeem what fate cannot. He is given a resting place at Colonus, a small town outside Athens, by the pious King Theseus, who also grants him citizenship (*Oedipus at Colonus*). There Oedipus mysteriously vanishes and is presumed to have died. The gods have decreed that his tomb will be held sacred and his spirit accorded semidivine status and posthumous power to protect the city Athens. The man who suffered a strikingly uncommon destiny receives an uncommon reward for piously submitting to events that were beyond his control.

The relationship between power and knowledge remains a complex and difficult area of human confusion in modern times. In the Oedipus plays, Sophocles defines essential knowledge, which surpasses any kind of *techne*, in patriarchal terms: A man needs to know who he is, not only in the sense commanded by the Delphic oracle (Know yourself, i.e., know that you are mortal), but also who his father is. The fate of

Oedipus does not, therefore, exemplify a sweeping generalization to the effect that epistemological ignorance makes a man morally fallible, but something more specific: By patriarchal definition, ontological ignorance gives rise to moral fallibility. Patriarchal orientations have informed the subsequent development of epistemology and moral thought in the West, as feminist philosophers now point out, and we shall return to some of their observations in a later chapter. Sophocles' play suggests some wide-ranging questions. Whose knowledge carries moral authority, and why? What is the relation between knowledge and power? In this Age of Information, when so much "knowledge" is available (Athens times twenty-seven hundred years), what kinds of knowledge do we need in order to make moral judgments and decisions?

In *Antigone* Sophocles sets man's common destiny, upheld by Antigone, against the political authority of the *polis* as interpreted by the king, Creon. The two protagonists, displaying the obstinacy characteristic of Sophoclean heroes, take extreme and inflexible positions.[57] King Creon has pronounced an edict forbidding the burial of his nephew Polynices, thereby denying the ritual which served to acknowledge the difference between mortals and immortals and to mediate the relationship between the living and the dead.[58] Polynices, whom Creon regards as an enemy of the state, and his brother Eteocles, brothers-sons of Oedipus, have fought for the rule of Thebes and killed each other. Fratricidal strife is another outcome of Oedipus's destiny, which confounded generation and, in turn, confused the order of the generations. Antigone refuses to obey the edict. "In my view," she tells Creon after she has been caught giving the corpse symbolic burial, "Zeus did not proclaim your orders; neither he nor Justice who lives with the gods below determined such laws among human beings. I did not think your orders so forceful that you, a mortal, could trample down respected and immutable laws of the gods" (450-455).[59]

Antigone values blood ties, men's necessary existence in nature, and divine patriarchal rule over obedience to civil authority. She upholds patriarchy on two levels: by acknowledging that the authority of the gods is greater than that of men (thereby affirming the difference between gods and men) and by defending the honor due to her brother, who belongs to the next generation of male rulers. Her motive for performing the forbidden act, she declares, is love, *philia* (523ff.). *Philia*[60] enables—or should enable—all sustained human ties, both public and private: those of brother and sister (Antigone, Polynices), brother and brother (Eteocles, Polynices), father and son (Creon, Haemon), husband

and wife (Creon, Eurydice), an engaged couple (Antigone and Haemon), ruler and citizens (Creon and the citizens of Thebes). Some of these bonds have already been corrupted in the preceding generation by Oedipus's destiny; all, familial and civil, are violated anew as a consequence of Creon's edict,[61] for he disregards ties of *philia*, except as they apply to the State, just as he fails to understand the correct priority of *nomoi*, laws or customs. The edict is a natural extension of his political philosophy: "You cannot know the soul or cast of mind of any man until it is tested through time-honored laws"(175-177).[62] He means the rule of law in civil society—a basic tenet of fifth-century Athenian political life—but fails to recognize that the time-honored laws of the gods, which affirm man's place in nature, have prior value.

The penalty for disobeying the edict is death, and Creon orders Antigone to be buried alive. As the bride of Death (lines 808ff.), she is deprived of marriage and motherhood, through which she would have perpetuated blood ties. Entombed, she anticipates death by hanging herself. If Antigone's position asserts the necessity of acknowledging life in nature, her choice—loyalty to the dead Polynices over bonds with the living, her sister Ismene and fiance Haemon—is a violation of nature, a predicament recalling that of Laius and Jocasta.

Antigone's attitude and actions resemble those of a Homeric hero, and the Chorus praises her, though a woman, in male heroic terms: "You die with great fame, attaining the lot of the godlike, both in your life and finally in your death" (834-838). They also say she has gone to the farthest edge of daring (another metaphor for male heroic action) and found justice (a male value, 853ff.).[63] The correctness of her moral judgment is recognized by the citizens (by report, 694-699), the Chorus (tentatively, 279), and Haemon (circumspectly, 628-763). We think of godlike Achilles, who defied the authority of another king because he had been dishonored. But Antigone is defending a principle, not a position in the hierarchy of powerful men. Achilles puts aside his anger at Agamemnon, enabling Greek victory over the Trojans and insuring his own eternal glory, and after killing Hector, he acknowledges men's common destiny to his enemy's father. Likewise, men of the *polis*, however elevated their status, are still mortal. Polynices, even if he should be considered an enemy of the state as Creon maintains, has not forfeited his mortality; the gods of the underworld require his spirit. The human community now organized as *polis*, with all its varied achievements, remains collectively obligated to acknowledge its mortality and the ultimate power of nature.

Antigone has been seen as a protofeminist heroine, model of an autonomous woman who understands and lays claim to political rights of citizenship denied to women in Greek society and dares to act against male political authority.[64] The Chorus describes her as *autonomos*, a law unto herself (821) and *autognotos* (875), acting from a self-sufficient impulse—literally, one known to and from the self. Autonomy in the modern sense, as philosopher Valerie Hartouni has argued,[65] can be exercised only by someone holding full membership in a political community—something no woman held in ancient Greece. It is an irony, one which the Chorus does not appreciate, that Antigone's affirmation of men's common destiny should be regarded as individualistic or antisocial. Antigone's chief virtue, loyalty, is stereotypically feminine. The two adjectives would be more aptly applied to Creon, for his view, which overrides ties to nature, family, and the gods, is a law unto itself. There is the danger that men in power may ignore a multiplicity of moral claims and subsume a singular and absolute moral order under the aegis of civil authority. Civil law does not cancel out the difference between men and gods or life in nature. Creon recognizes his terrible error too late: "I have come to fear that it is best to live out one's life observing established laws"(1112-14),[66] and he learns too late which "established laws" deserve greater respect.

The "Many Are the Wonders" choral ode of *Antigone* is a famous reflection on the necessity of acknowledging life in nature:

There are many things we call wonderful and terrible,
but none more wonderful and terrible than humankind.
This thing crosses the sea in stormy winter, cutting a path
through the engulfing waves; he wears down imperishable Earth,
greatest of the gods, his ploughs and mules turning up and down,
year after year. He traps the light flocks of birds, wild animals
of every kind, the fish of the sea with ensnaring nets—this resourceful man.
He has skills to take possession of the home of field animals, to harness
and drive the yoked horse, to outwit the powerful mountain bull.
He has taught himself language, thought quick as wind, the law-abiding ways
of the town, escape from the frosty open air and pelting rain. He meets
the future with a strategy for everything: Death alone he has not
contrived to escape, though he devises cures for incurable illnesses.
With a kind of cleverness—his contrivances—with skills beyond hope,
he creeps along, now toward evil, now toward good. Greatest is the city

which observes the laws of the land and the sworn justice of the gods;
an outcast the man who dwells with evil for the sake of daring.
He who would do this, may he not share my hearth or thoughts. (*Antigone* 332-375)

The progress of civilization, in the Chorus's estimation, is measured by man's acquisition of power:[67] control over Earth, the natural environment, and the seas; dominion over animals; the regulation of human behavior through the creation of socio-political communities and their institutions. Only death has proven resistant to all human manipulations, the one thing men cannot control no matter how intelligent and resourceful they are, no matter how hard they try. Despite (and, in a sense. because of) increased technical mastery and the growth of other kinds of knowledge now incorporated into fifth-century definitions of culture,[68] there is a discrepancy between man's expertise and his moral insight and conduct. These are the very terms in which we express our moral quandary today, in modern times.

Sophocles places the difference between men and gods at the heart of the problem. The man who fails to acknowledge it is an outcast: *apolis*, without a city, excluded from the bounds of culture. Creon, to whom the ode most immediately refers in the context of the play, was such a man. But Antigone, too, became citiless. She gave up her life to acknowledge the separation of men and gods, the first and fundamental difference, and by doing so was excluded from both nature and culture. Unlike Achilles and other Homeric heroes who sacrificed their lives for the sake of glory, she died in order to affirm that all men are mortal.[69]

Arlene Saxonhouse has drawn attention to another important aspect of the *Antigone*. From the extremity of their respective positions, both Creon and Antigone (*anti-gone*, against birth, against generation) deny the power of *eros* and generation, the outcome of heterosexuality. *Eros* is as necessary to the well-being of the city as is *philia*. Human intelligence must accept diversity in the world—the gods of the dead as well as the gods of the living, the female as well as the male, the *eros* that tells us we are incomplete, not autonomous—and it must not attempt to transform that diversity into simplicity. Such a denial is destructive of the *polis*, which cannot survive without the processes of birth that depend on the commingling of opposites, the erotic attachment of male to female.[70] *Eros*, the Chorus sings in lines 781-801, has power over gods, men, and beast. In the human world, it binds man and woman and also affirms mortality. *Eros* does not implicate the gods in death, but man born of woman is destined to die. Both Ismene and Haemon recognize the invincibility of its power, embodied in the goddess Aphrodite. When Ismene says to her sister, "We two are women and must not fight against men" (60-62), she acknowledges her subjection to male rule, which she fears; unlike her sister, however, she chooses life. Haemon, whose name means "blood," argues on behalf of Antigone against his father with great passion and tact and when he is unsuccessful follows Antigone in death. Queen Eurydice also commits suicide. What kind of a city denies *eros* and generation, as well as *philia*?

Sophoclean women are subject to moral order as defined by men's authority. Antigone understands, however, that the foundation of men's authority is the moral and religious order imposed by mortality, existential decorum, and pays the ultimate price for her understanding. Deianira and Clytemnestra (*Electra*) subvert male rule, and Jocasta in *Oedipus the King* intends to subvert it, for when she suspects the truth—that her husband is also her son—she tries to prevent Oedipus from discovering it. In *Electra*, the heroine refrains from acting to avenge her father's death, for she respects the proper role of woman as moral nonagent. Only divinely sanctioned vengeance enacted by her brother, Orestes, puts an end to her passionate suffering. Like Antigone, Electra is a woman whose life has been interrupted by a violation of the male code; until her father's death is avenged and her brother takes over the rule of the city which is rightly his, she is unable to proceed to the next stage of her natural life cycle, to become a bride. Both Electra's sister Chrysothemis and Antigone's sister Ismene see themselves as powerless because they are women, incapable of going against the authority of the *polis* and its male rulers. Eschewing heroic absolutism, they argue in favor of adaptation as the price of survival:[71] Their necessity is more than fate; it is compliance. Women who fail to know their place are potential threats, like Clytemnestra, who murdered her husband to avenge their daughter Iphigenia's death, and even Deianira, who tried to save her marriage. When a woman assumes power to think and act, there is a risk that she will become an agent of disorder and destruction. The necessity of confining women within the private sphere, where they can be more easily controlled, and the long-standing exclusion of women from public and political life are far-reaching reflections of this view.

In *Ajax* and *Philoctetes*, Sophocles considers how public recognition and mutual responsibility affect relationships among coequal men in the heroic community. The situations he poses, like that of *Antigone*, have implications for male leaders of the *polis*. Ajax, second only to Achilles in battle prowess, has just gone on a rampage and slaughtered a herd of cattle in a fit of madness sent by Athena, who deluded him into believing he was killing the chief Greek leaders at Troy—Odysseus, Agamemnon, and Menelaus. How could such a thing happen? Ajax had been dishonored by his peers when Odysseus persuaded them to award the arms of the dead Achilles to himself, rather than to Ajax. Odysseus's successful argument on his own behalf has already become an example of how powers of speech, Odysseus's forte since Homer, could be misused, with harmful and potentially disastrous consequences to the well-being of the community.[72] Ajax was not a man predisposed to be able to cope with disgrace. His response to loss of honor, *time*, was murderous rage, which Athena, Odysseus's champion, deflected onto the cattle. When Ajax (whose name means Agony, 430ff.) comes to his senses and realizes that by his own actions, he has brought a new disgrace upon himself, he is filled with remorse and pity for his wife and son and commits suicide.

Ajax has a history of denying that the gods play a critical role in the outcome of human actions; he does not recognize that, in the words of the prophet Calchas, "Whoever nurtures a mortal nature but does not mold his thoughts to human vulnerability, aiming too high and trusting in senseless strength, falls on acts which the gods doom to failure" (758-761). On two previous occasions Ajax has shown himself to be such a person. When his father sent him off to Troy, he advised his son to "take care to win with your spear, but always with the help of the gods" (764f.). Ajax retorted that even a man who is nothing can win with the gods; he will win without them. Again, when Athena stood by him in battle at Troy, he told her to go and help some other Greek; if he is fighting, the battle line will hold. He angered the goddess "by not thinking thoughts appropriate to a man"(777). Strength without sense is dangerous; perhaps the Greek leaders did show good judgment in awarding the arms to a man known from and since Homer as the embodiment of resourcefulness and intelligence and honored by Athena for these very qualities. After Ajax's suicide, his wife Tecmessa and his half-brother Teucer accept the outcome as the will of the gods (950,1036f.). There is a dispute, however, about the burial of the corpse. Teucer would bury it, not just to honor Ajax, but because the gods of the underworld must have their due. Agamemnon and Menelaus, not a little concerned with their own honor, would deny burial: Ajax was the son of a mere barbarian slave woman, out only for his own glory, an enemy not a friend, and insubordinate. It is Odysseus, the man who denied *time* to Ajax, who wins them over with sense and moderation, the very qualities which Ajax lacked.

The *Ajax* raises issues of male power within a discrete community of equals and seems to imply that a man must be recognized and valued within that group, given due honor. But he, for his part, must abide by communal norms, even when he is treated unfairly and does not receive due honor. Individual and community are interdependent, but the wellbeing of the community takes precedence. Moreover, a person whose self-esteem is wounded may suffer such severe psychic damage that he becomes mad, and he is then prone to violence and becomes a threat to all. If Ajax had murdered the leaders, the fate of the army and the entire expedition might have been compromised. In contemporary society, mental instability, madness, and acts of violence are often linked to low self-esteem (our way of describing a person's response to lack of honor and respect) and antisocial behavior. We no longer regard madness as an affliction sent by a divine power but understand it rather in hereditary, physiological, and psychological terms: impairment caused by lack of nurturance, economic deprivation, and, perhaps, the absence of social morality.

Philoctetes, like Ajax and Oedipus, has been cast out from the community of his peers; unlike them, he will be restored to it. Philoctetes was sent away after he unwittingly entered a grove sacred to the priest of Apollo and was bitten in the foot by a snake. His wound did not heal and its smell was so foul that the leaders of the Greek army at Troy banished him to the nearby island of Lemnos. At the opening of the play, Philoctetes has been in exile for nine years, during which victory has eluded the Greeks. According to a prophecy, victory will be achieved only when Philoctetes and his famous bow, a gift of Heracles, are brought back to Troy. He is destined to kill Prince Paris, the city will fall, and he will win great glory. The fulfillment of his destiny is also the fulfillment of the destined Greek victory.

Neoptolemus, son of Achilles, arrives on Lemnos with Odysseus, who has charged the young man with bringing Philoctetes back to Troy—by deception and deceit if necessary, but preferably by persuasion. When he meets the suffering hermit, Neoptolemus is filled with pity and indignation at the Greeks' treatment of the hero. At first he agrees to take him home to Greece. It is not in his nature to be deceitful, either in the service of fate or in obedience to Odysseus's command.

A sailor arrives and reveals the prophecy to Philoctetes, who adamantly refuses to return to Troy. The community of heroes cast him out when misfortune rendered him helpless and useless. He owes them nothing. Odysseus appears and wrests the bow from him, but the bow is useless without Philoctetes. Neoptolemus is torn: Though loyal to the army, he believes it is wrong to compel the miserable Philoctetes to return to Troy against his will. He reiterates his promise to take him home and argues that "the fortunes which the gods give to men must of necessity be borne, but those who willfully cling to their suffering deserve neither forgiveness nor pity" (1316-20). Philoctetes' suffering is passive; it is described by the same word, *ponos*, labor, that characterizes active, heroic labors, such as Heracles'. Suffering, too, is hard work.[73]

In the past Philoctetes had no alternative but to suffer; he was powerless to avoid transgression and banishment or to alleviate his pain and cure his wound. But he is too accepting of what he believes his fate to be. Why should he believe Odysseus's report of the prophecy? He has been misused before. The dilemma is resolved only when the immortalized Heracles appears *ex machina* and tells him that he must return to Troy and reenter the heroic life, which will engage his virtue and bring him glory.

Like Ajax, Philoctetes is an outcast from society. Ajax was marginalized first when he was devalued by his peers and then when he reacted with madness and violence to his treatment. Philoctetes was banished after involuntarily committing a religious offense. Although the Homeric warrior-hero fights for his own glory, Achilles' withdrawal from battle threatened the common enterprise. Sophocles presents the heroes Ajax and Philoctetes in the context of the community of heroes, and his presentation has implications, I suggest, for the community of Athenian citizens. A community of leaders must respect its individual members in order to maintain cohesiveness and stability. Both individual and community have a responsibiity to preserve social ties for the good of the entire group. The individual who is cast out may become a danger to the group or may, like Philoctetes, become embittered, no longer willing to participate in the group's endeavors.

Sophocles' insights into social cohesion and mutual responsibility have still broader implications. People who are marginalized suffer, their suffering may have serious and unexpected consequences, and they are a potential threat to the community. How does a society make its members feel valued and included, how does it inculcate a sense of responsibility to the community as a whole? In the context of contemporary American democracy, we address the needs not just of the community of select men but of all members. The same questions, however, apply. Feelings of alienation. expendability, and fragmentation are said to characterize the experience of man in modern and postmodern societies, especially in that there exists no community to be alienated from. While Others have always existed at the margins of society; preservation and recreation of community depends on their incorporation.[74]

Through discussions of Homer and Sophocles, I have suggested that in early and classical Greek thought, the human condition was defined by a primary difference, the separation of gods and men, immortals and mortals. That men share a common destiny—that they must die, that they are, without exception, confined within nature and time—is perhaps the single most important insight the Greco-Roman tradition offers us. Despite our differences, there is something we share, after all. But this definition is inherently negative: Man is defined by what he is not, by his lack. It is also discounted: Respect for the power of the gods and acknowledgment of mortality and other human limits are religious and moral imperatives, but our common destiny is a condition Greek men wished to deny and from which they sought to escape. The essence of being human is powerlessness.

The new fifth-century political man perceived the possibilities of human power and control as greater than what Homeric heroes and palace society had imagined. Knowledge, especially a wide range of uniquely human skills and capabilitites, seemed to enlarge the scope of those possibilities. Most characters in Sophocles, nevertheless, labor in states of epistemological and moral confusion, for ignorance goes to the heart of their *ponos*—both active, heroic labor and passive suffering—the conflicts they experience, the control they try to exercise. For Sophocles, neither intellectual knowledge nor expertise leading to man's greater control over his environment or physical existence are sources of moral knowledge. Sophoclean, like Homeric, man lives in ignorance, only he is, perhaps, more acutely aware of the complexity of his disability than his heroic ancestors were. The certainty of dying and the quest for transcendence that are Homeric preoccupations yield in Sophocles to the terrifying possibilities and obscure uncertainties of living which afflict even the most powerful of mortals.

The overriding importance which the early Greeks attached to man's powerlessness against death rendered universal membership in the community of nature a negative value. Impotence was thus written into early and classical Greek definitions of the human condition and not acknowledged for what, I suggest, it really is: fear, passivity, envy of superior imagined beings (the gods) who are what we are not, and rage against the force of a destiny (sometimes conceived as a female power) indifferent to men's purposes. Even today, after so much time has passed, we still assume that we want control but "can't" have it. Why is that? What kinds of control do we need, want, or feel entitled to? Are we really so powerless as the Greeks supposed? What if we saw ourselves and our condition differently?

By defining the human condition against death, Western culture has deliberately and habitually deflected attention away from life and many aspects of human existence; what happens during life, because it is transitory at best, has been accorded less value than striving to overcome death through transcendence of life. In early Greek culture, men's rage and fear against their powerlessness over death and their inability to control the outcome of their actions engendered a cultural response: an ethic grounded in the achievements of a select community of men.

Notes

[1] Emily Vermeule, *Aspects of Death in Early Greek Art and Poetry* (Berkeley and Los Angeles: University of California Press, 1979), p.121.

[2] E.M. Forster, *Howard's End*, Chapter 27.

[3] Jessica Mitford, *The American Way of Death* (New York: Simon and Schuster, 1963).

[4] The realms of the dead, visited by the living heroes Odysseus and Aeneas, are described by Homer in *Od.*11 and Vergil in *Aen.* 6. See also Vermeule, *Aspects of Death*, pp.128-130. For other aspects of Greek eschatology, see also Gherardo Gnoli and Jean-Pierre Vernant, eds., *La mort et les mortes dans les societes ancienne* (Cambridge: Cambridge University Press; Paris: Maison des sciences de l'homme, 1982); Froma I. Zeitlin, ed., *Mortals and Immortals*. Collected Essays in Honor of Jean-Pierre Vernant, (Princeton: Princeton University Press, 1991); and Christina Souvrinou-Inwood, *"Reading" Greek Death to the End of the Classical Period* (Oxford: Clarendon Press, 1995).

[5] Mary Daly traces death-centeredness to both classic and Christian sources

and calls this preoccupation of Western culture "necrophiliac. *"Gyn/Ecology. The Metaethics of Radical Feminism* (Boston: Beacon Press, 1978), pp.43-72, esp. 59f.

[6] G.E.R. Lloyd, *Polarity and Analogy. Two Types of Argumentation in Early Greek Thought* (Cambridge: Cambridge University Press, 1966). For the "Great Dichotomies" of Western thought, see Alice Jardine, *Gynesis. Configurations of Woman and Modernity* (Ithaca: Cornell University Press, 1986).

[7] The quotation is from p.24. Vermeule continues, "The Greeks are of course partly responsible for the western overestimation of the value of intelligence. The most familiar Greek virtue, *sophrosyne*, began as that quality of mind which would keep you safe and draw you back from the stupidity of the sleeping and the dead."

[8] Emily Vermeule reminds us, however, how much men and gods had in common. The gods experienced human emotions, including envy (*phthonos*) of men's good fortune, and they were unreliable and vulnerable. Of men, closest to a god was a hero: "a recognizable oxymoron, godlike, half-god, equal to the gods. . .but an unstable compound of irreconcilables, immortality and mortality, a gallant mind in a bloody and vulnerable body." *Aspects of Death*, Chapter 4, "Immortals Are Mortal, Mortals Immortal,"pp.118-144. The quote is from p.119.

[9] In *The Origin of the Gods. A Psychoanalytic Study of Greek Theogonic Myth* (New York: Oxford University Press, 1989), Richard Caldwell suggests, "From a psychoanalytic perspective, the wish of men (that is, children) to win the prerogative of the gods (that is, parents) is an oedipal desire; the paternal possession that the son wants, but fears he will be punished for wanting, is the mother (or, to put the same wish in other terms, the sexual power and freedom of the father" (p.137). Caldwell is discussing the early Greek poet Hesiod's *Theogony*, a work we shall consider in a later chapter. The Freudian, male-centered psychoanalytic model fits Hesiod's male-centered, mythic account well.

See also Margaret Miles, *Carnal Knowing. Female Nakedness and Religious Meaning in the Christian West* (Boston: Beacon Press, 1989), p.193, n2:

> Freud described the psychological roots of patriarchal domination in the relationship of the male infant to the mother, especially in the dual and contradictory needs of the infant, on the one hand, for recognition by the (m)other, and on the other hand, for independence from the (m)other. Classical psychoanalysis formulated individuation as a difficult and dangerous process of creating a self-other distinction, a development in which "merging was a dangerous form of undifferentiation, a sinking back into a sea of oneness". . .On the level of society, patriarchal institutions reflect the psychic needs of   the male infant—domination and control.

Miles cites Jessica Benjamin, *The Bonds of Love. Psychoanalysis, Feminism, and the Problem of Domination* (New York: Pantheon, 1988), pp.81-84.

[10] Recall, for example, Homer's Penelope, who avoids choosing a new husband from among her suitors on the pretext that she must weave a burial shroud for her father-in-law, Laertes.

[11] Oxford Latin Dictionary, s.v. Parca. *Fatum*, Latin "fate," was neuter, "that which had been spoken," from *fari*, speak. The speech of fate is beyond the power of human speech. See also Oxford Classical Dictionary, ed. 2, s.v. Fates.

[12] Robin Schott, *Cognition and Eros. A Critique of the Kantian Paradigm* (Boston: Beacon Press, 1988), pp.30-31, makes the plausible suggestion that Greek male culture transformed women as a class into *pharmakoi*, scapegoats: bodily, sensual, and sexual experiences were figuratively imposed onto women, who were then expelled from the community of men on the grounds that they were polluted and impure. See also Froma I. Zeitlin, "Feminine Figures of Death," in Zeitlin, ed., *Mortals and Immortals*, pp.95-109.

[13] "The Iliad. The Poem of Force," in Siaan Miles, ed., *Simone Weil. An Anthology* (New York: Weidenfeld and Nicolson, 1986), pp.178-215.

[14] Gregory Nagy, *The Best of the Achaeans. Concepts of the Hero in Archaic Greek Poetry* (Baltimore: Johns Hopkins University Press, 1979), pp.26-41 (Achilles as hero); pp.174-210 ("Poetic Visions of Immortality"); and pp.211-276 ("Praise, Blame, and the Hero"). See also Jasper Griffin, *Homer on Life and Death* (Oxford: Clarendon Press, 1980), esp. chapter III, "Death and the Godlike Hero," pp.81-102.

The word *kleos* is etymologically related to the verb *kluein*, hear (cf. Latin *fama* from the verb *fari*, speak). For the development of the concept of fame, see Simon Goldhill, *The Poet's Voice. Essays in Poetics and Greek Literature* (Cambridge: Cambridge University Press, 1991), "Intimations of immortality: fame and tradition from Homer and Pindar," pp.69-166; for *kleos* in the *Iliad* and *Odyssey* and the differences between *kleos* in the two poems, pp.69-108.

[15] Seth Schein, *The Mortal Hero. An Introduction to Homer's Iliad*. (Berkeley and Los Angeles: University of California Press, 1984), p.88. See also Jean-Pierre Vernant, "Panta Kala," pp. 1367-70, cited by Schein, Chapter 3, n10.

[16] James Redfield, *Nature and Culture in the Iliad. The Tragedy of Hector* (Durham: Duke University Press, 1994 [Chicago: University of Chicago Press, 1975]), p.71.

[17] Redfield, *Nature and Culture*, pp.102-103.

[18] Further on notions of pollution and purification in the *Iliad*, see Redfield, Chapter 5, "Purification," pp.160-223, esp. 218-220.

[19] Redfield, *Nature and Culture*, p.223.

[20] Nature in Homer offers paradigms of order as well as paradigms and ran-

dom incidences of chaos and disorder; see below, chap. 3.

[21] On this pattern, see Martin Mueller, "Knowledge and Delusion in the *Iliad*," in John Wright, ed., *Essays on the Iliad. Selected Modern Criticism* (Bloomington: Indiana University Press 1978), pp.105-123, esp. "Heroic knowledge is primarily a knowledge of death," p.106.

[22] Redfield, *Nature and Culture*, pp.218-219, observes that Achilles and Priam find a common bond outside of culture, in nature.

[23] The Niobe passage, *Iliad* 24.595-615.

[24] In *Ordinary Heroines: Transforming the Male Myth* (New York: Continuum, 1994), Nadya Aisenberg also argues that the heroic ideal is imprinted on Western culture.

[25] According to Athenian tradition, it was the sixth-century Athenian tyrant Peisistratus who first had the Homeric poems written down. In *The Singer of Tales* (Cambridge: Harvard University Press, 1960), A.B. Lord argued that the Homeric poems evolved from a long oral epic tradition. For the transition from an oral to a literate culture in antiquity, see Eric Havelock, *The Muse Learns to Write. Reflections on Orality and Literacy from Antiquity to the Present* (New Haven: Yale University Press, 1986); and *The Literate Revolution and Its Cultural Consequences* (Princeton: Princeton University Press, 1982).

[26] For the transition from Homer to tragedy in the *polis*, see Richard Seaford, *Reciprocity and Ritual. Homer and Tragedy in the Developing City-State* (Oxford: Clarendon Press, 1994).

[27] For the Greek theater, see Peter Arnott, *An Introduction to the Greek Theater* (London: Macmillan, 1959); H. C. Baldry, *The Greek Tragic Theater* (London: Chatto and Windus,1971), and Oliver Taplin, *Greek Tragedy in Action* (Berkeley: University of California Press, 1978).

[28] See Page duBois, *Centaurs and Amazons. Women and the Pre-History of the Great Chain of Being,* Introduction. On the social context of Greek tragedy, see Jean-Pierre Vernant, "The Historical Moment of Tragedy in Greece: Some of the Social and Psychological Conditions," and "Tensions and Ambiguities in Ancient Greece," pp. 23-28 and 29-48, respectively, in Vernant and Pierre Vidal-Naquet, *Myth and Tragedy*, trans. Janet Lloyd (Atlantic Highlands, NJ: Humanities Press, 1981); John Winkler and Froma I. Zeitlin, eds., *Nothing to Do with Dionysus?* (Princeton: Princeton University Press, 1989); and references in Eric Segal, *Oxford Readings in Greek Tragedy*, (Oxford: Oxford University Press, 1983), Preface, p.v, n1.

[29] Euripides, *Bacchae*, edited and with an introduction and commentary by E.R. Dodds (Oxford: Clarendon, 1960 [1944]), Introduction, p.xii.

[30] Charles Segal, *Dionysian Poetics and Euripides' Bacchae* (Princeton: Princeton University Press, 1982); and J-P Vernant, "The Masked Dionysus of Euripides *Bacchae*," chapter 14 in J.-P. Vernant and Pierre Vidal-Naquet, *Myth and Tragedy in Ancient Greece*, pp.384-405.

[31] For the the importance and functions of the theater in fifth-century

Athens, see Goldhill, *Reading Greek Tragedy* (Cambridge: Cambridge University Press, 1986), Chapter 3, "The City of Words," pp.57-78. For the theater as a vehicle for patriarchal thinking, see Sue-Ellen Chase, *Feminism and Theatre* (New York: Methuen, 1988), Chapter 1, "Traditional History: A Feminist Deconstruction," pp.5-19, esp. 11f.; Froma Zeitlin, "Playing the Other: Theater, Theatricality, and the Feminine in Greek Drama," in Winkler and Zeitlin, eds., *Nothing to Do with Dionysus?*, pp.62-94; and Arlene Saxonhouse, *Fear of Diversity: The Birth of Political Science in Ancient Greek Thought* (Chicago: Chicago University Press, 1992), Chapter 3, "Women and the Tragic Denial of Difference," pp.50-89.

[32] For the transition from palace to *polis* and from Homer to tragedy, see Richard Seaford, *Reciprocity and Ritual. Homer and Tragedy in the Developing City-State*.

[33] Victor Ehrenberg, *From Solon to Socrates. Greek History and Civilization during the Sixth and Fifth Centuries* (London: Methuen, 1968).

[34] Simon Goldhill, *Language, Sexuality, Narrative: the Oresteia* (Cambridge: Cambridge University Press, 1984), and *Reading Greek Tragedy*, pp.1-56.

[35] G. Kerferd, *The Sophistic Movement* (Cambridge: Cambridge University Press, 1981).

[36] "The festival, unlike theatre today, involved the majority of the city— even some women and children, notwithstanding the disbelief of "pious" Victorian scholars, seem to have attended the tragedies and comedies," Goldhill, *Reading Greek Tragedy*, p.76 and n62.

[37] "Emotion and Meaning in Greek Tragedy," in Segal, ed., *Oxford Readings in Greek Tragedy* p.12 (entire essay, pp.1-12).

[38] In *The Fragility of Goodness. Luck and Ethics in Greek Tragedy and Philosophy* (New York: Columbia University Press, 1986), Martha Nussbaum discusses the achievements and limitations of moral thinking in Greek tragedy and the superiority of Aristotelean reasoning as a tool of moral thought which is still useful to us today.

[39] Bernard Knox, *The Heroic Temper. Studies in Sophoclean Tragedy* (Berkeley and Los Angeles: University of California Press, 1969).

[40] For the conflict between two heroic types, the Homeric warrior-hero (the "intruder-hero," such as Achilles) and the "established king" (such as Agamemnon), see W.T.H. Jackson, *The Hero and the King* (New York: Columbia University Press, 1982).

[41] Sophocles wrote over 100 plays, of which only seven survive. Among the standard studies of his work (the bibliography is vast) are Brian Vickers, *Towards Greek Tragedy. Drama, Myth, Society. Comparative Tragedy*, vol. 1. (London: Longman, 1973); R.P. Winnington-Ingram, *Sophocles. An Interpretation* (Cambridge: Cambridge University Press, 1980); Charles Segal, *Tragedy and Civilization. An Interpretation of Sophocles* (Cambridge: Harvard

University Press, 1981).

[42] Arlene Saxonhouse, *Fear of Diversity. The Birth of Political Science in Ancient Greek Thought*, Chapter 2, "The Pre-Socratic Challenge," pp.40-49, and Chapter 3, "Women and the Tragic Denial of Difference: Three Versions," pp.50-89. The principle of Oneness is derived from the pre-Socratic philosophy of Parmenides.

[43] Froma Zeitlin, "Playing the Other: Theater, Theatricality, and the Feminine in Greek Drama," in Winkler and Zeitlin, eds., *Nothing to Do with Dionysus?*, pp.63-96.

[44] On the relation between *oikos* and *polis*, Jean-Pierre Vernant and Pierre Vidal-Naquet, *Tragedy and Myth in Ancient Greece*; Simon Goldhill, "The Great Dionysia and Civic Ideology," in *Nothing to Do with Dionysus?*, pp.97-129; and Oddone Longo, "The Theater of the Polis," pp.12-19 in the same volume.

[45] According to Philip Slater, *The Glory of Hera* (Boston: Beacon Press, 1968), the Heracles myth expresses Greek men's perception of women, especially mothers, as powerful and controlling.

[46] The prophecy: lines 77ff., 161-177, 821ff., ll50-73; Zeus's oversight, 112-140.

[47] In an attempt to save her marriage; even the gods are overcome by Eros, she reflects (436ff.; cf. Hera's prototypical seduction of Zeus, *Iliad* 14). For Eros as opponent of and opposite to civilization, see Sigmund Freud, *Civilization and Its Discontents*, and Robin Schott, *Cognition and Eros. A Critique of the Kantian Paradigm*, Part I, Historical Antecedents of Ascetic Philosophy: Classical and Christian Origins, pp.3-94.

[48] The charm is made from the centaur's blood or semen. Heracles killed him when he tried to rape Deianira, then Heracles' bride-to-be. For centaurs, see Page DuBois, *Centaurs and Amazons. Women and the Pre-History of the Great Chain of Being* (Ann Arbor: University of Michigan Press, 1982).

[49] Nicole Loraux, *Tragic Ways of Killing a Woman*, trans. Anthony Forster (Cambridge: Harvard University Press, 1987).

[50] duBois, *Centaurs and Amazons*, pp.96-106.

[51] *Oedipus the King, Oedipus at Colonus*, and *Antigone* relate the mythic history of the city Thebes. They are listed in chronological sequence. They were, however, composed and performed at different periods of Sophocles' life: *Antigone*, 442-441 B.C., *Oedipus the King*, 426-425, and *Oedipus at Colonus*, 404.

[52] Drunken rape and its consequences figure prominently in the plots of Greek New and Roman comedy; see below, Part II, Chapter 6.

[53] Goldhill, *Reading Greek Tragedy*, pp.205-221.

[54] Robert Parker, *Miasma. Pollution and Purification in Early Greek Religion* (Oxford: Clarendon, 1983).

[55] Homer, *Od*.9.19ff.

56 Ellyn Kaschak, *Engendered Lives. A New Psychology of Women's Experience* (New York: Basic Books, 1992), suggests that Antigone became the mythic paradigm of the dutiful daughter. See Chapter 3, "Oedipus and Antigone Revisited: The Family Drama," pp.55-88.

57 Bernard Knox, *The Heroic Temper. Studies in Sophoclean Tragedy.*

58 Hence, of course, the importance of funeral practices in archaic-classical Greek society; see Vermeule, *Aspects of Death*, pp.12-21.

59 Cf. Creon's misguided response when Antigone is apprehended: "To what fortune must I measure up?" (387). A mortal may become equal to fortune only by submitting to it.

60 On *philia*, see Emil Benveniste, *Indo-European Language and Society*, trans. E. Palmer (Coral Gables: University of Miami Press, 1973), and Simon Goldhill, *Reading Greek Tragedy*, pp.79-107, who discusses *philia* in *Antigone* (pp.89-106).

61 Bonds of *philia* may extend beyond the family to wider social and political ties: Oedipus is like a father to his subjects; see the opening lines of *Oedipus the King*.

62 Creon's political views are argued with his son, Haemon, Antigone's fiance (635-780). Haemon is very adroit, balancing protestations of filial piety against his plea on behalf of Antigone, whose position he supports. The king acknowledges his son's words of respect but asserts the obligation of citizens to obey their ruler, right or wrong. Haimon counters obligation with obligation. Creon should acknowledge his son's devotion to his father and the actions that prove it by listening to him. Creon rationalizes his position: He is at the top of the hierarchy of power, the command of father over son and of ruler over citizens (734 and 736). As Saxonhouse points out ("Tragic Denial," pp.70-74), both Antigone's sister Ismene and Haemon argue for recognition of the complexity of the situation, against Antigone's and Creon's absolute positions.

63 "Godlike" is the honorific epithet of heroes in the *Iliad*, esp. Achilles. For the "ends of the earth" metaphor, see below Chapter 3, on Pindar, *Nemean* 3. Antigone refers to herself in male terms (464; cf. 479, 96 [Creon]); see also Saxonhouse, "Tragic Denial," p.69 and n44.

64 Warren J. Lane and Ann M. Lane, "The Politics of *Antigone*," in J. Peter Eubens, ed., *Greek Tragedy and Political Theory* (Berkeley and Los Angeles: University of California Press, 1986), pp.162-182.

65 Valerie Hartouni,"Antigone's Dilemma: A Problem in Political Membership," *Hypatia* 1.1 (spring 1986): 3-20.

66 *Kathesteotes nomoi*, established laws, are laws which are grounded in right, *themis* (the words are are etymologically related). But before he arrives at the correct moral perception of his situation, Creon rages that his authority has been subverted by "a mere woman" (473ff., esp. 484-5), the same complaint Heracles makes in *Women of Trachis*.

67 Environmentalist Ynestra King discusses this passage in these terms in

"Healing the Wounds: Feminism, Ecology, and Nature/Culture Dualism," in Alison M. Jaggar and Susan R. Bordo, eds., *Gender/Body/Knowledge* (New Brunswick, N.J.: Rutgers University Press, 1989), pp.115-141.

[68] All the activities Sophocles lists—agriculture, hunting and fishing, sailing, the establishment of political communities and institutions—are male occupations.

[69] Cf. Saxonhouse, "Tragic Denial," p.70: "Marriage entails creation and the attachment to another; the piety Antigone espouses is an antilife piety and, like the male Homeric heroes, she becomes the warrior whose glory can be achieved only at the moment of death, in the very act of denying life and change, not in birth."

[70] Saxonhouse, "Tragic Denial," pp.75f.

[71] According to Chrysothemis, Aegisthus, consort of their mother Queen Clytemnestra, has threatened to bury Electra alive (lines 378-384)—Antigone's fate.

[72] Pindar tells the story of the arms of Achilles in *Nemean* 8.21-32, presenting it as an example of the perils of speech—lies and deceit—and the susceptibility of great men to envy.

[73] The other figure in Sophoclean drama whose suffering is extraordinary is Electra in the play which is named for her. Because she is a woman, Electra is prevented from avenging the murder of her father Agamemnon by her mother Clytemnestra, who has usurped the throne. Electra is consumed by grief, rage, and the desire to right the wrong which has been committed. Only the return of her brother Orestes, who kills their mother, restores patriarchal order: Orestes becomes king, thus succeeding to his father's rule, and Agamemnon's spirit is restored to its rightful place of honor.

[74] Adrienne Rich, "Disloyal to Civilization: Feminism, Racism, Gynophobia," in *On Lies, Secrets, and Silence. Selected Prose 1966-1978* (New York: W.W. Norton, 1979), pp. 275-310; and Mary Lynn Broe and Angela Ingram, eds., *Women's Writing in Exile* (Chapel Hill: North Carolina University Press, 1989), esp. Jane Marcus, "Alibis and Legends: The Ethics of Elsewhereness, Gender and Estrangement," pp. 269-294.

The virtue of virtue, the virtus, is force.
Annie Le Clerc[1]

Perhaps contemporary culture no longer requires the repression or repudiation of femininity to ensure its integrity. Or, perhaps, its own integrity is in such tatters that the return of its repressions is one of many symptoms of its madness. In either case, the 'break[ing] down' of the coherence of Western culture may be prerequisite to reassembling in a more viable and polyvalent form.
Moira Gatens[2]

Chapter 3

Transcending Mortality. From the Heroic to the Achievement Ethic

From man's deficiency, measured against the ineluctable powers of nature and the deathless gods, was born the dream of transcendence. He nurtures a heroic hope, to win honor (time) among his peers and fame (kleos) that will extend beyond his lifetime. The man who enacts his exceptional capabilities—the valor of the warrior, the judgment of the king, the wisdom of the poet or philosopher—to achieve something extraordinary deserves to outlive his own death. The actions that qualify a man for immortality are generally performed in a competitive context, judged by other men, and ranked according to their degree of excellence. In post-Homeric Greece, the male quest for achievement worthy of remembrance for all places and all time is extended from the battlefield to other areas of endeavor. Many of them have come to be understood, by traditional male definitions, as comprising civilization: the ideas, norms, and institutions of public, civic life; domains of knowledge; products or works (such as "the classics")[3] through which men's most valued perceptions and experiences are transmitted from one generation to the next. Heroic victory becomes achievement: military prowess, a broader range of talents, virtue in the archaic sense of power. The heroic ethic becomes the achievement ethic.

Competitiveness and striving for achievement—what I shall call the drive to primacy—are hallmarks of American culture. We relish the good fight, applaud the individual who wins out against all odds. We want to see the best man [sic] win. If you expect to get ahead, you—man or woman—had better cultivate a killer instinct. Thanks in part to mass media, we are obsessed with success and celebrity. We want them for ourselves, if only in our fantasies; watching the efforts and progress of others is a national pastime. The most frequently articulated aim of education is to make America first in the international arenas of science and technology, economics, and business. Believing that our ideology and way of life are best, we strive to impose them on the world community, for its own good.[4] It is a matter of national pride, this quest for primacy. We want to see possibilities for growth as boundless, a frontier that recedes as far as we can expand, an American manifest destiny of global dimensions. Even our approaches to domestic reform are agonistic. We declare war on everything: corruption in government and business, crime, poverty, drugs, environmental pollution; the language of combat pervades media advertising. This orientation and approach are deeply traditional.

Elaine Scarry has suggested that the achievements of culture, our power to "make the world," are responses to our power to unmake it through killing others or inflicting pain and torture on the bodies of others.[5] I am suggesting that the making of culture is also a response to man's feelings of powerlessness in the face of his mortality—his need to deny death and have control over his life—and his will to survive death by winning a place in collective human memory. This cultural orientation has informed many Western values, up to and including present-day attitudes to virtue, capability, excellence, and achievement.

Power as social reality and concepts of power were linked to moral goodness and human excellence in the Greek and Latin languages. Women, excluded from male domains of action and creation (Greek poiesis, making) and the values associated with them, were denied the opportunity to develop their full human potential. The principal model for defining achievement has been and is competition to determine primacy. Because competition has been valorized as the means to achievement, cooperation became the Other, and opposite, value, and the value of Others has been measured in terms of service and devotion to those engaged in competitive quests.[6]

Greek culture as a whole reflects the values and outlook of a profoundly competitive people,[7] and Greek concepts of virtue are imbued with an achievement ethic. To demonstrate greater arete than others, to achieve more or greater things, to attain greater fame, to attain to such great fame as to risk arousing the envy of the gods, even (the gods willing) to attain immortality: These are the preoccupations reflected in literature, informing combat in war, athletic competitions, the dramatic contests held in honor of Dionysus, the debates of the assemblies and law courts, philosophical inquiry (especially the Socratic trial of truth, elenchos), and the form of the Platonic dialogues. Anthropologist and classicist John Winkler has described this outlook as follows:

> The paramount concerns are generated within a framework of scarcity, competition, and intense mutual inspection . . . there is an implicit presumption that sexual identity does not organize the person but is peripheral to the central goals and worries which are focused on survival, public status, jockeying for place in social hierarchies at the expense of fellow competitors, the stability and prospering of patriarchal families in a hostile environment.[8]

The Greek word arete means manliness, excellence, moral virtue, power, and achievement[9], a conflation of meanings which left a lasting mark on Western moral and intellectual thought. Arete may be derived from the Indo-European root *ar- and etymologically related to areion, better, and aristos, best. The man who possesses arete is measured quantitatively and qualitatively in terms of his difference from other men. The etymological relation of these words to arsen, male, is uncertain, although the Latin counterpart of arete, virtus, is derived from vir, man.[10] Any linguistic connection to Ares, god of war, is also uncertain. Etymology aside, maleness, strife (such as that which stirs up battles, embodied in Ares), and degrees of excellence are associated in the world of Homer, and the association carries over in subsequent Greek thought.[11]

The achievement ethic translates "power to" into "power over," as victors and others who establish themselves as first—already a self-selected and privileged group—confirm their place at the apex of the social hierarchy, in positions of dominance over losers and other subordinates ("lesser" men, women, and slaves). Members of the class which performs, defines, and recognizes acts of achievement also claim the authority to name moral virtue. "Power to" as skill/ability and moral goodness are conflated, and both are vitiated by their association with power as "power over."

The Homeric warrior strives constantly to display qualities that show him to be better than others, or best among his tribesmen.[12] Achilles, quarreling with Agamemnon in *Iliad* 1, charges that although he is the better man, the braver fighter, the king always receives more honor and greater, more valuable prizes. Nestor and Odysseus are best in speech and counsel among the Greeks. Hector, protector of his city and valiant fighter, is best among the Trojans. Long stretches of narrative in the *Iliad* focus on *aristeiai*, the best or most valiant deeds, of a single hero. Passages discussed in the preceding chapter describe the culminations of such encounters. The *aretai* of Odysseus in the *Odyssey*, however, go well beyond the *Iliad's* primary definition of virtue as valor and victory in battle. Having proven his value in war as a persuasive speaker and brilliant strategist, Odysseus seeks his *nostos*, homecoming. His intelligence, craftiness, and powers of speech and endurance enable him to get home to Ithaca, albeit only after ten years of troubles and travel (Books 1-13), and to reintegrate himself into family and community (Books 13-24). Odysseus's extraordinary resourcefulness, loyalty, and persistence are the qualities of a heroic character, a man who meets life's obstacles with an agonistic spirit. To live gloriously, the example of Odysseus suggests, is to contend against a series of obstacles that impede one's path toward a goal and to overcome them. It is an attitude oriented to quest rather than conquest.

The association of competition and achievement is seen also in Hesiod, who, like Homer, composed his poems in the late eighth century (c.725 B.C.). Hesiod distinguishes two kinds of *eris*, strife or competition. They are personified and female, as abstract powers often are in archaic Greek thought. One is cruel; she stirs up evil battle and war. The other is good and praiseworthy, and she is

> much better to men. She moves even
> the resourceless (= uncompetitive) man to work. A man grows
> eager to work when he sees another who is rich and striving
> to plough and plant and place his house in order. Neighbor
> contends with neighbor, scurrying after wealth. This strife
> is good for mortals. Potter competes with potter, builder
> with builder, beggar casts an envious eye on beggar, singer
> on singer.   (Works and Days 19-26)

The desire to be first is what motivates men to act. In Hesiod's list, work is the equivalent of peacetime pursuits, and the war-work duo encompasses all valued spheres of action. Work, as Hesiod conceives it, is imbued with conflict and competition. While the strife of war is evil and destructive, competitive strife is good, since it produces the constructive works of civilization—agriculture, economic growth, and arts and crafts.[13]

The pre-Socratic philosopher Heraclitus took exception to Hesiod's distinction between (evil) war and (good) competition. "One must realize that war is common and conflict is justice, and that all things are destined to occur in accordance with conflict."[14] Cosmic justice, or harmony, arises from the conflict of opposites: all strife is necessary.[15] Conflict is the force destined to cause change; it is a good because warring opposites are generative: "War is father of all and king of all; and some he has shown as gods, others men; some he has made slaves, others free" (fr.LXXXIII Kahn). Generative power, dissociated from the female power to give birth and a cooptation of that power as bel mooney points out,[16] is transformed into an abstract force which operates in areas of male endeavor. In Heraclitus's view, birth becomes a kind of primeval and perpetual conflict which produces and sustains cosmic balance and justice. The view that competition is the force that drives constructive or generative activities is inherent in the achievement ethic. Conflict and competition are closely identified with one another, and all activity invested with value is seen as competitive.

The domain of achievement as defined by both Homer and Hesiod was an exclusive community of men. Women neither fought wars, nor did they engage in work that involved competition. Human labor deserving of recognition did involve competition; therefore, other work—women's birthing labor and labor that sustains life on a day-to-day basis—lacked value. Hesiod's notion of competitive strife and the definition of labor it implies were carried over into attitudes to political, intellectual, artistic, and cultural pursuits in classical Athens. The first sphere of action which had defined achievement was warfare. The next was panhellenic athletic competitions.[17] The earliest and best known were the Olympic Games (founded 776 B.C.). The games consisted of several events, including chariot racing, foot racing, discus and javelin throwing, and wrestling. Noble men and boys from all over the Greek mainland and islands gathered to compete. A successful competitor (or his proud father) might hire a poet to commemorate his victory, so as to be better known among other cultivated Greeks and not forgotten by future generations. Although the Theban poet Pindar (518-446 B.C.)

was not the originator of victory song, forty-five of his poems, more than from any other writer, have come down to us. They celebrate victories won at Olympia, Delphi, Nemea, and the Isthmus by such luminaries as the tyrants Hieron of Syracuse and Theron of Akragas and other noblemen from Sicily, the island of Aigina, seven cities of mainland Greece, and a few other places.

Pindar wrote about the connections among excellence, the power to excel, and competition, striving for primacy, and he perceived both in relation to mortal and moral limits. Pindaric *arete* is natural talent which a man has by virtue of his noble birth and which he cultivates and brings to fruition in order to distinguish himself. In contemporary terms, talent, hard work, and discipline are prerequisites for achievement. *Arete*, which is also the act of accomplishment itself, manifests itself before a community of like-minded men. Success makes a man stand out among his fellows, giving him exceptional reputation and visibility. Families and cities, too, may be first among equals. The communities Pindar addresses are almost exclusively male. Women and goddesses figure in his victory songs as consorts and mothers of important men, as patron deities of important cities, and as abstract powers that nurture their endeavors.

Pindar's victory songs are songs of celebrations and praise: of the skill and prowess of the victor, his success, his moral character (especially his acknowledgment that he owes his achievement to divine favor and that, for all his greatness, he is not a god) and his distinguished family and city, which have many outstanding past accomplishments to their credit. An act of achievement is performed by one man, but a community enables that act and estimates and confirms its value. There are several communities in Pindar's poems: the audience, the victor's family, his city, and a timeless community of panhellenic achievement. They are part reality, part myth and poetic fiction. The audience, consisting of the victor, family, friends, and invited guests, hears Pindar's poem sung by a trained chorus at the victory celebration, held after the victor returns home. This audience is assumed to be of one mind, full of admiration for the victor and happy to share in the honor he has bestowed on his family and city. Many of the noble families which produced victors traced their lineage to a divine ancestor (frequently, Zeus himself), and Pindar presents nobility not as a trait derived from possession of economic, social, or political power but as a quality of inborn nature (*phua* = *physis*, nature, including human nature). Descent from a divinity bestowed on a family (though not on every member) noble character and exceptional native talent. Pindar often relates stories about divine ancestors to give his listeners the pleasure of recalling their illustrious origins, and he recounts myths of the divine origins of the city's founders and prominent heroes. The city, like the audience and family, is addressed as a unity, for it shares a tradition of glorious achievements to which the present victory is the latest addition. Finally, there exists a community of panhellenic achievement extending back in time to the age of Homer and even before. The victor's accomplishments are said to match the greatest deeds of the past. All Greek-speaking peoples take pride in them, and they are the privileged heritage of future generations.

Human hopes and efforts, as well as the best of human achievements, derive their value from their conformity to moral and religious requirements. Pindar sometimes called his victory songs *hymnoi*, hymns, transferring the word, which originally meant songs of praise in honor of a gods, to men: By virtue of achievement, outstanding men become godlike. To be truly deserving of praise, however, they must acknowledge the limits of their own, merely human powers. Pindar regards all facets of men's striving, including his own (poetry and its aesthetics), from within the context of existential decorum, awareness of mortal limits. In so doing, he creates what we might call a decorum of achievement.[18]

We can best see the varied aspects of Pindar's ethic of achievement by reading a single poem together. I have chosen *Nemean 3*, composed for Aristocleides of Aegina, who won the pancratium (a combined boxing and wrestling contest) in about 475 B.C. The poem opens with an invocation to the muse to come and lend her presence to the victory celebration.

> Good lady Muse, our mother, I pray you
> come to Dorian Aegina, which opens its doors
> to strangers in the sacred Nemean month:
> the chorus of young men waits by the River Asopus
> to fashion honey-sweet songs of joy;
> they need your voice. Different acts
> have different thirsts, but victory in contest
> needs song more than anything else,
> most worthy to attend crowns and merit.
> Give unstintingly of our skill;
> Begin a hymn of praise to him who rules
> the cloud-swept sky. I shall share it

with their voices and my lyre.   (1-12a)

By invoking the muse, daughter of Zeus (line 10), in whose honor the Nemean contests were held, Pindar summons divine power for himself and the chorus who will perform his song.[19] He calls her "our mother," not because he means to stake a literal claim to divine ancestry, but because of her power to nurture his gift and the efforts of all who are devoted to *he mousike*. The reciprocal need of victory and song is the essence of the decorum of achievement: Song requires merit worthy of praise, merit requires wise and skilled praise.[20]

> She [the Muse] shall have a pleasant task,
> to honor a place where the ancient Myrmidons
> lived, whose long-famed community Aristocleides
> did not disgrace, in accordance with your favor,
> when tested in the most demanding of contests,
> the pancratium. The victory revel brings
> a wholesome cure for the brutal blows
> he took on the broad fields of Nemea.   (12b-19)

The link between the opening of the poem and this section is community. Pindar will share the muse's gift with his lyre and the chorus; Aristocleides forges a connection with the public honor of even the most ancient people of his homeland, the Myrmidons.

> If the son of Aristophon, whose deeds match
> his good looks, has gone to the limit of manhood,
> it is no longer easy to sail the trackless sea
> any farther, beyond the Pillars of Heracles,
> which the hero-god made famous witness
> to the limit of sailing. He tamed monstrous
> sea beasts. Alone, he sailed the shallow places
> and coming to the end of voyaging,
> revealed the earth's boundary.   (20-26a)

Through the metaphor of the ends of earth, marked by the mythic Pillars of Heracles [Straits of Gibraltar], Pindar indicates that the victor has reached the farthest limit of human achievement. Even the daring Heracles, who traveled farther west than anyone ever had before, discovered an impassible boundary. The victor's act compares favorably

Transcending Mortality. From the Heroic to the Achievement Ethic

with the mythic hero's. Since the poet's voyage of song travels a course analogous to the victor's, he, too, has attained a kind of limit, the limit of praise.

> Heart, to what alien headland are you
> guiding my sails? I bid you direct
> the muse to Aeacus and his race.
> "Praise the noble " — that's the essence
> of justice; a man shouldn't work at
> other people's loves. Strive from what you are.
> Your fate-given honor is sweet speech. (26b-32a)

Pindar shows how the sailing metaphor applies to himself, as well as to Heracles and the hero-victor. It would be impossible to praise the victor more highly, so he wants to change poetic tack and talk about the famous Aeginetan hero Aeacus and his descendants. Bestowing praise on deserving men is an act of justice, the one which Pindar's own nature enables him to do; his *arete*, itself an honor to possess, is to grant honor to others. *Arete* is a manifestation of a man's inborn nature, a point to which Pindar returns shortly.

> Long ago, Lord Peleus took joy in merits, too.
> Alone, without an army, he captured Iolcus,
> overcame sea-loving Thetis after a long struggle.
> Telamon in his broad strength took Laomedon,
> then bravely followed Iolaus against the Amazons
> with their bronze-tipped arrows, nor did
> man-taming fear ever quell the bravery of his heart.
> A man blooms like a fruit tree
> when he draws his acts from inborn virtue.
> He who has things only through learning,
> obscure, panting as he goes,
> walks with faltering step, confused,
> aimlessly testing ten-thousand virtues. (32b-43)

Pride in achievement, defined in terms of conquest, is a long-standing Aeginetan tradition, as the examples of Peleus and Iolaus show. What is the single most important indicator of a man's future success? Heredity, here called "inborn virtue." Inherited talent is what counts. Talent must be developed, skills must be honed, Pindar says elsewhere, but acquired skill alone makes for fruitless labor and leads a man nowhere.

> The play of blond Achilles, a child
> in Philyra's home, promised great deeds.
> He grasped the broad-bladed javelin in his hands,
> and it flew, swift as the wind;
> he slew fierce lions, felled bears,
> dragged their gasping carcasses to centaur,
> son of Zeus, when he was only six —
> later years, too. Artemis and Athena
> were astonished at his strength:
> He killed deer without hunting dogs
> or entangling nets, won with his feet.
> I have it from an old story-poem
> that Chiron, the centaur, raised Jason
> in his stone house, then Asclepius,
> to whom he taught the gentle-handed use
> of medicinal herbs. In time there was the wedding of
> Nereus' shining daughter, and he raised
> her mighty son [Achilles], expanding his spirit
> in all ways fitting, until he, sent to
> spear-shaking Troy over waves of sea and wind,
> would sit by to hear the war cries of Lycians,
> Phrygians, Dardanians. Then he tangled with
> armed Aethiopians and calculated how their leader,
> his first cousin, fierce Memnon,
> might never go home again. (43-63)

Achilles, hero par excellence of the Trojan war, illustrates how a man's nature determines what he is.[21] The hunting prowess he showed as a child prefigured his adult exploits as a warrior. Achilles exemplifies the best of native talent and early training, combined. It was clear even to Artemis, the huntress, and Athena, warrior goddess, that he was a mortal of exceptional ability. Pindar's description of Achilles at Troy also recalls the hero's terrible temper and cruelty. Because of his rage against Agamemnon, he sulked in his tent while others fought. He also plotted the death of his first cousin—a taste for conquest tinged with family blood. Achilles' savage and bloodthirsty nature, shown also in his abuse of Hector's body in the *Iliad*, was apparently not entirely amenable to Chiron's civilizing influences. But he was a winner, and one of the most godlike of men.

> The light of Aeacid achievement shines forth afar
> from here. Zeus, yours the blood, the contest,
> the song of young men glorifying this place.
> The victory cry is in harmony with Aristocleides,
> who cast this island forth into prominence with
> speech of good fame and Apollo's Thearion
> [a public hall] with shining hopes and memories.
> 70   In any trial, the outcome reveals
> what each outstanding man can accomplish.
> A child among children, man among men,
> later, elder among elders. We have each stage,
> in accordance with our mortal life span. The mortal age
> partakes of four virtues: The wise accommodate
> 75   to each circumstance as it occurs. In these skills,
> he [the victor] is not lacking. Fare well, friend.
> I send you this gift of honey and milk
> in full measure, a musical draught
> mixed with the breath of Aeolian flutes, late
> 80   though it is. The eagle is swift in flight,
> swoops down from afar, clutches his bloody prey
> in his talons, while jabbering daws coast below.
> For you, by the wishes of honored Cleo,
> because of your victorious spirit,
> from Nemea and Epidaurus and Megara
> light has shone forth. (64-84)

Light imagery introduces and concludes this final section of the poem. In both places, it is the shining light of achievement that extends outward without limit in space and time. The light of ancient Aeacid glory glows still; the light of Aristocleides' victories, won at Epidaurus and Megara as well as at Nemea, will, Pindar predicts, enjoy a similar transcendence.

    This contest honors Zeus in several ways: the victor traces his lineage to him, the Nemean games were held in his honor, and Pindar's song praises him as well as the victor. In reminding the god of his investment in this contest, family, and victory, Pindar also seeks his favor. The appeal is general but may also look to hope of victories in the future at even more prestigious competitions. It is not clear what the four virtues are nor how they are associated with the three stages of life. Pindar is not speaking of *arete* solely as merit revealed in athletic competitions, but of more general kinds of virtue. Good judgment, knowing what is appropriate to each stage of life and acting accordingly, is an important aspect of this virtue, and the victor, though still young, has already shown that he has it. Pindar next compares his song to a sacrificial offering of milk and honey, calling attention to the all-important religious dimension of his art and its power properly to judge goodness. His poem (which he is apparently late in delivering) soars like an eagle, bird of Zeus, which grips his bloody prey in his talons. The poet, a predator like Achilles, rises above lesser poets, who are compared to daws. Aristocleides, past Aeginetan heroes, Achilles, and Pindar have all risen to the top, the pinnacles of their respective fields of endeavor, and won out.

Pindar places Aristocleides and his other noble patrons in a tradition of male aristocratic achievement. In victory songs such as *Nemean* 3, Pindar expresses a new, post-Homeric ethos of achievement. The social context of achievement is a community of illustrious men. The merit of the outstanding individual, the victor, is the best fulfillment of human *arete*. A noble individual is the product of a noble family and community; he is born into the heritage of an illustrious past to enact the present moment, which equals it. This view of achievement and the strategies for recognizing it are archetypes. They became central to the ideology of patriarchy and are integral to the ways we continue to identify, evaluate, and reward merit in modern times.

How was achievement regarded in fifth-century Athens? The views of Homer, Hesiod, and Pindar provided the foundations for a tradition on which subsequent constructions of achievement were built. In *Whose Justice? Which Rationality?*[22] Alasdair MacIntyre identifies seven spheres of activity in the Homeric and post-Homeric worlds in which *arete* was exercised:

> warfare and combat; seamanship; athletic and gymnastic activity; epic, lyric, and dramatic poetry; farming both arable and the management of animals; rhetoric; and the making and sustaining of the communities of kinship and the household and later of the city-state. To this list architecture, sculpture, and painting were to be added, as were the intellectual enquiries of mathematics, philosophy, and theology.[23]

A man's skill in any of these spheres would be recognized by others who engaged in the same occupations and, in some cases, by his fellow citizens at large. Taken together, these activities, some of them involving specialized areas of expertise, comprised the collective cultural life of the *polis*. With the exception of household management, not one was an activity in which women were allowed to participate, an exclusion MacIntyre does not acknowledge.

Positive and negative paradigms of female virtue and fame were set in Homer. At the end of the *Odyssey,* the spirits of Penelope's slain suitors descend to Hades, where they meet the spirit of Agamemnon, killed by his unfaithful wife Clytemnestra and her lover Aegisthus. Agamemnon, hearing of Odysseus's homecoming, far happier than his own, exclaims:

> Fortunate son of Laertes, resourceful Odysseus,
> the wife you have possessed has truly great virtue (*arete*):
> So good were the thoughts of the exemplary daughter of
> Icarius. How well was she mindful of Odysseus, her lawful
> husband. Therefore, the fame of her virtue will never
> perish, and the immortals will fashion a lovely song for
> mortals about prudent Penelope. Not so the daughter of
> Tyndarus, who plotted evil deeds and killed her lawful
> husband. Hateful will be her song among men, and harsh will
> be the reputation that she will hand on the race of
> women, even to her who does good deeds. (*Od*.24.192-202)[24]

A woman's *arete,* exemplified by Penelope, is loyalty and fidelity to her husband and her "prudence." Though in a woman, prudence is often virtually synonymous with compliance, Penelope's resourcefulness and cunning are exceptional and make her a worthy match for her exceptional husband.[25] As we shall see later, a Greek woman's nature (*physis*) is defined according to a male-assigned code of sexual and social behavior. Woman is not thought of as having capacities or abilities, save the "ability" to be judged good or evil according to the criteria of that code.

In the fifth century, the ethic of achievement was extended from heroic and aristocratic warriors and athletes to a new and broader membership: Athenian male citizens embodying the collective entity Athens.[26] What was this new kind of *arete*, liberated from its traditional associations with noble birth? Who now could rightly claim to know and represent it? Prominent men of Athens and, of course, philosophers. When it came to principles of public morals—questions such as "What is virtue?" or "What is justice?"—Socrates would seem to be our man. Conventional wisdom, at least as described by him in Plato's *Apology* at the end of the fifth century, held that everyone more or less knew what values such as virtue, justice, or wisdom were, in the same way a carpenter knows woodworking and a doctor, medicine. But, Socrates objects, people seem to confuse ability or technical skill with wisdom or moral knowledge. No mortal, himself included, he argues, knows what virtue or moral knowledge really is. Only the gods know. It is possible, however, that he himself—now on trial on charges of corrupting the youth of Athens and impiety—knows just a little more than most (as the Delphic oracle has said) because he at least knows that he does not know. Without knowing what either virtue or moral knowledge is, Socrates the ironist argues, how can anyone know who does or does not have it? Socrates' show of dire scepticism about the value of human knowledge was, in part at least, a defensive strategy as well as an intellectual challenge to his fellow citizens. How could a man who professed such deference to the greater knowledge of the gods be found guilty of impiety? Easily, thought his fellow citizens, who knew that the philosopher was no arch traditionalist and condemned him to death. Socrates' trial and its outcome suggest that the difference between men and gods and the assumption that the gods were wiser than men was waning, and if traditional religious views were yielding to a more secular outlook, the need to defend them was felt all the more fiercely.

Thirty years earlier, in 429 B.C., the Athenian statesman Pericles delivered a public eulogy honoring the soldiers who had died in the previous year's fighting against Sparta. The substance of the speech is recorded by Thucydides, historian of the long conflict between the two cities usually referred to as the Peloponessian War. Whereas Pindar praised an outstanding individual who has honored his family and city, Pericles-Thucydides praises the citizen-soldiers, collectively, for their military-civic virtues. He also transfers the rhetoric of praise to the city-state as a social, political, imperial, artistic, and intellectual entity.[27] The dead citizen-soldiers collectively fill the role of the Pindaric victor; Athens, standing in for both family and *polis*, represents the tradition of achievement. The city-state, as Arlene Saxonhouse points out, is unified by a common vision and common goals; it "exists in the realm of speech, the creation of male intellect."[28] The fallen men have added to the past glories of the city, thus becoming part of its future fame. The power of commemoration to extend the fame of the war heroes informs the speech. Athenian collective *arete*, Pericles-Thucydides claims, already enjoys world renown; the speech itself merely articulates and reveals it, just as Athenians themselves have revealed their inborn virtue. In the democratic *polis*, all male citizens are presumed to have some form or degree of *arete*, no longer the exclusive prerogative of the mythic hero or noble-born aristocrat.[29] In the following paraphrase and summary of the speech, we shall see just how this rhetorical extension worked to valorize Athens and her male citizens.

In an adroit blend of fifth-century rationalism, sophism, and skepticism, Pericles' opening remarks forestall (imaginary?) criticism by addressing the difficulties of making a eulogy worthy of the dead. How does a speaker match noble deeds with fitting words? It ought to be sufficient to reveal the honor of men noble in action through action, the religious ceremony just concluded. Nor should the achievement of many be entrusted to one man, who may speak well or badly. How to speak with due measure, giving each aspect of the subject appropriate emphasis and treatment, in a matter where even the appearance of truth is uncertain. The man familiar with the facts may feel that the speaker's account falls short of what he knows or wants to hear, while the man who hasn't witnessed the event or known anyone who has listens, feels envious, and decides the speaker is exaggerating, if the deeds exceed what he thinks he could do himself.[30] These remarks serve to express the speaker's awareness of the power of language and its possible misuses:

> It is just and proper that our ancestors receive the honor of remembrance on this occasion. They inhabited this land for a long time, passing it on a free country from generation to generation through their virtue. They deserve praise, as do the fathers of everyone present today. They acquired the rule of empire through dint of effort—an empire which the present generation has transformed into a state self-sufficient in peace and war. Pericles will reveal the constitution and character that have made the city great; afterwards he will praise the dead (2.36)

All who have gone before shared in collective Athenian *arete*, yet here is a new and important sphere of action: the acquisition of imperial power, established in Pericles' lifetime (in part as a result of his policies) and the justifiable dominion of one sovereign state over another.

> Praise of the city: Pericles next describes the basic principles of Athenian democratic society: equality before the law in private disputes, and, in respect to public worth, each man is valued not by his social class or wealth, but by his *arete*. The religious and cultural life of Athens enriches and recreates her citizens, and because of her size and greatness, the city enjoys good things from all over the world. While Spartans are mere uncultivated brawn (they value only physical development and a sparse life-style and culture), Athenians fight for a noble way of life. They love beauty with economy and wisdom without weakness. Wealth is valued for what it can accomplish. Everyone participates in public affairs and informs himself in public debate before acting. Acts of courage are motivated by considered judgment. Unlike other people, Athenians exercise their *arete* toward others with generosity and without calculating self-interest. (2.37-40)

Pericles first mentions what has remained a basic principle of Western law since it was established at Athens, the equality of all (male) citizens under the law (*isonomia*). He next sweeps aside the archaic notion that *arete* is the special prerogative of aristocrats; all citizens can and should use their individual talents on behalf of the city. Athenian cultural and intellectual life is richer than that of other cities, its citizens are more cultivated, public spirited, economically judicious, and nobler in character than other peoples:

> All things considered, Athens is an education [= model] to all Greece. Her *arete* is such that she is stronger/ nobler than her reputation; an enemy does not feel shame to be defeated by her, nor do other states which are subject to her feel they are ruled by unworthy men. The men who have died were worthy of the city. Their fate revealed their own *arete*, both as first sign and ultimate proof of it, regardless of their individual virtues and vices. Those who survive them should cultivate the same spirit. Every citizen should think about the power of the city every day, and become a lover of her. He should consider her deserving of his *arete*, his best and most noble efforts. Those who have died will be remembered everywhere: The whole earth is the grave of famous men. The living must now imitate them, recognizing that good fortune is freedom and freedom courage; the threat [from Sparta] should not be minimized. The thoughtful man would find death that came from weakness a worse evil than death that came in the midst of strength and hope shared with fellow-citizens—scarcely noticed. The parents of the dead should take comfort from the fact that

they share their sons' honor. Younger men, sons or brothers of the dead, must now enter a contest (*agon*) to equal or surpass their relatives' glory, and it will not be easy. (2.41-45)

Athens's *arete*, Pericles claims, makes her worthy of dominion over other states. He conflates power as virtue with power as force, particularly in creating the fiction that enemies and subject states bow willingly to Athens because of her superior qualities. He enjoins citizens always to hold the city's power in their minds, and also to become her lover, contending on her behalf as a Pindaric athlete competed to achieve victory.[31] Parents and male relatives of the dead share in their community of achievement. Competition to achieve is a legacy handed down from one generation to the next.

Finally, Pericles addresses the widows of the fallen men. Using the same terms of praise that inform the entire speech, he brilliantly subverts and distorts them to give them negative and opposite meanings:

If it is proper for me to mention something about the virtue (*arete*) of the women widowed in this war, I shall reveal everything with a brief word of advice. For you, the basis of a great reputation is not to be inferior to your given nature, and for your fame with regard to either virtue or blame among men to be as small as possible. (2.45)

The widows do not share in the Athenian community of achievement or in the glory of the fallen men in the same ways as the fathers, sons, and brothers do. Because they are excluded from action, they cannot become emulators or rivals of that glory. Women's *arete* is, like that of men, determined by "their given nature," which is inherently different from men's. Women's nature (and therefore, *arete*) seems to be of a single kind. That is, all women have the same nature and it is determined by their gender. Since all women do not have the same reputation, there may be some individual differences among women. Yet the differences are confined by the upper limit of their collective nature, a kind of glass ceiling. A woman's special excellence is not made manifest through any inborn ability or productive action; it is revealed solely through her social (though not exclusively sexual) behavior. Moreover, Pericles subverts the expected relationship between virtue and praise as it applies to outstanding men. Great *arete* deserves praise in equal measure. Only the most adroit speaker of praise is able successfully to raise the specter of vice or blame.[32] Praise rescues arete from a fate worse than blame—

silence.[33] The widows should not aspire to a great reputation, but to the smallest possible one, regardless of the measure of their virtue. Even virtuous women should be scarcely seen or heard. Pericles offers no praise to the widows, calling attention, as one might, to their moral support of their men, to their sacrifice on behalf of the *polis*, or the honor that sacrifice has earned for them, because praise seeks the maximum, the superlative, and the material the women offer for praise is inherently minimal.[34]

Pericles translates many of the terms of the achievement ethic we observed in Pindar's victory songs to adult Athenian male citizens and to Athens as culture, society, and State. The city-state is valorized as a collective, heroic entity,[35] and, ideally at least, adult male citizens strive to enhance its excellence and primacy. Collectively, they work to that end, and in this sense they exercise a kind of cooperative *arete*, although competitive *arete* has been both their means and their goal. Additionally, Athens competes with Sparta and other city-states for primacy of empire and wins imperial power, which she deserves to hold, now and in the future, because of the kind of society she is and the kind of culture she has: the best. Pericles' arguments rationalize the domination of one political entity over another on the grounds that its ideology and institutions are inherently superior. His description of Athens as a nation-state aptly fits Benedict Anderson's definition of an "imagined political community." Anderson connects the rise of the idea of nationalism in the eighteenth century with beliefs about death and immortality: A man is mortal, a nation eternal. Self-sacrifice on behalf of the community gives a man a small share in its immortality. This is very much what Pericles argued many centuries earlier.[36]

War. *Arete*. Competition. Work. Achievement. Success and Fame. Transcendence over death to gain immortality. These are the values that govern exclusively male endeavors enacted in a collective and public context. They constitute an idological legacy which was imposed on society as a whole. Before turning to the exclusions of this legacy in the next two chapters, let us sum up and think about what we have been discussing. The texts we have looked at make the following arguments. The aristocratic warriors of the Homeric age, the aristocratic rulers depicted in tragic drama, and the aristocratic contenders in the panhellenic games were believed to have inborn powers (to fight, to rule, to compete: *arete* as capability) derived from their birth, class, and gender. They also were believed to possess superior moral virtue *(arete* as ethical value) and judgment, and they were seen, therefore, as moral examples. They held the power to define virtue in both senses, and they embodied it. Military engagement, as both single combat between two opposing warriors and as a contest between armies, determined who was first; the first was also the best: a winner. Winners in both war and athletic competitions honored their families and communities and were, in turn, honored by them. Victors and other outstanding men joined a wider community of achievement, they served as models for future generations, they deserved to be remembered for all time. Athenian democracy forged a link between military and other competitive activities and the civic spheres. Citizen-soldiers, as ideally described by Pericles, strove to enoble the city through their prowess and to rule wisely: the best men, heroes.

How does the achievement ethic manifest itself in our culture and society today? Let us think about five overlapping areas: the valuation of competition and its supposed opposite, cooperation; the legacy of the Greek notion of *arete* and its confusions of capability, power, and moral virtue; the idea and practice of work (relative to productivity and achievement); the achievement ethic and power as domination; and the human cost of the ideal of transcendence.

Striving toward excellence confers a kind of heroic status. Single-combat in battle was the prototype for determining the comparative *arete* of two men and establishing the primacy of one, the victor, over the other, the vanquished. It established a model for revealing excellence through competition. According to Hesiod, men also compete in their everyday work, in such peacetime activities as farming and artisanship. The determination of excellence and men's nonheroic striving to establish degrees of expertise and social rank are linked. Athletic contests such as the panhellenic games institutionalized competitive strife in peacetime. The ideology of the conflict between nation-powers, Athens and Sparta, is expressed in the same terms. Although the aim of war is to inflict injury, in most peacetime contests injury does not occur in the form of death or bodily harm. Rather, losers suffer other kinds of injuries: loss of the rewards of winning—status, money, power, and reputation, and loss of self-esteem. This dynamic, our cultural legacy, permeates our own social norms and practices. As we reconsider values today, we may ask ourselves: Do we want to perpetuate this ethic? Do we want the kind of society in which gains and losses, benefits and deprivations are major forces in determining the course of people's lives?

The admission of women into competitive arenas and domains of achievement has been and still is a prime social issue in the twentieth century. Cultural attitudes toward women's nature and capabilities, which, as we shall see in the next chapter, are indebted to Greek and Roman views, are a major obstacle. Do women have a nature, and if it is not what tradition says it is, what is it? Today, we look for further enlightenment about human, both male and female, nature, from the sciences and social sciences, particularly genetics and sociobiology.

Since women, the most significant Others, have been socialized to care for and serve the needs of others, it is not surprising that many women regard the intrinsically hostile and adversarial stance of military and other competitive activities as alien, especially given, to use Janice Moulton's phrase, "the unhappy conflation of aggression with success."[37] It is a commonplace in our culture that excellence is revealed through competition and that it is, in fact, seldom attained or recognized by any other means.[38] Moreover, we, like the Greeks, see competition as opposed to cooperation, in defiance of the fact that in many areas of human endeavor, goals can be achieved only through the combined and shared efforts of many. By tradition, cooperation is at best a secondary value. Some might say it is what those who don't have what it takes to be first fall back on. Cooperation in the competition-cooperation dichotomy does have its place: Men in a civic setting where competition is the dominant value must cooperate for the sake of civil order or to unite against an outside enemy. Referring to the power of the "weak," women and slaves, however, cooperation becomes a euphemism for subordination and compliance. As the Other value, it is the value of Others devoted to serving the quests of those who compete and achieve.

This simplistic and antithetic ordering of values helps us to understand why it is difficult to think anew about difference in a democratic society: dominate or be subordinate, nurture or succeed, compete or cooperate, live your daily life or reach for immortality. Are these the only alternatives?

Arete as "power to" manifests itself in labor or work (active *ponos*), and, as we have said, the most valued work is that which leads to achievement. Because "power to" was conflated with "power over," prowess in battle with conquest, achievement was inevitably associated with domination. Thus, the achievement ethic became—and still is— also an ethic of domination. In the Greco-Roman world, women were not perceived as having *arete* as excellence or capacity, they did not compete, and they did not achieve. The association of excellence and power both reflected and perpetuated a definition of social and moral authority based in dominance: over those allegedly without *arete*; within the hierarchy, dominance over those with allegedly less *arete*.

The achievement ethic informs notions of productive work and productivity we have received from classical antiquity. It assumes a hierarchy of power built upon merit, and this arrangement determines the conditions under which outstanding work is produced, the pool of potential producers, and the avenues for bestowing and receiving recognition. What is called excellence is achieved when new work emerges that meets the standards of an elite group because it reinforces their point of view and values.

Merit and meritocracies in America today—especially in educational institutions and in professional, business, and government organizations—are the domains of prerogative and privilege. Excellence as power has long masqueraded as merit, and still does wherever the traditional ideology of achievement prevails over productive work. Ideals of economic justice and equal access and opportunity for all compel us to recognize that this is the case. As the main ethic of the dominant Western culture, the achievement ethic holds that only productive work has value, and that some kinds of productive work have more value than others. The most valued work in a market economy is work that generates capital. To the extent that members of the workforce do so, they are valuable. This modern variant of the achievement ethic discounts values outside the domain of economics, market value.

Nonproductive labor—work which contributes merely to sustaining everyday, physical existence and which women and nonprivileged men have long routinely performed[39]—has long been discounted. Thus manual (in our society, blue- or pink-collar) labor has a lower status than professional and other white-collar jobs. Work that engages the mind has greater value than physical labor, a reflection of the cultural valuation of mind over body. Women's reproductive labor, moreover, although it combines a bodily activity and a creative act par excellence, has also been discounted.

Shall we choose to value the achievement ethic to the same degree and in the same ways it has been valued in the past? We are searching for an accommodation between productive ane reproductive labor in terms other than the traditional male/female division. We are only just beginning to consider the hidden assumptions about work implicit in the achievement ethic, and public debate resounds with practical, everyday issues affecting the well-being of many people, especially families with minor children. Today, women are present in the work force in great numbers, but they earn less than men. If they have children, they have major difficulties finding adequate and affordable childcare. Women who want to stay home with their children may not be able to afford to do so, and if they are single heads of households and do so, they have no income. Women in the work force have long encountered a glass ceiling which prevents them from rising to higher-income, decision-making positions in the public sphere—business, industry, and government. Many men, too, find themselves at odds with the achievement ethic, on temperamental or philosophical grounds. And although men traditionally have access to achievement (and women do not), many are excluded through poverty, lack of access to education, class, and race. Some people choose to march to a different drummer and adopt alternative life-styles, turn to Eastern philosophies, take "the road less traveled" (M. Scott Peck), or "follow their bliss" (Joseph Campbell). We call these values alternative or countercultural. In a later chapter we shall see that countercultural trends are also part of the Greco-Roman legacy.

The heroic and achievement ethics were formulated to glorify powerful men privileged by birth, class, and gender. Those with power also held moral authority, they embodied and named moral virtue, and they defined and prescribed values for others. The aristocratic monopoly on *arete*—despite its extension to Athenian adult male citizens—was both an avenue to power and the outcome of already possessing it. But even the best men did not have the *arete* of the gods. They could not master death, they suffered from existential blindness (a limited ability to foresee the consequences of their actions and the outcome of events), and they were prone to be sabotaged by inner forces such as pride and anger. The quest for achievement is an attempt to overcome human fallibility and vulnerability, as well as a wish to transcend death.

Powerful men forged and enforced social values in Greek (and Roman) society, yet it was clear to some Greek thinkers, such as Homer and Sophocles, that there was a discrepancy between moral capability and the achievements of civilization. We perceive the same discontinuity and have, I suspect, come to regard it as one of the failings of the human condition. As a society, we are ambivalent about the relation between achievement and moral virtue. Like the Greeks, we search for examples, or role models as we now call them. We expect a higher standard of ethics from the more prestigious members of society, such as government or religious officials, those invested with authority. Many, especially young people, look up to sports and entertainment celebrities as models. Is it really possible, we wonder, to be in the thick of the fray and to get to the top—and still be good? We would all like to think so. No one has absolute control, we ruefully admit, least of all over himself.

Must we accept the Greek vision of the human condition as one defined by powerlessness? Are the best responses to the fact of death passivity, a kind of moral abdication, and escapism? Must power and control be equated with achievement, immortality, and the perpetuation of male rule? I do not think so. Is there a moral foundation for an inclusive human community, different from the values of the community of individuals who achieve? We all belong to the community of nature. We all die. But it is also true that we all live. According to the achievement ethic, in order to overcome death, man must escape from embodied existence, from nature itself. We shall see in the next two chapters how that aspiration fostered a cultural dichotomy between nature and culture and how women, excluded from achievement and designated as the primary Others, were confined within nature and (became scapegoats for) the vulnerabilities of bodily existence.

Notes

[1] Annie Leclerc, *Parole des femmes*, in Elaine Marks and Isabelle de Courtivron, eds., *New French Feminisms. An Anthology* (New York: Schocken, 1981), p.82.

[2] Moira Gatens, *Feminism and Philosophy. Perspectives on Difference and Equality* (Bloomington: Indiana Unversity Press, 1991), p.121.

[3] "Classics" from Latin *classis*, a class of citizens determined by ownership of property; a military levy; fleet. Feminists are now questioning the authority of cultural constructs expressed in civic and military terms. See, e.g., Judith Hallett, "Feminist Theory, Historical Periods, Literary Canons, and the Study of Greco-Roman Antiquity" in Nancy Sorkin Rabinowitz and Amy Richlin, *Feminist Theory and the Classics* (New York: Routledge, 1993), pp.44-72.

[4] On the the conduct of American foreign policy as moral mission, see Mona Harrington, *The Dream of Deliverance in American Politics* (New York: Knopf, 1986).

[5] Elaine Scarry, *The Body in Pain. The Making and Unmaking of the World* (New York: Oxford University Press, 1985).

[6] On the alleged two kinds of power or virtue (*arete*), see Alasdair MacIntyre, *Whose Justice? Which Rationality?* (South Bend, IN: Notre Dame, 1988), Chapters 2-4; and A.W.H. Adkins, *From the Many to the One. A Study of Personality and Views of Human Nature in the Context of Ancient Greek Society, Values, and Beliefs* (Ithaca: Cornell University Press, 1970), and *Merit and Responsibiity* (Oxford: Clarendon Press, 1960). Adkins, who discusses competition and cooperation as opposites, concludes that the former is very prominent in Greek culture, while there is little evidence for "cooperative" virtue, which he characterizes as the "quieter" virtue and, not incidentally, more suitable for a woman. Douglas Cairns, *Aidos. The Psychology and Ethics of Honor and Shame in Ancient Greek Literature* (Oxford: Clarendon Press, 1993), pp. 50-51, 66-68, 83-87, and 100-103, finds the competition-cooperative distinction of limited use in understanding Greek culture, since both come into play in the feeling of *aidos*, which is concerned with "how things look" and "what people say," in other words, with *time*, honor.

[7] Alasdair MacIntyre, *Whose Justice? Which Rationality?*, pp.27ff., discusses the place of the *agon* in Greek and, in particular, Athenian culture. See also Philip Slater, *The Glory of Hera* (Boston: Beacon Press, 1968), pp.36-37. In *Shame and Necessity* (Berkeley and Los Angeles: University of California Press, 1993), Bernard Williams suggests, as I do, that Greek ethical ideas are very similar to our own. Contrary to the claims of Bruno Snell, E.R. Dodds, A.W.H. Adkins, and others, early Greeks conceived individuals as having a unified moral identity, they had experience of guilt as well as shame, and they also had notions of moral responsibility. Williams questions the view (originally Dodds's) that the early Greeks had a shame culture. In a shame culture, men do what is right because they are ashamed not to and strive for success in order to avoid the disgrace of failure. The implicit confusion of morality and achievement is inherent in the Greek language as well as in these critical interpretations. While Williams believes that the importance of competition and competitive virtue in Greek ethics has been overestimated, I think that achievement measured through competitive activities was central to Greek ethics from its beginnings and that what I am calling the achievement ethic pervaded ancient culture.

[8] John Winkler, *The Constraints of Desire. The Anthropology of Gender in Ancient Greece* (New York: Routledge, 1990). The quotations are from pp.27 and 43, respectively.

[9] Liddell-Scott-Jones, *Greek-English Lexicon*.

[10] Ernout-Meillet, *Dictionnaire etymologique de la langue greque ancienne*; Walde-Hofmann, *Etymologische Worterbuch der lateinische Sprache*. For designations of the man of *arete* as *areion* and esp. *aristos*, see Gregory Nagy, *The Best of the Achaians. Concepts of the Hero in Archaic Greek Poetry* (Baltimore:

Johns Hopkins University Press, 1979), pp.26-41.

[11] Seth Schein, *The Mortal Hero* (Berkeley and Los Angeles: University of California Press, 1984), p.80. Nel Noddings, *Women and Evil* (Berkeley and Los Angeles: University of California Press, 1992), pp.179-183, discusses connections between war and striving in Greek thought.

[12] On *eris*, see Nagy, *The Best of the Achaeans*, Chapters 11, "On Strife and the Human Condition," pp.213-221, and 19, "More on Strife and the Human Condition," pp.309-316.

[13] For discussion of this passage, see Mihae Spariosu, *Dionysus Reborn* (Ithaca: Cornell University Press, 1989), "Introduction. Play, Power, and the Western Mentality," pp.12-14. Sparioso discerns in Hesiod the beginnings of "a dialectic between play and work" and "the long process of separating play from unmediated power and violence" (p.14).

[14] Fr. LXXXII Kahn, in Charles Kahn, *The Art and Thought of Herclitus* (Cambridge: Cambridge University Press, 1979), pp.205-210.

[15] Kahn, p. 207, section 4, doubts the reading *chreomena*. As my translation of fr. LXXXII indicates, I believe that his suggestion "are ordained (as by an oracle)" is correct.

[16] "Beyond the Wasteland," in Dorothy Thompson, ed., *Over Our Dead Bodies. Women Against the Bomb* (London: Virago, 1983), p.7, cited by Sara Ruddick, *Maternal Thinking. Toward A Politics of Peace* (Boston: Beacon Press, 1989), p.270, n26.

[17] The tradition of holding competitive games in honor of a dead man is seen in Homer's *Iliad* 23 (Achilles' friend Patroclus); Vergil's Aeneas holds funeral games for his father, Anchises, in *Aeneid* 5.

[18] For the epinician poetry of praise and its social, economic, and literary, and religious contexts, see Frank J. Nisetich's Introduction to his translation of *Pindar's Victory Songs* (Baltimore: Johns Hopkins University Press, 1980), pp.1-77; Leslie Kurke, *The Traffic in Praise: Pindar and the Poetics of Social Economy* (Ithaca: Cornell University Press, 1991); Kevin Crotty, *Song and Action: The Victory Odes of Pindar* (Baltimore: Johns Hopkins University Press, 1982).

[19] For the cooptation of female creative and generative powers into patriarchal theory, see Page duBois, *Sowing the Body. Psychoanalysis and Ancient Representations of Women* (Chicago: University of Chicago Press, 1988), pp.7-17 and 169-183.

[20] E.L. Bundy emphasized the reciprocal relation of these two kinds of *arete* in *Studia Pindarica* (Berkeley: University of California Press, 1986), originally published as *Studia Pindarica I and II* (1962).

[21] The victor's *arete* is, variously, his inherent (and inherited) talent and his

nobility of birth and spirit, which, together with divine favor and hard work, lead to his achievement and success.

[22] Alasdair MacIntyre, *Whose Justice? Which Rationality?*, "The Division of the Post-Homeric Inheritance," pp.30-46.

[23] *Whose Justice? Which Rationality?*, p.30. The ranking itself is canonical, as Nadya Aisenberg has pointed out to me.

[24] For discussion of this passage. see A.W.H. Adkins, *Merit and Responsibility* (Oxford: Clarendon Press, 1960), p.37 and n9, and Sarah Pomeroy, *Goddesses, Whores, Wives, and Slaves. Women in Classical Antiquity* (New York: Schocken, 1975), pp.21f.

[25] John Winkler, "Penelope's Cunning—And Homer's," pp.129-161 in *The Constraints of Desire. The Anthropology of Sex and Gender in Ancient Greece* (New York: Routledge, 1990).

[26] To be an Athenian citizen was to be an autochthonous male: Nicole Loraux, *The Children of Athena. Athenian Ideas about Citizenship and the Division of the Sexes*, trans. Caroline Levine (Princeton: Princeton University Press, 1993), pp.111-143. (originally published as *L'enfance d'Athene* [Paris, 1981]).

[27] For the encomiastic tradition as applied to the *polis* and its role in creating the language of civic ideology, see Nicole Loraux, *The Invention of Athens. The Funeral Oration in the Classical City*, trans. A. Sheridan (Cambridge: Harvard University Press, 1986).

[28] Arlene Saxonhouse, *Fear of Diversity. The Birth of Political Science in Ancient Greek Thought* (Chicago: University of Chicago Press, 1992), pp.117-122. The quotation is from p.121.

[29] Nicole Loraux, *The Invention of Athens*, points out that Athenians appropriated *arete* and made it an autochthonous quality. As Saxonhouse also argues, the city replaces the family, thereby displacing women and generation from women with birth from the land. For *arete* as a fifth-century Athenian value, see Alasdair MacIntyre, *After Virtue* (South Bend, IN: Notre Dame University Press, 1981), Chap. 3, and Elizabeth Spelman, *Inessential Woman. Problems of Exclusion in Feminist Thought* (Boston: Beacon Press, 1988), Chap. 1.

[30] For the problem of the accuracy of the spoken word, see Thucydides, Book 1, chapter 22.

[31] Note the transference of *eros* as sexual pursuit to the pursuit of achievement.

[32] Pindar, for example, does so to point out the vulnerability of the outstanding man to the envy of those whose achievements are inferior to his. The just poet of praise forestalls envy, or tries to do so, by telling the truth—how good the victor really is.

[33] The poet of praise rescues achievement from silence and hence oblivion. For the interconnected themes of praise, truth, envy, and silence, see also *Nemean* 8.19-44.

[34] On women in Pericles' speech, see also Arlene Saxonhouse, *Fear of Diversity*, pp.4-5, 50-51, 58-59, 151, 233-234.

[35] Nel Noddings, *Women and Evil*, pp.189f., observes that "an ideology of individualism supports the competitive, adversarial way of life," and that this, "the warrior model," "masquerades as a community model" in ancient Greek culture.

[36] Benedict Anderson, *Imagined Communities. Reflections on the Origins and Spread of Nationalism* (London: Verco, 1983), pp. 15-19. Moreover, "'official nationalism' was from the start a conscious, self-protective policy, intimately linked to the preservation of imperial-dynastic interests . . .The one persistent feature of this style of nationalism was, and is, that it is official—i.e., something emenating from the state, and serving the interests of the state first and foremost" (p. 145). On the common language of imperialist ideology, see Edward Said, *Culture and Imperialism* (New York: Knopf, 1993), pp.15-19, 43-61, and passim.

[37] Janice Moulton,"A Paradigm of Philosophy: The Adversary Method," in Sandra Harding and Merril B. Hintikka, eds., *Discovering Reality. Feminist Perspectives on Epistemology, Metaphysics, Methodology, and Philosophy of Science* (Dordrecht: Reidel, 1983), pp.149-164. The quotation is from p.149. Moulton points out in the conclusion of this essay that the conflation is not only unhappy but unnecessary.

[38] See the remarks of Sandra Harding in "Why Has the Sex/Gender System Become Visible Only Now?" in Harding and Hintikka, *Discovering Reality*, p.314:
> [A]s recent re-evaluations of the history of science have revealed, scientific discoveries are not the "Eureka!" accomplishments of individual geniuses which traditional history and philosophy of science would lead us to believe. Rather, they seem to be slow and collective processes of "paradigm shift" marked by dawning recognitions of the following sorts. The known problems for available theories remain unsolvable within those theories. Observations which cannot be accounted for in a systematic way by the existing theories probably should be regarded as significant indicators that the existing theories' concepts and methodologies are too impoverished to enable us to grasp important regularities in nature or social life. Alternative theories can be developed which will account systematically for the previously observed regularities as well as for the new and "recalcitrant" observations, and which will open new and fruitful research issues. Paradigm shifts have frequently occurred in the context of broad social movements aimed at redistributing political power. Of

course, the "discovery" of the sex/gender system has occurred in the context of the Second Women's Movement.

[39] Olive Schreiner, *Women and Labor* (London: Virago, 1978 [1911]); Dorothy Smith, "A Sociology of Women," in Julia A. Sherman and Evelyn Torton Beck, eds., *The Prism of Sex. Essays in the Sociology of Knowledge* (Madison: University of Wisconsin Press, 1979), pp.135-187: "In general, women's work routines and the organization of their daily lives do not conform to the `voluntaristic' mode or to the model upon which an agentic style of sociology might be based. Women have little opportunity for the exercise of mastery and control" (p.151) and "We can see then how the silencing of women . . . suppresses not only women but the work they represent and the dimensions of existence which locates, among other things, that fear of death which Schultz holds as the fundamental anxiety. The fear of death is the final announcement to the thinker that his occupancy of the conceptual mode of bifurcated consciousness is necessarily temporary. He is precipitated into time. Women's lack of authority to speak, their exclusion from the circle of those who make the tradition, who make the discourse, means that the work that suppresses the concrete and material locus of consciousness is also silenced" (pp.169f.).

For work as a determinant of power in contemporary society, see also Iris Marion Young, "Five Faces of Oppression," in Thomas Wartenberg, ed., *Rethinking Power* (Albany,NY: State University of New York Press, 1992), pp.187ff.

> Woman threatened man's virility, his valor, and his life.
> Robert Parker[1]

> Ancient Greek philosophy showed that alterity, otherness, is the same thing as negation, therefore Evil.
> Simone de Beauvoir[2]

> It is as if women were the keepers of a dirty little secret that humanity emerges from nonhuman nature into society in the life of the species, and the person. The process of nurturing an unsocialized, undifferentiated human infant into an adult person—the socialization of the organic—is the bridge between nature and culture. The western male bourgeois subject then extracts himself from the realm of the organic to become a public citizen, as if born from the head of Zeus.
> Ynestra King[3]

> Thus [in Platonic and Aristotelian thought] woman's lack of spirituality, her lack of a full-fledged active intelligence, justifies her social subordination as it rationalizes her moral inferiority. Biologically and metaphysically deficient, she lives at the level of matter, where her moral and social aspirations are accordingly fixed.
> Hilde Hein[4]

Chapter 4

Construction of the Other 1. Flight from Nature, the Body, and Woman

The desire to escape from death that informed Greek culture also required escape from life, a concomitant quest: to avoid being caught up in the web of nature, to reduce living "in" a body to an absolute minimum, and to distance male selfhood from woman, the designated representative of all the allegedly negative implications of being human.

Althought everyone perforce belongs to the community of nature, the male community of achievement sought as much as it dared to discount the inclusiveness, homogeneity, and anonymity such membership was thought to imply. From this orientation arose the major polarities which have shaped Western thought:[5] female and male, nature (earth) and culture, the body (sensations, emotions) and mind (reason). The terms of each pair were associated with one another, connections apparent in early Greek myth and thought: female/nature/body and male/culture/mind. Thus, these oppositions were present in Greek thought well before Plato and Aristotle, and, indeed, well before the beginnings of Greek philosophy. In this chapter we shall explore these antitheses. We shall also see how mind and body came to be dissociated, and the mind (together with its most valued capabilities: language, reason, and judgment) associated with masculinity and the body (sensations, emotions) with femininity.

The valuation of maleness, culture, and mind and the denigration of their so-called opposites reflects a pervasive obsession with control in Greco-Roman thought. When nature has been regarded as an untrustworthy paradigm for values, the very reason has often been that life in nature—embodied existence—is implicated in multiplicity, complexity, diversity, fluidity, inconsistency, mutability, and transcience. As creatures of nature, everyone is implicated in bodily existence—its needs, pleasures, pains, and other sensory and emotional experiences. Mind (reason, intellect) and spirit have long been considered the most godlike—and most stable and lasting—aspects of man. The body, on the other hand, being both prone to corruption and apt to corrupt, is implicated in unstable and destabilizing forces. Creatures of time, we are subject to constant change, a multiplicity of internal and external experiences. Merely by virtue of being human, we are not one but many; we see and are seen differently at different times. Shifting appearances may (or may not) reflect shifting realities. The longing for values that either are or ought to be immutable, lasting, and universal is a very ancient desire, and it is at odds with the essential quality of human experience. It is not by chance that reactions against culture in both ancient and modern times have often been expressed as a desire to return to nature: the longing for an integrity fragmented by civilization, for a utopia removed from the arbitrary or allegedly corrupt and corrupting requirements of culture.[6]

How did it happen that values derived from universal membership in a community of nature did not become part of dominant Western ethics?[7] Some scholars of European prehistory suggest a partial answer. The archeologist Marija Gimbutas, for example, has shown that in the pre-Indo-European and pre-patriarchal culture of Old Europe, the principal divine power was a goddess who presided over "eternal transformation": endless cycles of generation, death, and regeneration and renewal. "The obvious analogy [to the goddess] would be to Nature itself; through the multiplicity of phenomena and continuing clues of which it is made, one recognizes the fundamental and underlying unity of Nature. The Goddess is immanent rather than transcendent and therefore physically manifest."[8] The work of Gimbutas and others is very suggestive to contemporary feminists, theologians and ethicists in particular, but it is not entirely clear to what extent neolitic cultures offer an alternative model to later, Indo-European, male-dominated culture.[9]

In the Greco-Roman view, implication in nature and natural process is not only unavoidable and therefore necessary, but also inherently dangerous. Major life changes are often rooted in natural events. Anthropologist Arnold van Gennep has pointed out that it is the function of many religious rituals to help people negotiate change by easing them through processes of separation, transition, and reintegration into the community.[10] An aim of many Greek rituals, Robert Parker notes, is purification, "the desire for [restoration] of order" disrupted by the presence of some sort of pollution.[11] Major sources of pollution are birth, death, and "the works of Aphrodite." Birth and death are not controlled events: "the dead or dying man and the parturient woman have lost control of their bodies . . . the accompanying rites of passage can be seen as reassertions of control."[12]

* * * * *

Human excellence (*arete*) rises up like a tree in the green dew,
elevated among wise and just men to the liquid sky. (Pindar, *Nemean* 8.40)

By an irony of existence Greek men found impossible to forget and difficult to forgive, insensate, nonverbal, nonrational, nonpurposive vegetative life possesses powers of generation and regeneration denied to all mortals, both male and female. The fertility of the earth, the renewal of natural process are enviable forces. But, Pindar claims in this passage, *arete* rises to the dwelling place of the Olympian gods and the eternal stars through the praise of good men, just as a tree grows heavenward. Pindar's comparison coopts the generative power of nature and further suggests that immortal praise has the advantage over it: a tree does not live forever, but praise and the name of good men very well may.

To Martha Nussbaum, these lines express a hope that it is possible to escape existence in nature, which she regards (and believes we all regard) as passive:

> A raw sense of the passivity of human beings and their humanity in the world of nature, and a response of both horror and anger at that passivity, lived side by side with and nourished the belief that reason's activity could make safe, and thereby save, our human lives—indeed must save them, if they were to be humanly worth living.[13]

The aspiration to rational self-sufficiency ("this splendid and equivocal hope") "is a central preoccupation of ancient Greek thought about human good." Her reading of the Greek ethical tradition valorizes Platonic-Aristotelean *logos*, reason, over other facets of human nature and incorporates many dualisms prominent in the thought of these two philosophers: pure, active, rational, godlike, immortal, singular, immune to change, abstract, as opposed to polluted, passive, irrational or nonrational, transitory, multiple, mutable, particular.[14]

The antithesis between generation in nature and cultural creation seen in Pindar found its most famous classical expression in Plato's *Symposium*. The philosopher distinguishes between "common Aphrodite," erotic love, the ability human beings share with animals to produce a new life by an act of bodily love and so to perpetuate a family and the species; and the nobler "heavenly Aphrodite," the ability of a few men, inspired by the love of other men, to engage in creative acts of mind and spirit. The artistic and intellectual products of male creativity bring men closer to the gods and immortality and are themselves enduring.[15] Reproduction is the only form of creativity of which women are capable and the only form which they are permitted. Since women are body (matter), unlike men, who are spirit (mind), they belong in nature.[16] Woman, like the earth, generates; men create. The products of her labor, human beings, are "all the same"; the products of male creativity are individual and unique.

While the dichotomy between male culture and female nature is seen in all periods of Greco-Roman thought, it is especially evident in the identification of earth with the female body, the dominant Greek image of sexuality and generation, as Page du Bois shows in *Sowing the Body. Psychoanalysis and Ancient Representations of Women*.[17] This identification, far from validating Freud's castration theory,[18] suggests male fear of expendability, for if earth and woman are autonomous and self-sufficient—able to produce and sustain life without the participation of man—wherein does a man's value lie? The earth/body/woman assimilation is reflected in many Greek religious rituals and myths. Earth and woman are conceived as having great powers: to give or withhold, conceal or bring forth, store up or scatter, and perform actions that may work good or ill for men. In the Homeric poems the earth receives seeds and "produces, gives, and contains" nourishment; it also receives the dead. Sexual intercourse of the gods which takes place on earth affects and ensures the earth's fertility. At *Iliad* 14.346-349 Zeus and Hera make love on Mt. Ida and the earth flowers in response. The union of the corn goddess Demeter and the hero Iasion in a thrice-ploughed field (*Odyssey* 5.125-128, *Theogony* 969-971) produced a son, Ploutos, Wealth. Ritual sexual intercourse, "sacred marriage" (*hieros gamos*), took place as part of state cult practice in some classical city-states, and women played key roles in Athenian religious cult practices of Demeter and Dionysus as intermediaries between nature and culture.[19]

The language of metaphor, as du Bois shows, also reveals the identification of woman and nature. In sources referring back to prehistoric and preagricultural times, woman's body is compared to a field. With the introduction of agriculture, it is likened to a furrow. Later, with the rise of artisanship, the female body is compared with stone, oven, and writing tablet. The generative powers of both earth and woman were thus translated to male modes of production and products through a series of appropriations, which culminates, du Bois suggests, with Plato's transference of erotic and reproductive language to the pursuit of philosophy. Plato's strategy marks the beginning of "a monotheistic, idealistic metaphysics," which charaterizes Western male theory.[20] Greek male culture aspired to escape from nature and the body so that men could realize their godlike qualities as fully as possible. In civic life, the greatest *arete* of man was *logos*, the faculty through which he attained control most comparable to the power of the gods.[21]

The major literary sources for early Greek notions about the disjunctions between gods and men, men and women, and culture and nature are the works of the late-eighth-century B.C. epic poet Hesiod. In the prologue of the *Theogony* (Origins of the Gods), the Muses, daughters of Zeus, appear to Hesiod as he shepherds his lambs on Mount Helicon. Addressing him as one of the "shepherds of the wilderness, shameful, wretched creatures, nothing but bellies (*gastera oion*," 26), they inspire him to sing of the future and the past and the race of blessed gods. "Nothing but bellies," Marilyn Arthur points out, encapsulates "the human condition . . . man's inscription into the world of needs and desires, of temporality and partiality. The need to be fed stands as a symbol of helplessness, of the condemnation to an eternal cycle of longing and fulfillment."[22] Mankind is helpless, hapless, and near hopeless, if it were not for the Muses' inspiration. The knowledge they impart— to know more than the immediacy of the present moment—is a blow against man's vulnerability and evanescence. Their gift, Hesiod's poem, is a defense against life in nature circumscribed by time.

In the body of this poem, Hesiod first presents a cosmogony and theogony, accounts of how the universe was formed and how the gods came into being. He then relates the familial-political contest among the gods for the rule of the universe and turning to mortals, describes the creation of woman (the second sex, chronologically speaking), the separation of gods from men, and the five ages of man, a graduated moral decline. Loss of association with the gods coincided with the first appearance of woman, for until woman came on the scene, men lived in a paradisiacal age of gold.

Cosmological Origins: Difference and Order in Nature[23]

How did the universe come into being? Hesiod's narrative is shaped by the assumption that existence in nature arises from difference. Difference is the outcome of separation and assumes the law of identity: To be is to not be something else.[24] The process of differentiation, moreover, creates order.

First (*Theogony* 116ff.) there was Chaos, a gaping, undifferentiated void. Earth (Gaia; Ge in classical Greek), followed next, along with Tartarus (part of the underworld), and Eros. Through parthenogenesis, Earth bore Ouranos (Heaven) and other children; then, through sexual union with her brother-son-husband Ouranos, she bore many more children, of whom the most important in the family saga about to unfold were Iapetus, Rhea, Themis, and Kronos. Ouranos, jealous of his sons, hid them in the earth and would not allow them to see the light of day.

Earth fashioned a sickle and incited her son Kronos to castrate his father and thereby succeed to his rule. The goddess Aphrodite (who, like Pandora, the first woman, subdues men and gods through charm and deceit; see below) was born from the sea foam into which Ouranos's genitals had fallen. Kronos was also destined to be overthrown by his own son; therefore, he swallowed down all the children his wife Rhea bore him, until Rhea plotted with her parents (Earth and Heaven) to save the next child; when Zeus was born, she hid the infant and gave Kronos a stone wrapped in swaddling clothes to swallow. Thus did Zeus survive to "overcome his father by force of hand, deprive him of honor (*time*), and rule over the deathless gods" (490f.). With the reign of Zeus, "who knows eternal counsels" (550, 561), the succession of power from father to son engineered by wives and daughters through acts of retaliation is brought to an end. But transference of power from one generation of the gods to the next becomes moot: Though challenged from time to time, Zeus never has to relinquish his rule to a younger male, the expression, perhaps, of a powerful male fantasy. Mortal men are not so lucky, but one thing is clear: Female partiality and deceit are a threat to the orderly transference of power from one generation of males to the next. Zeus's eternal reign is characterized by justice (*dike*), persuasion (*peitho*), and speech and reason (*logos*), rather than by force (*bia*). This new arrangement establishes "congruence between the sexual and political spheres,"[25] and Zeus the father of gods and men holds supreme rule in both. The patriarchal divine pantheon described by Hesiod mirrors the familial and political institutions of Greek society.

Gaining control over female power was a prerequisite for the order of (male) rule. Replacement of parthenogenesis by sexual reproduction was also necessary, for as long as Earth brought forth new life "without aid," she was autonomous, self-sufficient, and self-willed. When left to its own devices, furthermore, female power brought forth some dire entities. According to Hesiod, black Night bore the following parthenogenically: hateful Doom, black Fate (Ker), death, sleep, and the race of Dreams. Next, Blame, painful Grief, the Hesperides, Destinies (Moirai), the avenging Keres (also known as fates; Clotho, Lachesis, and Atropos) "who give human beings good and evil and pursue the transgressions of men and gods with terrible rage,"[26] Nemesis, Deceit, Friendship, woeful Old Age, and flinty-spirited Strife (Eris).[27] Most of these female-born entities held power over men's lives and threatened male autonomy. The introduction of sexual reproduction is presented as having had equally dire consequences, however (see below). The fantasy of avoiding generation from females altogether is reflected in myths of autochthony, the birth of founding ancestors and original inhabitants of a place from the land itself. Athenian and Theban traditions claimed birth from the soil of their cities, claims which also served to validate their right to possess and rule the land.[28]

Origins: The Consolidation of Male Power

The triumph of Zeus introduces a stable divine patriarchal hierarchy infused with a new and just order. As described by Hugh Lloyd-Jones: "The early Greek concept of order required that each god and man should receive his proper *time* [honor]; and besides meaning justice, *dike* meant the preservation of the established order."[29] *Dike* is concerned with the apportionment of recognition proper to a man's or a god's status, a measure of his power.[30] Through concern for the proper estimation and distribution of honor and power, this concept of justice among men is tied to the achievement ethic. The new justice replaces the old one based on retaliation and punishment, and consists in "the emergence of symbolic exchange and balanced reciprocity."[31] Relationships among men, public and private, are mediated by the rule of law and economic and social equity, and free men are equal under the law. Women do not participate as equals under this new system, however, for they are not allowed to become agents of exchange or reciprocity.

There is evidence, however, that order and justice were not always imagined as residing in the power of Zeus or in power relations among men. In early literary passages, *dike* describes the "way" or manner of the world and all things in it—of a mountain torrent, colt's mane, wolf, divine kings in Aeschylus, Sophocles, Pindar, and Homer, respectively.[32] In *Themis. A Study of the Social Origins of Greek Religion*,[33] Jane Ellen Harrison looked to myth for clues to earlier social constructions of the *dike*. The name of the goddess Themis means "the way of man in society." Themis gave birth to Dike because it was the way of man to so conceptualize the way of the world.[34] Dike was associated with Ploutos, Wealth, king of the underworld, so named because Below the Earth was a source of boundless renewal. Here "indications" of Themis's divine laws, as distinguished from human laws, originate. In time, Dike came to be associated with violators of "the way," so that the common noun *dike* took on the meaning "vengeance." It was also appropriated to human law, law courts, and trials.[35] Before Dike was coopted into patriarchy (Harrison's view as well as mine), myth and early usage reflect an orientation[36] to an established order, one inherent in the universe and encompassing the natural, divine, and human worlds. "What was established" and "the way of all things" were determined by female powers which drew their limitless strength from Below the Earth.[37] As early as Hesiod, the powers of both were denied and subordinated. At *Theogony* 901, as well as Pindar, *Olympian* 13.6-8, Dike was the eldest daughter of Themis and Zeus. Her sisters were Eunomia (Social Harmony) and Eirene (Peace); these personifications are not only born from Zeus but hold power in accordance with his rule, and they nurture male social and political institutions.

Up to this point, our discussion of Hesiod and his mythological account has shown: (1) the importance of separation in early Greek abstract thinking, validating the views of both Freud and feminists that separation has long been central to Western male thought;[38] (2) the essential connection between processes of separation and definitions of difference; (3) gender as a key determinant in processes of separation and the creation of order, as well as in emerging definitions of difference; (4) emphasis on freedom from the control of female powers and the necessity, in turn, of gaining and keeping control over them; and (5) the relation between male honor and self-esteem, the status of a god or man within a hierarchy of power, and early concepts of order and justice.

Two important goddesses favorably disposed to male authority are enrolled in the new divine pantheon established under Zeus.[39] Athena, patron goddess of Athens, was born armed as a male warrior from the head of her father Zeus after he swallowed her mother Metis, Counsel, thus incorporating female judgment into himself. Athena's tendency to identify with paternal and male power is reflected in Aeschylus, *Eumenides* (734ff.), where the goddess defends Orestes on the charge of matricide on the grounds that a father is the true parent of a child, a mother merely the soil in which his seed grows.[40] The second, the goddess Hekate (*Hymn to Hekate*, *Th* 411-452), especially honored by Zeus, represents the power of female nurturance, "the willing sponsorship of the activities of human life," who "poses no threat to the divine patriarchy."[41]

Pandora, the First Woman, Prototype of the Race of Woman[42]

Until the third generation of Olympian gods, the reign of Zeus, the race of mortals was all male, and mortals and immortals enjoyed a harmonious relationship. Then Zeus ordered the gods to create woman (a story related in both the *Theogony* and *Works and Days*), who should be sent to mankind as punishment for Prometheus's gift of fire to men (*WD* 37): a beautiful evil (*kalon kakon*, *Th* 85), and a snare from which there is no escape (*dolos . . . amechanos*, *WD* 83). As in the Ouranos-Kronos-Zeus succession story, this myth tells of generational conflict between males: Prometheus, son of Zeus's brother Iapetus, tries to deceive Zeus and subvert his will (*WD* 105, *Th* 613-616); mortals have the misfortune to be caught in the middle of their power contest. Prometheus's wiles deceived Zeus twice. First came the deception of the sacrifice, originally intended to heal a rift between gods and mortal men (*Th* 535). The animal sacrifice was divided into two portions, of which the better half, the meat and organs, should have been assigned to the gods. Prometheus tricked Zeus into accepting the worse portion, consisting of bones covered with fat, however, while the meat and organs went to the mortals. In retaliation, Zeus refused to give heavenly fire to men. When the young rebel nevertheless smuggled fire down to earth, Zeus took revenge by asking all the gods to use their various skills to create woman, to be a scourge to men. The arrival of woman introduced sexual reproduction, which thus became the price of civilization.[43] These events are also the source of the permanent separation of men from gods, for up to this time, a Golden Age (see below), gods had associated freely with men.

Woman was created as a deception in return for deceptions. Formed from earth and water, like a pottery vessel, into the likeness of a chaste maiden (*Th* 571f.) but with a face like a goddess's (*WD* 60ff.), her beautiful appearance and luxurious attire conceal her shameless (*kuneon*, literally, doglike)[44] mind and deceitful nature; she tells lies, her words are wily. When Pandora opens the jar the gods have given her, she releases war, the necessity of labor, painful childbirth, disease, and death, which now becomes an evil. Through and from her, a host of evils come upon mankind (*WD* 90-105), so that men toil like worker-bees, while women, like drones, stay home and store up the labor of others into their bellies[45] (*Th* 590ff.; bellies, *gastera*, 599). Women have another interior hollow space, the womb. The belly, the womb, the tomb, the earth: all are associated with man's inescapable implication in birth, hunger, and death. From Pandora comes the race and tribe of women (*Th* 591), all of one kind.[46] Woman is henceforth associated with the weaknesses of the flesh, mortality and death.[47]

Hesiod's Myth of Moral Decline: The Five Ages of Man

In *WD* 109-201 Hesiod describes the moral condition of men through five generations. After the perfect goodness of the Golden Age, the race declined, until Hesiod's own time, an age of Iron, with a brief reprieve during the Age of Heroes. By the last of these periods, he claims, moral order has been severely compromised because men no longer obey the will of Zeus (or his justice).

(1) The Golden Age consisted of a race of mortals created by the gods under rule of Kronos. Human life was all celebration, without work, suffering, or evil. Earth (*aroura*, tilled or arable land) supplied all in abundance, generously. Men were loved by the gods and nurtured by the earth. Under the oversight of the gods, all were good and their lives were pleasant and easy. Everything changed after the separation of men from gods and with the arrival of woman.

(2) Men of the Silver Age were also created by the gods, but they were less noble by far. They were unlike the preceding generation in body and spirit. Humans were nurtured by their devoted mothers for 100 years but when finally mature, were hybristic and prone to injure one another. They were destroyed by Zeus because they were impious and refused to sacrifice to the gods. The nurturance and oversight of mothers, however prolonged, failed to produce respect for the gods, moral order, or social harmony.

(3) The Bronze Age men were created by Zeus the Father from manna ash (trees or spears). They were lovers of Ares, god of war, and violence. They had great physical strength and destroyed one another with their own hands. They were nameless after death. Violence enacted outside of social order does not deserve immortality.

(4) The Age of Heroes[48] was created by Zeus "on the bounteous earth," and men were more just and better, a godlike race. Some were destroyed by war at Thebes and Troy and concealed by death, like the bronze men. But others were granted life after life and transported by Zeus to the ends of earth, where they dwell forever on The Blessed Isles. There, earth brings forth bounteously for them. The Golden Age is recreated not on earth but at the ends of the earth, where grain-giving Earth produced honey-sweet fruit three times a year. No longer the benefactress of all, she favors only a small group of men singled out by

Zeus as noble.

(5) The Age of Iron was also created by Zeus. This is the present (Hesiod's) age, filled with endless work, suffering, and death, but (and here Hesiod changes verb tense and speaks of the future) though the gods will bestow heavy burdens on men, they will also mix some good with evils. For the most part, however, Hesiod presents a dystopian vision of present and future. Father and children, guest and host, companion and companion will not be alike (bonded by similar thoughts? values?); brothers will not be dear to one another, as before. Men will dishonor their parents, destroy one another's cities. The principle of reciprocity will be ignored: No one will acknowledge that he owes a debt or should repay a favor to the man who keeps his oath or is just or good. The evil man will win praise. Misappropriation of praise and blame will subvert the right use of *logos*, while the man who uses *logos* rightly will not be respected. *Dike* will be "in the hands"—might will be right; there will be no shame, only slander and envy. At last, Aidos (Respect, Scruple) and Nemesis (Retribution) as personified and divinized moral forces will desert men and retreat to the company of the gods. Without them, men will have no defense against evil. Consigned to a physical and material existence, men are at the mercy of the irrational forces (of woman and nature? themselves?) which bring out the worst in them.

Hesiod affirmed that justice and right in human society are grounded in the final moral authority of a supreme male god. Greek myths which tell the origins of nature and society relate the emergence of male culture and concomitant dominion over supernatural female powers and woman. The twin necessities of mastering nature and controlling woman are men's curse. Their salvation lies in culture. Because of her origin, as Nicole Loraux and Page duBois point out, woman belongs "in nature" and is an outsider within the *polis*. Men are not all of one kind: they have diverse *aretai* and are members of the *demos* (people) and *polis*.[49] Because she never changes, generic woman belongs to myth, where she was created, while men act in the arena of history.

"Human" society was originally all male, civilization a male creation. Once woman introduced a variety of evils into both, men could but dream of a world without women. As Marilyn Arthur puts it, "Only in the cultural realm [the realm of *logos*],[50] in the world of the Muse, the bard, and the king do they [men] have the possibility of constructing a fiction of a world without women, a world freed from corporeality, a fiction of transcendence."[51] *Logos*, the ordering power of language and the authority of reasoned speech, creates social order. The Muses, daughters of Zeus, confer language and knowledge on the poet; Zeus himself oversees kings, and through his oversight, kings have the judgment and authority to determine right and justice for their peoples. The accession of Zeus marks the defeat of Earth and the subordination of her power and influence to his reign. In subsequent Western thought, the sources and messengers of *logos* have varied, but the primacy and value of male-determined *logos* have not.

Man's necessary association with generic woman and her essential evil is a negative condition, detrimental because it places him at the mercy of external and internal forces difficult or impossible to control. Bodily existence in and of itself is a hindrance to control. The main affects of the body are pleasure and pain, both of which are, paradoxically, associated with evil. Pleasure, in particular erotic pleasure, is an evil because it grounds a man in a self-absorbed present; pursued with sufficient rigor, it deflects a man from achievement. Embodiment also consigns a man to pain: the pain of the physical labor Hesiod's Iron-Age man must perform in order merely to sustain his life, as well as suffering and diseases of all kinds and, ultimately, the pain of dying and death itself. Pain is an evil for the same reason that pleasure is an evil: It imprisons man within the present (and the material existence of a self restricted within time). Woman (Pandora) first brought pain to men, though woman, too, became subject to pain, the labor of childbirth.

In the Greco-Roman view, sexual *eros*, an irrational force[52] so powerful it overcomes even gods, is a hindrance to the pursuit of achievement and an obstacle to virtuous conduct. Michel Foucault reflects the dominant classical formulation of "the problem" of pleasure: "Pleasurable acts are situated in an agonistic field of force difficult to control";[53] the key to proper sexual conduct is "domination of oneself by oneself,"[54] the very strategy Plato proposed in his *Republic*. Plato described man's *psyche* as composed of three parts: reason, emotions, and the *thymos*, or power to act. In the soul of the just man, reason, assisted by the *thymos*, governs the emotions, and justice consists in the dynamic established by this distribution of power. Aristotle's more flexible guiding principle, the Golden Mean, is an adaptation of archaic Greek notions of propriety and moral limit. It looked to such "reasonable" criteria as moderation and appropriateness as guides to governing the uses of pleasure: Cultivation of deliberative reason and habits of moderation and self-discipline are learned responses under the control of thoughtful men.

Another strategy for reconciling reason and pleasure is the translation of pleasure from physical and sensual experience to the exclusive domain of male culture—intellectual or philosophical experience.[55] The creation of culture, Freud argued, required the transformation of *eros*[56]; the impulse to coopt and transform *eros* predates the rise of philosophy. In the opening lines of *Nemean* 8, Pindar conflates sexual desire and the desire to pursue *arete*. Lady Season (Hora, personification of timeliness in natural processes) is said to preside over the destinies of men and women in the springtime of their lives. "It is a fine thing for a person to be able to achieve the better (= nobler) *erotes* and not depart from decorum in any action" (4f.). Timeliness in nature should serve as a paradigm for human conduct. The young are ripe for *eros*, and Zeus's sexual union with the nymph Aigina sets a positive, if exalted, example, for it produced the hero Aiakus, founder of a noble race, and noble races—both peoples of a city and members of a family—aspire to and perform nobler deeds. The boy victor of this poem illustrates the maxim, for he is descended from a noble race and has performed a noble action. He will also, in time, mature, perhaps to sire sons who will follow in his footsteps and to perform new acts of prowess.

Vergil translates *eros* to the achievement ethic with even greater boldness and exclusivity. The second half of the *Aeneid* (Books 7-12), modeled on Homer's *Iliad*, is the story of Aeneas's war in Italy. Vergil invokes neither a generic muse (as Homer did) nor a muse specific to the task (Clio, for example, whose special interest is *res gestae*, valiant deeds of historical significance), but Erato, the muse traditionally associated with erotic poetry. His choice is an act of appropriation:

> Come now, Erato, I shall set forth the kings, the times,
> the state of things in Latium long ago, when Aeneas'
> folk, an army, beached on Ausonian shores. I shall recall,
> too, how the first battle began. You, you, goddess,
> advise your poet-seer. I shall speak of dire wars,
> battle lines drawn, kings courageous to the death,
> the Tyrrhenian force, all Hesperia compelled to arms.
> A greater panoply of events appears to me,
> I begin a greater work.   (*Aeneid* 7.36-45)

Vergil has already shown how *eros* as erotic passion, embodied in and exemplified by Queen Dido, disrupts and subverts social order at Carthage. Dido's passion, moreover, threatened to divert Aeneas from reaching Italy and initiating the destiny of the future Roman race. Aeneas has now arrived in Italy and must win a place for the Trojan refugees among the native peoples. *Eros* must be subjected (sublimated, according to Freud) to the service of noble endeavors of noble men, and Vergil requests that (a presumably reconstituted) Erato serve as patron goddess to the second half of his epic, which will glorify Roman military, political, and moral achievements.

Membership in the community of nature is an emblem of man's vulnerability, his needs and desires, dependencies and connections, emotions, sexuality and other sources of pleasure, pain, the very life experiences most human beings share with one another. All the liabilities traceable to membership in the community of nature threaten to deprive men of their individual identities and integrity and to deflect them from pursuing achievement and immortality. They also pose obstacles to a man's control over himself and his circumstances, and beyond the individual, to the well-being and order of society, which depends on control in the form of male rule.

A man who possessed and exercised *arete* achieved some measure of separation and control. Escape from earthly and embodied existence (whether through denial or devaluation) enabled him to realize his godlike aspect to the greatest possible extent. As the *polis* and its understanding of the powers of *logos* evolved, moral philosophy, which focused on virtue, reason, and happiness, emerged. Plato and Aristotle extended the sense of *arete* as moral goodness, for the most part incorporating well-established polarities of gender difference. The hegemony of reason in the Platonic tripartite soul and the guiding force of deliberative reasoning in Aristotle were hallmarks of thinking men. Thus, moral thought was formulated for the benefit of men in terms of their moral concerns, and intellectual and moral knowledge and gender were interconnected.

Like Plato and Aristotle, later philosophers of the Hellenistic and Roman periods (Stoics, Epicureans, and Skeptics) focus on the individual's dual quest for virtue and happiness. How can he be in charge of his behavior and in control of his life? These schools of thought were the self-help and recovery movements of postclassical Greece and of Rome, where they continued to flourish; the pains and problems of human existence, like medical conditions, were amenable to treatment.[57] These ethical outlooks are based on virtue, which was considered to be part inborn disposition and part social training. They are based also on practical reasoning, for being good is not just a matter of brute discipline and self-control. All recognize that virtue involves emotions, pleasure and pain, as well as reason; all believe that a person can cultivate his own moral judgment and ability to live well.[58] The pursuit of virtue is not necessarily compatible with conforming to social norms or towing the line of society's power brokers. In fact, in the Stoic view, power—wealth, political or social status—and even health are considered "indifferent" goods, secondary to possession of virtue. In Epicurean thought, the quest for power is a positive hindrance to living a virtuous life. Thus, Hellenistic philosophy established notions of virtue independent of norms and legitimized the option of critiquing and dissenting from dominant values.

Some scholars believe the principles that Hellenistic philosophers and their followers advocated applied (or, at least, could have applied) to women as well as to men. In *The Therapy of Desire*, for example, Martha Nussbaum presents the positions of the various schools through the hypothetical experiences of an imaginary female student Nikidion.[59] Why, after all, shouldn't a thoughtful Greek or Roman woman have been considered capable of cultivating virtue, especially since this was a private endeavor? There is some evidence that she was, particularly if she had access to education or to educated men. She would have been obliged, however, to adopt a male point of view: These philosophies assume a quest for control and frame their arguments in terms of male concerns and experiences. The polarities seen in earlier works are perpetuated in these later ethical systems. What forms do they take? How are nature, woman, and embodied existence regarded? Both Stoicism and Epicureanism professed the principle, living in accordance with nature. What did that mean?

* * * * *

Living in Accordance with Nature. The Stoic View

Our discussion of Stoic thought will focus on the work of the Roman philosopher Seneca.[60] I choose Seneca because of his influential place in the Western classic tradition,[61] because his writings are available and accessible today, and because discussing his thought gives us an opportunity to begin to talk about Rome and Roman beliefs. We might have expected Seneca's 124 letters to his friend Lucilius and his philosophical essays to reflect his struggles to guide the mercurial young Nero, whom he tutored and advised and who could hardly be counted among men of reason, through the chaotic consequences of his own vices and the intricacies of public affairs. Instead, the philosopher rises above the fluctuating fortunes of court personalities and intrigues to argue theoretical guidelines to the practice of moral philosophy.[62]

Stoic ethics was adrocentric.[63] Reason (*ratio*, Greek *logos*) or mind, the highest and most godlike facility (Letter to Lucilius 41), manifests itself in exclusively male activities: philosophy, politics and public affairs. Only men of reason understand and are in harmony with nature, god, or fate, and only men of reason are truly wise. Such men are scarce, however, since most men aspire to what Stoics called "preferred indifferents," such as health or wealth, not to the cultivation of virtue.[64] Thus, the Stoic view is an exclusionary ideal. Anyone may aspire to this ideal, but, in reality, though all men belong to nature and nature is rational, most men and virtually all women do not choose to make virtue their priority. Women tend to be weak and emotional and are born to obey men who are born to rule.[65] The universe is overseen by a god who is the supreme repository of reason; nature is organized in accordance with the same reason. To be wise is to participate in the reason of both. Because he is rational, man is superior to other livings beings, over which he naturally holds ruling authority.[66]

Rational mind and spirit are antithetic to body, its affects, and most pleasures. *Corpus habet; et arbores*, man has a body, but so do trees, Seneca says dismissively (Letter 76.9). *Nemo liber est qui corpori servit*, No man is free who is a slave to the body (Letter 92.33; cf. 2.2). Like Plato, Seneca considers the body the lodging or prison of the soul, which, once released from its bonds, will enjoy eternal peace and bliss.[67] True freedom—Seneca's reformulation of the cherished Roman political concept *libertas*—is to serve philosophy (Letter 1.8.8, *The Happy Life* 4.5, *Integrity of the Wise Man* 19.2). Reason defines and is a guide to the virtuous life, the only path to happiness. Seneca, like other Stoics, relegates emotions or affects, which are corruptions of nature, and pleasure, the cornerstone of Epicurean ethics, to the realm of distraction, disorder, and at worst, vice.[68] Ideally, the virtuous person is *apathes*, free from emotion. The very word *pathe* reflects the view that emotions are things you suffer, in passivity, and over which you lack control.

You can't let your happiness depend on ordinary pleasures and joys; they are both uncertain and brief (Letter 59.14ff.). Most tend toward excess and are contrary to nature/reason. There are, however, "good" feelings: joy (reasonable elation, opposed to pleasure), caution (reasonable avoidance), and wishing (reasonable wanting).[69] The pleasures of the wise man, because derived from his commitment to virtue and reason, are superior (Letters 23.2, 27.3, 59.2 and 14, 72.8; *The Happy Life* 3.4, 4.4; *Anger* 2.6.2). Even animals experience some pleasures. You should also try to rid yourself of desires for unnecessary things. Nature in her wisdom has bestowed many benefits on the human race and has supplied everything for our needs: food, shelter, clothing, and physical comforts. Inveighing against luxury was native to all Roman moralists, and Seneca is no exception.[70]

By conflating nature and reason, the Stoics masculinized nature. Even generation is dissociated from earth, female deities, and women, and radically transformed: The creative force in nature is Generative Reason (*logos spermatikos*), related to all other forms of *logos/ratio* in the universe, including creative human powers.[71] Arts, crafts, and trades were all invented by *ratio*, but this is reason of an inferior sort, belonging to the hands and body, and not to be confused with philosophic wisdom, which comes from the mind/soul (Letter 90.20ff.)

Although Senecan virtue, like Greek *arete*, is male-defined and -identified, his community of wise men[72] differs from the community of achievement seen in Homer, Pindar, or Thucydides. The association of reasonable men who share an ideal of virtue is not a political entity. Social and political standing have no bearing on moral status; thus, a slave may confer moral benefit on his master and the mind of even a slave may be free (*Benefits* 3.18), while the only person who truly deserves to be called "king" is the wise man. Although the Stoic outlook tended to be what Julia Annas calls "depoliticized,"[73] Roman Stoics considered that their principles either coincided or were compatible with old Roman virtues. Some believed they were morally obligated to employ their virtue in the service of society and the State.

Stoic ideals were self-sufficiency, detachment, autonomy—the familiar male valuation of separation. All life's gains may be seen as (potential) losses and death as a kind of liberation from the possibility of either gain or loss (*Consolation to Marcia* 20). While Fate holds the power to take away life, and at least you and your loved ones can die only once, Fortuna may take away the other things you cherish at any time and as often as it pleases her (Lady Luck is, of course, female). Detachment from the assaults of Fortune, a powerful goddess whose religious cult at Rome was older than the city itself, was prerequisite to happiness. In spite of his intellectual detachment, however, the Stoic should employ his virtue toward the betterment of society as a whole. He should also strive to distance himself from all things that deflect him from the pursuit of his work. The body (beyond the necessity of tending to basic needs), emotions, and pleasure are associated with fluctuations of fortune, everything that is subject to change, a threat to balance and stability. Pleasure is one of the four kinds of emotions (pleasure, desire, care, and fear), all of which are transitory, disruptive, and contrary to (man's best) nature.[74] The pleasures of the wise man, because they are derived from his commitment to virtue and reason, are superior (Letters 23.2, 27.3, 59.2 and 14, 72.8; *The Happy Life* 3.4, 4.4; *Anger* 2.6.2). "Virtue is dignified, untiring, imperturbable; pleasure is groveling, effeminate, fleeting," in Eduard Zeller's summary of the Senecan view.[75]

Many Stoic motifs are evident in the essay Seneca wrote to his mother Helvia to console her when he had experienced a severe blow of fortune: He had been sent into exile on the island of Corsica by the Emperor Claudius. The rhetoric of the essay is especially interesting, for Seneca is obviously very attached to his mother, so in order to compliment her on how well she is bearing up, he must argue that she is a virtuous woman because she is more like a man and is not behaving like a woman at all. A female Stoic battles the same enemies as a male but faces a greater challenge because she begins the fight with a weaker nature. Most women cannot use reason to set a limit to their grief, while Helvia has the makings of a real trooper.[76] A person who has suffered many losses, as she has, has learned how to be wretched. Using the first of a series of military metaphors, Seneca claims that she is like an old soldier. He will teach her how to conquer her grief heroically (3-4), he says, though what he in fact tries to do is to argue it almost out of existence by denying that banishment is a misfortune. The wise man relies entirely on himself and is himself like a soldier, ever on guard against the enemy Fortuna (5). Since the order of nature is the same the world over and we take our virtues with us wherever we go (8), no place on earth is really foreign. We do not need our birthplace, costly luxuries, high public office. All we really need is *ratio*, and it overcomes all other desires and all vices (13). Helvia, lacking the weaknesses of a woman, never wanted luxuries, ran a strict household, was proud of her many pregnancies, and used no cosmetics (16). Therefore, she is made of strong enough stuff to be moderate in her grief. Unlike other women, she should take refuge in philosophic studies, as she has in the past.

Helvia's real problem is that she misses her son—their conversations and shared studies, in which she took part "with more than a woman's pleasure and more than a mother's involvement" (15). But she should think of him as happy now, for his mind is truly free. It rises above the universe to contemplate the mysteries of nature and, from this vantage point, "enjoys the most beautiful sight of divine things, and mindful of its own immortality traverses everything that was or will be for all the generations of time" (20).

* * * * *

In trying to defend itself against death, Greco-Roman male culture also chose to defend itself against life: everything that threatened its secure and separate identity and autonomy, everything that seemed to oppose men's aspirations to power and achievement. Reason, judgment, wisdom, order, justice, language, and male-centered institutions are cultural defenses against a many-headed hydra: the changeful, unpredictable, unstable, vulnerable, corruptible, distracting and disruptive, irrational, temporary and evanescent. This orientation appears both in early, mythic, and in later, philosophical, thought. Greek male culture's definitions of Otherness, like its self-definitions, reflect a persistent obsession with control. Subject to the natural world into which his body was integrated, man tried to but could not exclude disruptive forces from the society he created. The image of Hesiod's chaos may represent man's greatest fear: a dark (unseen and unseeable) interior, a gaping space, a place where there is no differentiation, from which a dire, hidden power may strike out to overturn the order he has labored to create. At worst, such a force lies in wait within even the best of men, ready to sabotage his inner and outer control. Thus, perhaps the meliorative fantasy that man's inner space is occupied by pure mind, whereas inside a woman there is only a womb, and mortality.

In the next chapter, we look at what kinds of strategies served to mediate differences in ways which allowed these opposing powers to coexist, though not as equals. We shall also discover some countercultural attitudes toward difference, thinkers who subverted dominant values by making Others or Otherness their primary term. Finally, we shall see how the philosopher Epicurus, in an interpretation of the principle to live in accordance with nature very different from the Stoic view, attempted to integrate nature and culture, but did so only by radically redefining and withdrawing from the dominant culture.

Notes

[1] Robert Parker, *Miasma. Pollution and Purification in Early Greek Religion* (Oxford: Clarendon Press, 1983), p.101.

[2] Simone de Beauvoir, *The Second Sex*, trans. H.M. Parshley (New York: Vintage Press, 1974), p.73.

[3] Ynestra King, "Healing the Wounds: Feminism, Ecology, and Nature/Culture Dualism," in Alison Jaggar and Susan Bordo, eds., *Gender/Body/Knowledge* (Rutgers: Rutgers University Press, 1989), p.139; entire article, pp.115-141.

[4] Hilde Hein,"Liberating Philosophy: An End to the Dichotomy between Matter and Spirit," in Carol C. Gould, ed., *Beyond Domination. New Perspectives on Women and Philosophy* (Totowa, NJ: Rowman and Allenheld, 1983) p.125.

[5] Alice Jardine, *Gynesis. Configurations of Women and Modernity* (Ithaca: Cornell University Press, 1988); Sherry Ortner, "Is Female to Male as Nature Is to Culture?" in Michelle Rosaldo and Louise Lamphere, eds., *Women, Culture, and Society* (Stanford: Stanford University Press, 1974), pp.67-87.

[6] See, for example, T. Jackson Lears, *No Place of Grace. Antimodernism and the Transformation of American Culture, 1890-1920* (New York: Pantheon, 1981).

[7] The objection may appropriately be raised that the values I am seeking are salient features of the Western Christian tradition. I can answer only that these are not the values which guide conduct in capitalist North America in the late twentieth century. Our concerns touch on many ethical areas, from the uses of our environment to the possession and uses of social, political, and economic powers.

[8] Marija Gimbutas, *The Language of the Goddess* (San Francisco: Harper and Row, 1989), p. 316. See also Sarah Pomeroy's discussion of Isis as a pan-

goddess in the closing pages of her *Goddesses, Whores, Wives, and Slaves. Women in Classical Antiquity* (New York: Schocken Books, 1975).

[9] Rosemary Radford Reuther (*Gaia and God. An Ecofeminist Theology of Earth Healing* [Harper SanFrancisco, 1992]), pp.145-165, argues convincingly that we do not yet know enough about the existence and possible organization of societies that may have been matriarchal to draw firm conclusions about them. For women in neolithic cultures, see Stella Georgoudi, "Creating a Myth of Matriarchy," and Nicole Loraux, "What Is a Goddess?," pp.449-463 and 11-45, respectively, in Pauline S. Pantel, ed., *History of Women in the West*, trans. Arthur Goldhammer (Cambridge: Harvard University Press, 1992), vol. 1.

[10] Arnold van Gennep, *The Rites of Passage*, trans. M.B. Vizedom and G.L. Caffee (Chicago: University of Chicago Press, 1960).

[11] Robert Parker, *Miasma*, p.31. Purification is "a science of division," separating and retaining what is better and expelling what is worse (Plato, *Sophist* 226d) (p.18). For birth, death, especially death resulting from homicide, and "the works of Aphrodite, see Chapters 2-4.

[12] Parker, *Miasma*, p.63. Cf. p.92: lack of control over sexual desire deflected both men and women "from their essential virtues."

[13] Martha Nussbaum, *The Fragility of Goodness. Luck and Ethics in Greek Tragedy and Philosophy* (Cambridge and New York: Cambridge University Press, 1986), pp.3-4. Cf. "We have reason. We are able to deliberate and choose, to make a plan in which ends are ranked, to decide actively what is to have value and how much. All this must count for something. If it is true that a lot about us is messy, needy, uncontrolled, rooted in the dirt and standing helplessly in the rain, it is also true that there is something about us that is pure and purely active, something that we could think of as `divine, immortal, intelligible, unitary, indissoluble, ever self-consistent and invariable' [Plato, *Phaedrus* 80B]. It seems possible that this rational element in us can rule and guide the rest, thereby saving the whole person from living at the mercy of luck" (p.3). Human beings are subject to "internal obstacles to self-sufficiency, our bodily and sensuous nature, our passions, our sexuality" (p.7).

[14] But Aristotle, building on the notion of *kairos*, also emphasized the importance of the particular in ethical decision making. Control over change, Jean-Pierre Vernant points out, is expressed in the Greek myths of Hestia and Hermes. The goddess Hestia is in charge of the hearth, center of the Greek house, and "symbol and pledge of fixity, immutability, and permanence." She is associated with Earth, which was thought to be motionless. Mutable woman is confined to the house, made to be stationary. Hermes, by contrast, was associated with "movement and flow, mutation and transition, contact between foreign elements." Man acquires control of mutability. Jean-Pierre Vernant, *Myth and Thought among the Greeks* (Boston: Routledge, 1983), Part V, "Hermes-Hestia: The Religious Experience of Space and Movement in Ancient Greece," pp.127-175. The quotations are from pp.128ff.

Construction of the Other 1. Flight from Nature, the Body, and Woman   97

[15] For feminist readings of the *Symposium*, see Giulla Sissa, "The Sexual Philosophies of Plato and Aristotle," in Pantel, ed., *A History of Women in the West*, vol. 1, pp.46-81; Page du Bois, *Sowing the Body. Psychoanalysis and Ancient Representations of Women* (Chicago: University of Chicago Press, 1988), pp.181-183; Elizabeth Spelman, *Inessential Woman. Problems of Exclusion in Feminist Thought* (Boston: Beacon Press, 1988), Chapter 1, esp. p.29; and Robin Schott, *Cognition and Eros. A Critique of the Kantian Paradigm* (Boston: Beacon Press, 1988), pp.10-15, and Chapter 1 passim.

[16] For the dichotomy between matter and spirit in Aristotle, see Hilde Hein,"Liberating Philosophy: An End to the Dichotomy between Matter and Spirit," in Carol C. Gould, ed., *Beyond Domination, New Perspectives on Women and Philosophy* (Totowa, NJ: Rowman and Allenheld, 1983), pp.123-141, esp. 125-128.

[17] Page duBois, *Sowing the Body. Psychoanalysis and Ancient Representations of Women* (Chicago: University of Chicago Press, 1988).

[18] For duBois's discussion of Freud's readings of Greek culture, see *Sowing the Body*, pp.18-22.

[19] Froma Zeitlin, "Cultic Models of the Female: Rites of Dionysus and Demeter, *Arethusa* 15 (1982): 129-157.

[20] du Bois, *Sowing the Body*, pp.40-42. The quote is from p.4. For metaphors of the female body, Part II, Chapters 3-7.

[21] Jean-Pierre Vernant, *The Origins of Greek Thought* (Ithaca: Cornell University Press, 1982 [1962]), pp.49ff.

[22] Marilyn B. Arthur, "Poetics and Circles of Order in the. *Theogony* Prooemium," *Arethusa* 16.1-2 (1983), p.104.

[23] The standard commentary on the *Theogony* is that of M.L. West. In the summary and discussion which follows, I am indebted to Marilyn B. Arthur, "Cultural Strategies in Hesiod's *Theogony*: Law, Family, Society," *Arethusa* 15 (1982): 63-82, and "The Dream of a World without Women: Poetics and Circles of Order in the *Theogony* Proem," *Arethusa* 16 (1983): 97-116; Ann L. Bergren,"Language and the Female in Early Greek Thought," *Arethusa* 16 (1983): 69-95 ; Pietro Pucci, *Hesiod and the Language of Poetry* (Baltimore: Johns Hopkins, 1977); and J.-P. Vernant, *Myth and Thought*, Parts I and II.

[24] On identity, see Morwenna Griffiths and Margaret Whitford, eds., *Feminist Perspectives in Philosophy* (Bloomington: Indiana University Press, 1988), Introduction, pp.6f, 14, 23; and Margaret Whitford, "Luce Irigaray's Critique of Rationality," pp.109-130. "The unconscious is a realm in which the laws of identity and non-contradiction do not apply. So when Irigaray writes that for the female imaginary, too, the laws of identity and non-contradiction (A is A, A is not B) do not apply either, it may sound like a dangerously irrationalist description of women that merely reinforces a traditional denigration. The practical value of these principles, without which rationality would be incon-

ceivable, is so evident that it appears unquestionable. The logic of identity is the prerequisite of any language or any society at all. However, the point is that there will always be a residue which exceeds the categories, and this excess is conceptualized as female." (pp.119f.) (Whitford refers to Irigaray, *The Sex Which Is Not One*, p.78.)

[25] Arthur, "Cultural Strategies," p.64.

[26] The Moirai, the more common embodiments of destiny in classical thought, were stripped of their powers to make moral judgments and punish evil when Zeus came to power.

[27] The progeny of Eris are equally dire; see lines 226-232.

[28] Nicole Loraux, *The Children of Athens: Athenian Ideas about Citizenship and the Division of the Sexes,* trans. Caroline Levine (Princeton: Princeton University Press, 1993; French ed., 1981). See also du Bois, *Sowing the Body*, pp.44-45 (Athens) and 55-56 (Thebes).

[29] Hugh Lloyd-Jones, *The Justice of Zeus.* Sather Classical Lectures, vol. 41 (Berkeley and Los Angeles: University of California Press, 2 ed., 1983 [1971]), p.4 and n16.

[30] "The noun *dike* occurs seven times in the *Iliad* . . . It means . . . either a judgment given by a judge or an assertion of his right by a party to a dispute. . . *Dike* originally meant the `indication' of the requirement of the divine law, *themis*." Lloyd-Jones, *Justice of Zeus*, Chapter 1, "The Iliad," n23. See also Eric Havelock, *The Greek Concept of Justice* (Cambridge: Harvard University Press, 1978), pp.193-217. *Dike* in Aeschylus, *Oresteia*: Simon Goldhill, *Reading Greek Tragedy* (Cambridge: Cambridge University Press, 1986), Chapter 2, "The Language of Appropriation," pp.33-56.

[31] Arthur, "Cultural Strategies," p.73.

[32] Jane Ellen Harrison, *Themis. A Study of the Social Origins of Greek Religion* (Cleveland: Meridian Books, 1962 [1912]), pp.515f.

[33] Harrison, *Themis*,"Themis, Dike, and the Horae," pp.514-535.

[34] The name Themis and common noun *themis*, right, custom, are derived from the Greek verb *tithemi*, put, place, set, establish. On the etymologies of both *themis* and *dike*, see Lloyd-Jones, *The Justice of Zeus*, pp.186f. and n23.

[35] Liddell-Scott-Jones, *Greek-English Lexicon.*

[36] Interestingly, Harrison, *Themis*, pp.526ff., compares *dike*, "the way," with Persian and Chinese philosophical concepts.

[37] For the relations between Themis and Gaia (Earth), see Harrison, *Themis*, pp.385ff. and 480ff.

[38] See below, Part III, Chapter 8.

[39] Aphrodite also joins the pantheon, but, because of her sexual charm and deceitful nature, she is a threat to male order.

[40] For male-female and other polarities in Aeschylus, *Oresteia*, see Froma Zeitlin, "The Dynamics of Misogyny: Myth and Mythmaking in the *Oresteia*," in John Peradotto and J.P. Sullivan, eds., *Women in the Ancient World. The Arethusa Papers* (Albany: State University of New York Press, 1984), pp.159-191. See also Arlene Saxonhouse, "Aeschylus' *Oresteia*: Misogyny, Phylogeny, and Justice," *Women and Politics* 4.2 (summer 1984): 11-32; and Goldhill, *Reading Greek Tragedy*, pp.1-56, 147-154, and passim.

[41] Arthur, "Cultural Strategies," pp.68-71.

[42] Pandora: Bergren, "Language and the Female," p.75; Pucci, *Hesiod*, Chapter 4, pp.82-126; and Nicole Loraux, "Sur la race des femmes,"*Arethusa* 11 (1978): 43ff.

[43] du Bois, *Sowing the Body*, pp.46f.; Loraux, "Sur La Race," p.53.

[44] For the association of generic woman with negative animal-like qualities, see Semonides, "Satire on Women," and similarly, Phokylides (du Bois, *Sowing the Body*, p.29).

[45] Linda Sussman, "Workers and Drones: Labor, Idleness and Gender Definition in Hesiod's Beehive," in Peradotto and Sullivan eds., *Women in the Ancient World*, pp.79-93.

[46] Nicole Loraux, "Sur la race des femmes." For Hesiod's myth of the races, see J.-P. Vernant, *Myth and Thought*, Part I, Chapters 1 and 2.

[47] Froma I. Zeitlin, "Feminine Figures of Death in Greece," and Jean-Pierre Vernant, "Death in the Eyes. Gorgo, Figure of the Other," in Froma Zeitlin, ed., *Mortals and Immortals. Collected Essays in Honor of Jean-Pierre Vernant* (Princeton: Princeton University Press, 1991), pp.95-109 and 111-138, respectively.

[48] It has been suggested that the Age of Heroes is a corruption in the manuscript, added to account for Theban, Trojan, and other legendary heroes.

[49] Loraux, "Sur la race," p.53; for women as outsiders within the *polis*, see du Bois on Medea, *Centaurs and Amazons. Women and the Pre-History of the Great Chain of Being* (Ann Arbor: University of Michigan Press, 1982) and *Sowing the Body* passim.

[50] Arthur, "Poetics," pp.105-111.

[51] Arthur, "Cultural Strategies," pp.78-79.

[52] Women are associated with madness and the irrational; see Ruth Padel, "Women: Model for Possession by Greek Daemons," in Averil Cameron and Amelie Kuhrt, eds., *Images of Women in Antiquity* (London, 1983), pp.3-19; and Padel, *Whom Gods Destroy. Elements of Greek and Tragic Madness* (Princeton: Princeton University Press, 1995) passim.

[53] Michel Foucault, *History of Sexuality*, trans. Robert Hurley (New York: Pantheon, 1980), vol. 2, *The Uses of Pleasure*, p.250.

[54] See esp. Part 2, Chapters 2 and 3. Foucault discusses *kairos*, pp.57ff., and *enkrateia* (self-control), pp.63-77.

[55] The classical impulse toward asceticism: Robin May Schott, *Cognition and Eros. A Critique of the Kantian Paradigm* (Boston: Beacon Press, 1988), Part I, "Philosophical Origins of Ascetic Philosophy: Platonic Views of Women and Eros," Chapters 1 and 2.

[56] Sigmund Freud, *Civilization and Its Discontents* (London: Hogarth Press and Institute of Psychoanalysis, 1957).

[57] Martha Nussbaum describes this analogy in *The Therapy of Desire. Theory and Practice in Hellenistic Ethics* (Princeton: Princeton University Press, 1994): "Philosophy heals human diseases, diseases produced by false beliefs. Its arguments are to the soul as the doctor's remedies are to the body" (p.14).

[58] Julia Annas, *The Morality of Happiness* (New York: Oxford University Press, 1993), Chapter 2, "The Virtues," pp.47-131, and passim.

[59] A Nikidion is said to have been a pupil of Epicurus (Diogenes Laertius, *Lives of the Philosophers* 10.7).

[60] Besides Seneca, our primary sources for Stoic thought are Cicero, *De Finibus* (The Limits of Good and Evil), Book III; Stobaeus (not yet available in English translation); Diogenes Laertius, *Lives of the Ancient Philosophers*, Book 2 (Loeb edition); Marcus Aurelius; and Epictetus.

[61] Nussbaum, *The Therapy of Desire*, Introduction, esp. pp.4-5; A.A. Long, *Hellenistic Philosophy* (London: Duckworth, 1986 [1974]), pp.233-235; and (the Roman Stoics) Miriam Griffin, "Philosophy, Politics, and Politicians at Rome," in Miriam Griffin and Jonathan Barnes, eds., *Philosophia Togata* (Oxford: Clarendon Press, 1989), pp.8f.

[62] See esp. Seneca, *Providence*. Also Annas, *The Morality of Happiness*, "The Stoics: Human Nature and the Point of View of the Universe," pp.159-179; Eduard Zeller, *The Stoics, Epicureans, and Skeptics* (New York: Russell and Russell, repr. ed. 1962), p.223; and Elizabeth Rawson, "Roman Rulers and the Philosophical Adviser," in *Philosophia Togata*, Chapter 9, pp.233-257.

[63] Annas, *The Morality of Happiness*, pp.140f. But cf. her comment on "appeals to rational reflection": "it was as open for a slave or a woman to become virtuous as for a prosperous citizen . . . given their [the Stoic] views of virtue and what it is to acquire it" (p.446). See also Philip M. Ris, "Seneca on reason, rules, and moral development," in Jacque Brunschwig and Martha Nussbaum, eds., *Passions and Perceptions. Studies in Hellenistic Philosophies of Mind*. Proceedings of the Fifth Annual Symposium Hellenisticum (Cambridge: Cambridge University Press, 1993), pp.285-312.

[64] Annas, *The Morality of Happiness*, pp.177ff.; and I.G. Kidd, "Stoic Intermediates and the End for Man," in A.A. Long, ed., *Problems in Stoicism*

(London: University of London, Athlone Press, 1971), pp.150-172.

[65] *Integrity of the Wise Man* 1 and 2, *Consolation to Marcia* 1.1, and see below.

[66] Gerard Watson, "The Natural Law and Stoicism," in Long, ed., *Problems in Stoicism*, pp.216-238, esp. 222f.

[67] *Consolation to Marcia* 23, *Consolation to Helvia* 11.6ff.; Zeller, *Stoics, Epicureans, and Skeptics*, pp.219-222.

[68] Of the emotions, Seneca argues in his essay on anger, anger is the most vicious, foul, and rabid. It is also the emotion most opposed to reason. See Nussbaum, *The Therapy of Desire*, Chapter 11, "Seneca on Anger in Public Life," pp.402-438.

[69] Annas, *The Morality of Happiness*, pp.61-66, and Nussbaum,*The Therapy of Desire*, pp.359-401.

[70] Whom, Seneca asks, do you consider wiser, the man who has contrived some feat of engineering (a field in which Romans excelled, of course) or

> he who can prove to himself and others that nature has made nothing hard or difficult for us, that we can live without a marble worker or engineer, we can clothe ourselves without the silk trade, that we could have everything we need from what earth bears on her surface. If the human race were willing to listen to him, it would know that the cook is as unnecessary as the soldier. (Letter 90.15; cf. 19). Seneca places less value on Roman achievements in engineering and commerce and the conquest of empire than on the quest for virtue. See also *Consolation to Helvia* 9.

[71] A.A. Long, "Freedom and Determinism," in Long, ed., *Problems in Stoicism,* pp.173-199, esp. 178f. See also Carolyn Merchant, *The Death of Nature. Women, Ecology, and the Scientific Revolution* (New York: Harper and Row, 1980), pp.23f.

[72] For *societas*, human community, see *Benefits* 4.18.3, and Letter 90.

[73] Julia Annas, *The Morality of Happiness*, pp.302-311 and 106f.

[74] Letters 59, 92; Zeller, pp.243-252.

[75] Zeller, p.237.

[76] Long-drawn-out grief is due to false belief (*Marcia* 7), whereas even animals do not grieve indefinitely; it is also womanish (*muliebre*: *Marcia* 1.1 and 16, *Consolation to Polybius* 6.2).

The tragedy of the *Bacchae* shows the dangers that are involved when a city retrenches within its own boundaries. If the world of the same refuses to absorb the element of otherness that every group and every human being unconsciously carry within themselves, . . . then all that is stable, regular, and the same tips over and collapses and the other, of hideous aspect, absolute otherness and a return to chaos, comes to appear as the sinister truth, the other authentic, and terrifying face of the same. The only solution is . . . for the city as a whole, in and through the theater, to make it possible for the other to become one of the dimensions of both collective life and the daily life of each individual. The victorious eruption of Dionysus is a sign that otherness is being given its place, with full honors, at the center of the social system.
J.-P. Vernant[1]

Communities function under natural constraints and continue to function only so long as they respect the ground of nature.
James Redfield[2]

Chapter 5

Construction of the Other 2: Connections and Beyond

We have explored some expressions of the Greco-Roman impulse toward a single, authorized viewpoint both in myth and in later, philosophic thought: nature, woman, and the body were construed as foil, associated with the dark powers of mutability against which shining achievement and its ethic were defined. Yet, the powers of Others and Otherness, connections that bridged the impulse toward separation, could not be denied: recognition of similarities that link opposites; resolution of conflict or competition among differences through mediation; identification with, even adoption of the Other; and, finally, the most extreme orientation, dissent from or rejection of accepted polarities in favor of an altogether different world view. The presence of women in the *polis* was necessary in order to perpetuate the family and the body of citizens. Physical survival itself required adaptation to the terms of living which nature dictated. Psychic survival depended on managing the multiple and complex demands of man's interior space.

It was, therefore, also a basic tenet of Greek thought that culture could thrive only if it incorporated—however reluctantly—the powers of nature. Although Hesiod, as we saw in the previous chapter, described life-in-nature as fraught with labor and suffering, he also depicts a nature which may, though no longer bounteous and all-giving, be of great help to men in their labors, if they pay attention to her recurrent processes and patterns and use them as guides. If we must live in nature, he says in *Works and Days*, better in than out of harmony with her. Her lessons, moreover, may be translated into principles for living, moral and religious beliefs and practices. Time and timeliness (*hora*, season or seasonal change)[3] point the way to informed regulation of farming activities: timely sustenance, ploughing, planting, wood-cutting, and sailing. Everything in good time, in good order. And with due or right measure, a response tailored to fit a set of contingencies or variables. "Keep due measure; appropriateness is best in all things" (694). Processes of change in nature suggested a moral principle: accommodating activity or speech to time or circumstance, one source for what we now call propriety or appropriateness.[4] Hesiod extends his principle to social relations—when to marry and beget children, how to order one's life, how to treat neighbors, how to act among the villagers.[5] In the following passage, Hesiod castigates his brother, who apparently did not share his values:

> Big fool that you are, Perses, I'll talk sense to you.
> You can get badness easily and plenty of it,
> the road is smooth and very close by.
> The immortal gods put the path of virtue
> off at a distance and paved it with our sweat.
> Long and straight is the road and hard at first.
> . . . .
> But despite your high birth, always remember
> and follow my advice, Perses, so that hunger
> may hate you and Demeter, abundant and respectful,
> will love you and fill your barn with food.
> Hunger keeps company with the lazy man.
> Both gods and men hate a parasite, who,
> like the stingless drones, wastes the labor
> of the bees by eating and not working.
> Plan your actions with proper measure,

to fill your barn with seasonable food.
As a result of labor, men grow rich in flocks
and crops, good workers are much dearer to the gods.
(Works and Days 286-291, 298-309)

Hesiodic virtue is far removed from valor on the battlefield and heroic excess. It is a work ethic (one which may have anachronistic Puritan resonances to American ears) which aims not at immortality but at economic self-sufficiency or, better yet, prosperity, and the good opinion of the gods. Nobility of birth does not exempt a man from this standard of virtue nor does humble birth exclude him. In the world of the farmer, the opposite of virtue is not defeat but sloth. Lazy men are like drones, nonworker bees, and are therefore no better than women.

Hesiod's insight was that similarities, order and sequence, and recurrent patterns in nature are useful paradigms for human actions. Through the formulaic language of oral epic poetry and use of similes, Homer, too, forges connections and explores relationships between separate categories (gods, men, animals), and, within the human world, between people separated by gender or class.[6] Repetition of so-called traditional modifiers—rosy-fingered Dawn, the wine-dark sea, swift-footed Achilles, resourceful Odysseus—shows that there is continuity within these worlds. Word-for-word descriptions of repeated actions, such as preparing a meal or arming for battle, draw attention to the rituals of Homeric existence.[7] In the *Odyssey*, the artful arrangements of the Phaeacian royal palace and garden (Book 7) and Laertes' orchard (Book 23) are also reminders of correspondences between natural order and ordered human existence.

Most Homeric similes[8] highlight qualities or experiences which integrate human beings into nature. In the *Iliad*, warriors are often compared to the most majestic animals—lions, boars, and eagles—as a way of highlighting their heroic strength and prowess. The comparison of Odysseus to a mountain lion (*Od*.6.131ff.),[9] on the other hand, shows both hero and beast at the mercy of the elements and their own need. This Odyssean lion is not a predator attacking his prey, but a defenseless, naked man who crawls out from his bed of leaves in search of food as a rain-soaked lion is driven from his lair by hunger. Later, however, (22.401ff., 23.45) after the slaughter of the suitors, Odysseus is compared to a lion spattered by the blood of an ox he has killed.[10] The suitors, by contrast, lack the virtues and even the animation of animals.

They are compared to dead rats 21.375, cattle maddened by the gadfly's sting 22.302ff., and dead fish 22.385-389.[11]

Kinship and unity are important values in the *Odyssey*, and many similes are closely connected with the central theme of the poem, loss and recovery of home and family. Athena, Odysseus, Penelope, their son Telemachus, swineherd Eumaeus, and nurse Eurycleia share an affinity Homer calls likemindedness, defined by character, bonds of affection, and shared values. Husband and wife, though separated for twenty years, share the same goal, reunion and restoration of their marriage and position within the Ithacan community, and both are resourceful and crafty people. Athena, face to face with Odysseus, confesses that she loves him because he is like her, inventive and crafty.[12] Especially poignant are the similes that embellish the reunions of Odysseus with his son Telemachus and wife Penelope. Father and son fall into one another's arms weeping "like hawks whose nestlings have been stolen by farmers" (16.216-218). Even animals know the pain of loss. The hero lost his "nestling" through long absence at war, as his son lost his parent and paradigm of heroic manhood. But unlike the hawks, hero and son have been reunited, and they are stung by their mutual deprivation and long-hoped-for recovery.[13] The simile which describes the reunion of Odysseus and Penelope mirrors the couple's likemindedness. Penelope welcomes her husband home as shipwrecked swimmers, exhausted by the sea, welcome the safety of land (23.233-240). To both of them, near-loss of their marriage is like near-loss of life. Although it is Odysseus, not Penelope, who experienced shipwreck at sea, they are bound together by such strong empathy that it is as if she, too, had experienced this terror, and both, having survived, are at last reunited as one. Two swallow images in books 21 and 22 remind the reader that the mortal Odysseus and the goddess Athena are united by corresponding *aretai* and a common purpose.[14] Homer's similes integrate mortals into the natural world. That is where we belong, and there are, moreover, qualities, feelings, and experiences we share with creatures above and below us in the hierarchy of being. From what we have in common grows empathy, which crosses natural and supernatural boundaries.

These facets of Hesiod and Homer acknowledge connections among beings usually regarded as separate; there is analogy within the overall context of polarity. Nevertheless, powers construed for the most part as antithetic, however secondary and subordinate, remained potential threats. One way of controlling nature, woman, and embodied existence was to incorporate them into society and culture, to empower yet tame them in ways that would serve male values. Myths and cult rituals of honoring the divinities Dionysus and Demeter were important vehicles for mediating these claims. Dionysus was worshiped in mystery rites held outside the *polis* in the wild; tamed, he was also honored within the city at public dramatic festivals.

Unlike most other divinities, Dionysus had no fixed seat of worship, an indication perhaps of his fundamental instability. He was originally a missionary god, a stranger whose efforts to introduce his cult from Asia met with strong resistance.[15] Dionysus embodied the life force in all nature. Associated with generation, growth, and change, it manifests itself literally as fluid, figuratively as fluidity. The god's power causes "an instantaneous and sudden surge of natural energy":[16] sudden and unexpected motion; earthquake; inexplicable shaking of roofs; jumping, leaping, sprinting, spurting, and boiling; mass fits of 'hysterical' dancing; and movements of the heart and of the phallus, including ejaculation. According to Aristotle (*The Movement of Animals*), the purpose of voluntary motion [action] is either to pursue what is pleasurable or to avoid what is painful (8.701b). The promptings of the heart and phallus, however, since they are subject to thought and imagination, are likely to give rise to involuntary motion. The movements they initiate may or may not take place in accordance with reason, *logos* (11.703b-704a).[17] Aristotle is not, of course, speaking about Dionysus, but he describes in scientific terms qualities attributed to the god and their unfavorable effects on men.

Dionysus's identity is located in Otherness, but it is also his essential nature to evade definition. The god collapses difference and the logic of difference; he is both illogical and nonlogical: beyond and outside of *logos*.[18] Worshipers of the god, both willing and unwilling, were said to be "filled with his spirit" (to be *entheos*, to have the god within them). Through the transformative experience of inspiration, they became one with him and with nature. He dissolved boundaries and united opposites: male and female, young and old, far and near, presence and absence,[19] Greek and barbarian, wisdom and madness, civilization and the wild,[20] humans and animals, animate and inanimate. Worshipers (maenads, bacchants) were mostly women, Others. In the god's so-called mystery rites, they served as mediators between Otherness and the psychic and civic order of civilized life. In this role, they were allowed to abandon the homes and domestic duties to which they were ordinarily confined.

Dionysus punishes those who deny his divinity and resist his worship by inflicting delusion and madness upon them. Such were King Pentheus and his mother Agave of Thebes, whose fate was depicted by Euripides in the *Bacchae*.[21] Through the power of the god, an individual submerged himself into nature, he embraced the suspension of *logos*, and he was liberated from all the terms of power and authority defined by culture.[22] The worship of Dionysus, Euripides' play argues, is a cultural necessity. The fate of Pentheus attests that failure to acknowledge internal irrational forces, to relinquish control and dissolve cultural boundaries, wreaks psychic and physical destruction. Otherness, as J.-P. Vernant points out, has a place within the city, and it must have a place in order to ensure the city's well-being. We observe, however, that Otherness is supposed to appear only when it is allowed to do so and to go only where it is told; its presence and the duration and circumstances of that presence are decided and controlled by the powers of the dominant culture.

In Euripides' play, King Pentheus opposes his authority, reason, order, and probity to the claims of the god, who, with his long, flowing hair and dress, incorporates both sexes and simultaneously attracts and repels him. The king enchains and imprisons this creature and is outraged but not converted when Dionysus appears to turn himself into a bull, causes the palace to shake and fire to rise up from his mother Semele's tomb, and his prison to crumble. Pentheus is also unconvinced by the miracles the bacchants, including his own mother, are said to have performed on the mountain. The women (an eyewitness, a cowherd, reports, 660-774) look and act wild. Dressed in fawnskins girded up by snakes, they suckle young deer or wolf cubs. When they strike the ground with the god's staff, the thyrsus, water, wine, or milk gushes forth. When they dance, all of nature moves with them. They would attack the cowherds and shepherds who are spying on them, but the men escape and the women attack the herd instead, tearing cows and bulls apart with their bare hands. Moving on to a village, they seize fire without being burned, steal children, and wound men with their thyrsi but are themselves invulnerable. After, the snakes lick the blood which has spattered on their faces.

Stricken by the god, Pentheus experiences double vision—two suns and two Thebes. Now he sees like a woman, who perceives both her own and the dominant, male point of view, and the god persuades him, in this altered psychic state, to dress as a woman.[23] Thus disguised, he goes to the mountain to spy on the bacchants. Unable to recognize Otherness within himself, he fantasizes that the bacchants, released from social constraints, engage in lewd acts, to which he feels a strong voyeuristic attraction. He climbs a fir tree for a better view but is sighted by the women, who pull the tree down with their bare hands and attack him. Mistaking her own son for a lion cub, Agave tears him limb from limb, mimicking a ritual act in which the embodied god is dismembered by celebrants and then regenerates himself. The *Bacchae* enacts the necessity of honoring life in nature and the life force with which women especially are in touch. Worship of Dionysus is a kind of wisdom, even though when viewed from the perspective of the order that culture imposes, it appears to be madness. But failure to acknowledge the powers of nature, woman, and irrational states of mind—denial of the god—is the greater and far more dangerous form of madness. To "honor" Dionysus is, simultaneously, to yield to and to acquire his power.

The mysteries that honored both Dionysus and Demeter-Persephone celebrated transcendence of mortality through natural and divine powers of generation and regeneration. Like the "secrets" of these powers, mysteries were known only to initiates (*mustoi*, from the verb *muein*, to hide). Emphasizing eternal bliss and joy after life, they promised a continuation of divine protection after death. Probably the earliest, those held at Eleusis in honor of the goddess Demeter, goddess of growing grain, and her daughter Persephone,[24] celebrated the annual rebirth of nature, represented by the return of Persephone from the underworld where she lived with her husband Hades, to visit her mother for six months of the year. Mother-daughter love survives marriage, which in Persephone's case took the form of rape, and earth, though it appears dead, survives to generate new life, especially to revivify grains that nourish human life. Ceremonies enacted or revealed cyclical processes of nature and the paradox of life in death, embodied in Persephone herself. Unlike the mainly female band that attended Dionysus, Eleusinian celebrants were not mainly women; initiation was open to all willing to undergo the required psychological preparation.[25] "*Sympatheia* of souls and rituals," Walter Burkert observes, may "deeply move or even shatter the constructs of reality"; participation offered "a chance to break out of the enclosed and barren ways of predictable existence."[26] Cult rituals of Demeter that were part of Athens's official state religious calendar (not mystery rites) also served to promote the survival and prosperity of the city through the mediation of its women.[27]

Mystery rites, Richard Seaford has suggested, are the opposite of puberty and marriage rites, rituals through which the city "tames" girls, transforming their "wild" "animal" natures and thereby removing them from their essential state of liminal savagery. What Seaford calls "fatal confusions (of gender differences, of human being and sacrificial animal)" were central to Dionysiac cult from its beginnings.[28] The rape of Persephone, central to Demeter's myth and cult, was a paradigm for marriage in classical Athens, a state which the bride resisted and one in which she experienced an imagined (symbolic) death through sacrifice.

> [Persephone's] extended liminality, at once mortuary and bridal . . .is perpetually renewed in the temporary mystic liminality of initiands celebrating her return in an annual festival [at Eleusis] . . .
> Perpetuation of liminality [is] involved in the movement from household ritual (marriage and funeral) to polis cult (maenadism, hero-cult)
> . . .The perpetuation of liminality [is] also its collectivization,its transformation from an agent of potentially dangerous household solidarity into an agent of salutary collective solidarity.[29]

Seen in this light, integrating women into the institutions of the *polis* preempts competition from the family and household, which are, accordingly, subordinated to civic life.

* * * * *

To live in nature—with greater or lesser degrees of comfort and affinity—is also to live in a body, and women bore the burden of embodiment. There were, however, men who embraced countercultural qualities or values associated with the Other. To embrace the Other was to reject the achievement ethic, especially the glorification of *arete* as valor, in favor of either an ethic of pleasure or, in some cases, an altogether different definition of achievement.

As often, we begin with Homer. In the *Odyssey*, Odysseus visits the Phaeacians, a people who detach virtue from valor, recognize no conflict between virtue and pleasure, and cultivate a variety of excellences. Although they do not engage in warfare, they celebrate the heroic exploits of others in song, and they are highly skilled in the arts (artisanship and metallurgy, music and dance), as well as in seafaring, some sports, and agriculture. Their king, Alcinous, explains the Phaeacian view of life to Odysseus, whom a nobleman has accused of cowardice when he is too preoccupied with his homecoming to be much interested in athletic contests. Odysseus, angered, picks up a discus and throws it much farther than any other competitor had done, then challenges almost everyone to almost everything. The king praises Odysseus's virtue and tries to smooth things over:

> But come now
> and take my word to heart, to tell other heroes
> when you dine again in your own hall
> with your wife and children, recalling
> our virtue, the deeds Zeus has given us
> since the days of our ancestors.
> We are not notable boxers or wrestlers,
> but we are fastest in foot and boat races.
> And feasting, music, and dance are dear to us,
> fresh clothes, warm baths, and bed. (8.239-249)

Homer perhaps has his tongue in his cheek when he lets the king slip easily from the special skills and strengths of his people to their love of comfort and pleasure. To the Phaeacian way of thinking, the differences between the exercise of virtue and the pursuit of pleasure are inconsequential. It is therefore probably not by chance that the queen, described as having qualities of leadership and judgment associated only with men in Greek culture, holds exceptional status in the Phaeacian community. If born male, she would have ruled as king; as it is, she is consort to her uncle, who is descended from the younger branch of the royal line, while she is descended from the elder. It is through her influence that her people live in harmony. She is still subordinate to her husband, however, and does not participate in the all-male assembly or its decisions. Does Homer imply that a people who honor a woman ruler and do not cultivate warrior skills are less competitive than Greeks and therefore achieve a lesser degree of excellence? Perhaps, although Homer also glorifies Odysseus's *arete* in order to anticipate his physical prowess in the climactic contest of the bow (Book 21), which leads to the defeat of the suitors and the reestablishment of his identity and authority at Ithaca.

In Greek, though not in Phaeacian society, generic woman, Pandora's daughters, was dangerous not only because she embodied deceit, mortality, evil, and changeability; she was also an incitement to and purveyor of pleasure. The praise and pursuit of *eros* was antithetic to the values of the dominant culture, a force of subversion from within. But the threat did not come only from women. At all periods of antiquity, there were men, especially writers of short lyric poetry, who sang the praises of enjoyment—an anachronistic "Gather Ye Rosebuds" school. Their attitude is celebratory and playful. Since life is brief and youth, the season of enjoyment, even briefer, the poets of pleasure argue, we ought to live in and for the moment, an attitude best known through Horace's famous phrase, *Carpe diem*. The pleasures of that youthful moment are drinking and making love and poetry: wine, women, and song.[30]

Pleasure, being in and of the body, senses, and emotions, is inherently democratic, experienced by all and accessible to all. It is immediate, having no greater end than enjoyment of the here and now. To devote yourself to pleasure meant "yielding" to sensory experience, the body, passion. Given the logic of this pursuit in Greco-Roman terms, it might even mean, for better and for worse, yielding to unreason and madness. Implicit in "Gather Ye Rosebuds" poetry are the paradoxes that immanence—being in the moment—is an avenue to transcendence when immortalized in poetry and that a vivid moment of sensory or emotional experience deserves to be preserved in human memory as much as an act of valor or other (by some definition heroic) achievement. Many enthusiasts of pleasure make no claim, however, that enjoyment has to be the reward for anything other than itself. Archilochus (625 B. C.?), one of the earliest poets to write in the first person, is probably implying a war-celebration/pleasure antithesis when he boasts his skills in twin spheres, fighting and writing poetry:

> I am two things: a fighter who follows the Master of Battles,
> and one who understands the gift of the Muses' love.

Anacreon states his literary preference as a choice between these mutually exclusive alternatives:

> I have no love for the man who,
> lying next to the bowl brimful with wine,

> tells of quarrels and tearful battle;
> give me one who, commingling the glorious gifts
> of the Muses and Aphrodite,
> celebrates beloved enjoyment.

As a matter of fact, one does not need to go to war or engage in athletic competitions in order to fight:

> Bring water, boy, bring wine,
> bring a garland of flowers;
> I would box a round
> with Love.

By the time of the Roman poet Ovid (first century B.C.), the antithesis has become a cliche, and variations on the theme "Make love, not war" are common in his collection *Amores* (Loves). In the first poem of this collection, Ovid declares he was about "to hold forth on arms and violent wars in the weighty meter (of epic poetry: dactylic hexameter), but Cupid "giggled and stole a foot from the second line" (the result was elegiac meter) and commanded him to write about love. In another poem Ovid compares the lives of the soldier and the lover:

> Every lover is a soldier, and Cupid also bivouacs.
>   Believe me, Atticus, every lover campaigns.
> The time of life for war is the time for Venus, too:
>   an old soldier, an old lover—both disgraces! (*Amores* 1.9.1-4)

Ovid draws out the comparison: Both hold nightwatches, endure hardships, have enemies, lay sieges; "Mars is uncertain, Venus no sure thing, either" (29).

If pursuing love was play, not work, it was arduous, nonetheless, and demanded the stamina of youth. Aging Ibycus feels unequal to the occasion:

> Again Eros, languid, glances at me
> beneath dusky lids,
> then, with his million charms,
> tosses me into Cypris' fatal net.
> Truly, I am shaking: a champion racehorse,

prizewinner but now old,
drawing the car with fast hooves
into the lineup.

Though these poets praised the moment and its pleasures, they did not offer men, much less women, anything like integration into life-in-nature and its cycles as an alternative to traditional male pursuits. Women belong in the community of nature, but even there they are perceived as objects of erotic interest for only a short phase of the life cycle, and then, poets also tell us, they were often in competition with boys.[31] In the pleasure-seeking mode and in the company of unequal partners, men give themselves over to sensuality, emotions, and non- or irrationality. Here, the body is permitted to exist and be acknowledged. Here, men abandon control and take a leave of absence from serious endeavors, such as intellectual, moral, and political pursuits. "With his big hammer, smithy Eros clobbered me/again and washed me in an icy torrent." "I'm in love again, and yet I'm not,/I rage with madness, then again I don't." In the second poem (not a fragment), Anacreon expresses about as succinctly as possible the association of erotic love and madness and the belief that they confound reason. It wasn't always fun or amusing. As Catullus put it in poem 85: "I hate and I love. How this happens, I cannot say./ I know only that it does, and I am crucified."

The poet Sappho of Lesbos also dissociated herself from the standard antithesis between virtue-achievement and pleasure but rejected countercultural male attitudes as well. In an poem addressed to a woman friend, perhaps a fellow artist, Sappho uses heroic, male *arete*, defined in terms of Homeric and post-Homeric warfare, as foil for her own preference, beholding a beautiful love object:

Some say a host of horsemen, some of infantry,
others of ships is the most beautiful thing
on the dark earth, but I say
    it is what you love.
It is easy to make this clear
to everyone: Helen, very beautiful
and very stricken by love, deserted
her most noble husband
and went to Troy—sailed, forgot
her daughter and dear parents

completely. . . . . .
    lead her astray.
(2 lines missing)
now reminds me of Anactoria,
    also far away,
        whose lovely walk and bright shining
face I would rather see than
Lydian chariots and foot soldiers
    armed for battle.

Sappho is subject, and her own point of view, the basis of her authority.[32] She contrasts the sight that gives her pleasure, the woman she loves, with the presumed male preference, the sight of military forces in battle formation. In merely naming the latter, Sappho displays nothing of her special poetic skill, vivid and detailed visual description, for these objects are neither splendid nor inspiring in comparison with Anactoria. But lovely Anactoria is not now present to Sappho's sight. Like Helen, she is far away, away from home (Sappho). Beautiful love objects may have minds of their own and these minds may lead them astray. Helen, for example, should have cherished home, husband, child, and parents, but she fell in love with Paris and abandoned them. So, we infer, Anactoria abandoned Sappho, who continues to direct her gaze toward this lovely young woman, even though she is no longer present. Feelings and their complexities, psychological forces, and aesthetic perception are interior, personal, outside the purview of male *arete*; they are, nevertheless, equally worthy of poetic commemoration. Sappho is one of the few surviving women poets from antiquity explicitly to contrast her own point of view, preference, and feelings with a traditional male outlook. We see in her antithesis intimations of other polarities (objective/subjective, exterior/interior) that have become part of traditional definitions of male/female difference.

The *locus classicus* of countercultural opposition to the achievement ethic is the Hellenistic philosophy of Epicurus. Like the Stoics, Epicurus derived ethics from the physical world—the structure, order, and processes of nature.[33] Like the Stoics, Epicurus advocated self-cultivation and self-sufficiency, a posture of philosophical detachment; unlike the Stoic, the Epicurean posture of detachment deliberately leaned away from dominant social and cultural norms. The writings of Epicurus have come down to us in only fragmentary form, but his views were set forth with powerful art and argument by the Roman poet Lucretius.[34] Writing in epic meter and in the didactic tradition of Hesiod, Lucretius set out to show how happiness, the good life, and peace of mind depended on an understanding of the way nature worked, specifically an atomic theory of physics first proposed by the natural scientist-philosopher Democritus. We think of value theory as belonging to the province of philosophy, and modern scientific studies have devalued and objectified nature (what is known) and the investigator of nature (the knower).[35] But Lucretius worked within a tradition that united poetry, philosophy, and science: Empedocles, a pre-Socratic philosopher, discussed natural science in epic verse, and Hesiod's didactic epics, written before Greek science came into existence, were philosophical.

Understand the true "nature of things" (the title of Lucretius's work; Epicurus's essay on physics, *On Nature*, is lost), and you will maximize enjoyment of life and be free from baseless fear and other obstacles to achieving the best state of being, tranquillity of mind and body, *ataraxia*. To study his philosophy, you memorize Epicurus's maxims, think about them, discuss them with friends and colleagues who are engaged in the same quest as you. Understanding is something that evolves. Epicurean teaching promised as much control over one's self and life circumstances as was humanly possible, but there were strict limits to how much control anyone could expect to have.[36] As summed up by Philodemus, another follower, Epicurean teaching proposed a four-fold remedy to human misery: "God is nothing to fear, death is nothing to dread, the good is easy to secure, the dreadful easy to endure."[37]

Lucretius's *natura* is female; no force in the universe is more powerful, and she replaces the divinities of Greco-Roman religion and myth. Epicureans believed that gods as traditionally conceived exist, but care nothing for human affairs; they deserve to be called gods only because they enjoy complete and uninterrupted tranquillity. As *rerum . . . creatrix*, the creator of things (1.629, 2.1117, 5.1362), nature is analogous to *Aeneadum genetrix . . . alma Venus*, nurturing Venus,[38] mother of the race of Aeneas, whose aid Lucretius invokes in creating his poem, and who is the cause of all generation, fruitfulness, abundance, and loveliness:

> Mother of the race of Aeneas,
>   pleasure of mortals and gods,

nurturing Venus:
beneath the gliding signs of the sky,
over the ship-supporting sea,
on the fruit-bearing earth,
you make everything teem with life
since through you every race of living things
is conceived and born into light.
The winds and clouds flee your coming, goddess,
for you the ingenious earth sends up sweet flowers,
for you the broad sea laughs,
the calm sky, bathed in light, glistens.
Once the spring day appears,
once the fertile west wind gains gentle strength,
the flying birds mark your coming,
their breasts pierced by your power.
The beasts of the field caper through lush grasses,
swim rushing streams, seized with pleasure,
each follows wherever you lead.
Until on seas, in woods, rapid rivers,
the leafy homes of birds, green stretches of field,
you strike ingratiating desire in every creature,
to make each create a new generation of its own.
And since you alone govern the nature of things,
and nothing rises to the bright shores of light
without you, nothing joyful or lovable comes to be,
I seek you as my ally in writing this poem, in which
I am trying to explain the nature of things
to our Memmius, whom you, goddess, have favored
so that he excels at every time in every way.
For his sake, goddess, give lasting charm to my words.
(*The Nature of Things* 1.1-28)

Lucretius's introduction is ingratiating (hopefully to both the goddess and Memmius, his addressee and reader; certainly to readers today) as well as traditional; it would, in fact, seem to contradict Epicurean beliefs about the gods. Why does Lucretius seek Venus's favor? Let us say for the time being that she is a symbol of natural and artistic, generative and creative powers. But there is an additional puzzle. Venus, as mother of Rome's legendary founder Aeneas, is presumed to have a special interest in the well-being of the Roman Republic. The Memmius whom Lucretius addresses has been identified as a distinguished nobleman who devoted himself to public service during two turbulent decades prior to the end of the Roman Republic.[39] Lucretius acknowledges civil unrest at Rome in the conclusion of the prologue, a prayer to Venus to subdue Mars (1.29-43). Epicureans thought that participation in public and political life, the pursuit and possession of wealth, power, and what passes for achievement and success in most men's estimation were likely to be obstacles to inner peace. Lucretius will show that nature, though destructive as well as creative, is the greatest ruling power, far greater than any king, mortal or immortal, or political empire.[40]

Too often, mortals, indoctrinated into conventional beliefs of religion and myth, live in terror of god-sent catastrophes—natural disasters such as fire, flood, and drought—and of divine punishment for wrongdoing in an afterlife. Those who understand and accept the realities of physical existence fear neither the gods nor death. Knowing how nature works frees people to enjoy the pleasures of this life, the only life there is, because the human mind/spirit perishes with the body at the time of death. In a vivid and well-known passage, Lucretius conjures an indignant Nature, impatient with the all-too-common human tendency to desire the impossible and disdain the possible. Personified, she adopts the conversational tone of satire to dispense some trenchant moral advice:

> Why, mortal, do you take such pains to wallow
> in grievous suffering? Why do you weep and wail
> at death? If the life you had was gratifying,
> why has everything slipped through your fingers
> like water from a cracked jar, and been lost
> without ever having been appreciated?
> Be level-headed, not stupid;
> welcome carefree rest and depart
> like a guest from a banquet, sated with life. (3.933-939)

After one has lived for a time, Nature continues, life offers no new pleasures. One should not expect to have the same ones extended indefinitely. It is especially unseemly for bad-tempered old codgers, who no longer enjoy life and maybe never did, to complain. The old must make way for the young: "To no one is life given in perpetuity; to every person, for use unto death" (971). We cannot control death nor should we regard it as an evil. And when we contemplate the time before and the time after our own life spans, we see how insignificant we are, how restful the lasting sleep to come.[41] Well-known myths that tell of punishments in the afterlife express truths about human nature, not divine power. Tityos is the man racked by obsessive love in *this* life, Sisyphus a man condemned to a life of torment because his appetite for power can never be satisfied. Even the greatest benefactors of the human race—the omnipotent Persian King of Kings, the Roman general and statesman Scipio, Homer, the philosophers Democritus and Epicurus—all have died.

What, then, do we want out of life? The correct measure of and for any person is need, which nature alone determines.[42] Lucretius compares the security philosophy provides against stressful contests for wealth and power with the safety of a person who stands on shore watching a storm at sea. Nature demands only "that the body be free from pain, the mind enjoy pleasure free from care and fear." She does not feel deprived without lavish banquets and opulent appointments but prefers a grassy, shaded spot by a quiet stream in the company of few friends. Luxuries are useless; embroidered coverlets do not dispel a fever faster than simple cotton. Memmius may thrill at the sight of legions practicing military maneuvers on the Campus Martius or warships patrolling the seas, but neither wars nor battles free a man from the fear of the things over which he has no power.[43] So much for the glories of Rome invoked in the poem's prologue. The reward for detachment from worldly values is psychic autonomy and peace, not the kind of peace Venus could bestow by subduing Mars, not the kind of peace that would result from the quelling of political unrest.

The one arena in which men can hope to exercise control is philosophical understanding: Nature has set a fixed limit to all aspects of existence, and to mortal existence in particular. There is no conflict between embodied existence and reason/mind/spirit because the human body, its life force (*anima*), and its mind/soul (*animus*) are all composed of atoms: minute, indestructible, indivisible particles endlessly combining and recombining. Those of the life force and mind/soul are lighter in weight and less dense than those of the body. The aggregate of atoms which form any object may disperse into space for any number of reasons, among them the ending of a natural process or life itself. All of these different atoms scatter at the time of an individual's death. Thus, there is no dichotomy between body and spirit because both are mortal and at death, both "die," or are, rather, released into the universal pool of matter to become available for recycling into something new.[44] Moreover, new matter is always being formed, old is disintegrating, parts of complex objects are constantly shifting. The world as we know it has perished, is perishing, will continue to perish. Therefore, our only possible wise choice is to accept mutability and impermanence as the condition of human life and incorporate it into our quest for happiness.

The source of all atoms is Earth itself, called *mater*, mother, and is described by a striking synthesis of earth, body, and woman imagery. The inexhaustible generative powers of Earth, Lucretius explains, gave rise to the religious cult of the Great Mother, Magna Mater (2.600-660):

> quare magna deum mater materque ferarum
> et nostri genetrix haec dicta est corporis una. (2.598-599)
> Therefore, she, and she alone, is called the great
> mother of gods and mother of beasts and begetter
> of our body.

The universe itself is a single organic entity subject to the cycle of birth, growth, maturity, decay, and, ultimately, death, and thus will come to a natural end (a belief shared with Stoics). This is the perspective from which we should view human affairs.

In mainstream classical thought, man hopes to escape nature by creating civil society and a culture associated with it. Epicureans, rejecting the dominant values, concluded that the only possible way to live in accordance with nature was to live one's life in the private domain. To try to exist in the public sphere required participation in public values, which were implicated in a quest for wealth and power, especially political power. In order to be true to nature and themselves, Epicureans withdrew from society. In fact, Epicurus gathered friends and disciples at his house in Athens (The Garden), and his followers tended to form their own "families" or communities (though there is no indication that Lucretius belonged to one). In these circumstances they could be free from disturbing and distracting influences, maximize enjoyment of life and self-development, and cultivate friendships through philosophical pursuits.[45]

Epicureanism presented an alternative value system to the conventional, dominant one which emphasized standards of "success" and "greatness" not unlike those we know today. Epicurean philosophers aspired to the best of human wisdom and happiness, bestowing on themselves an outsider status which others may have found quaint, if not ludicrous. Cicero, known for his philosophical eclecticism (with strong Stoic and Peripatetic leanings) had little use for Epicureanism because it devalued everything to which he aspired. His close friend Atticus, with whom he had a long and voluminous correspondence, was drawn to Epicurean thinking, however, but the attraction doesn't seem to have been a hindrance to their friendship.

It is not surprising that women, confined to the private domain within patriarchal culture, were not excluded from Epicurean communities. Women were, by implication, capable of thought, friendship, and the self-control necessary to live the philosophic life, which entailed a somewhat austere hedonism.[46] The Epicurean view does not make women the scapegoats for sexuality on the traditional grounds that their very existence and nature constitute a dangerous incitement to evil and a source of corruption to men.[47] In his discussion of sexuality and desire (*venus*, the power of Venus) in Book 4 (1029ff.), however, Lucretius stresses the power and dangers of sexual pleasure: it causes acute *tarache* (opposite of *ataraxia*) but becomes an obstacle to tranquillity if completely denied. *Venus* makes fools of men, deluding them about the beauty or desirability of their beloved. Men and women share equally in pleasure, and what we would call the genetic makeup of each child comes from both parents equally.[48]

Nature is not only creator, like Venus and Earth (the Great Mother), but destroyer as well. Book 2 concludes with the prediction that Earth will die, worn out by old age (1105-1174). The poem ends with an excruciatingly detailed description of devastation brought on by plague (6.1090-1286),[49] which kills or blights all living things, destroying the hard-won fruits of a man's labor. To urge anyone to take nature as guide to all expectations and conduct turns out, then, to be no facile recommendation. Who is able to contemplate plague and the dissolution of the world with equanimity? Only such a person could be said to achieve tranquillity and deserves to be called happy.

Epicurean teaching argued that values and knowledge are interdependent and that values arise from the foundation of nature. It rejected values of the dominant culture, death-centeredness and the achievement ethic. Nature imposes equal status on all people. Mortality, the workings of the physical world, and basic human needs are common to everyone without distinction. Gender difference is Otherness but takes its meaning from the broader context of nature, which is characteristically diverse, multiple, complex, and changeful. Traditional constructions of gender difference are given no place in the realm of values.

The Roman lyric poet and satirist Horace combined the Epicurean valuation of pleasure with the "Gather Ye Rosebuds," make-love-not-war themes of early Greek lyric. He also fused the supposed opposites virtue and pleasure into an oxymoron, the virtues of pleasure. He incorporated many traditional Roman and some Stoic values into his poetry as well. His "here and now" is thus a more complex philosophical and artistic creation than any we see in his poetic models. One of his best-known poems is the *Carpe diem* ode, 1.11, in which he urges a young woman to enjoy the present moment because our life span is the merest moment in time:

> Don't ask, my clearest Crystal, what end the gods
> have given me or you, don't play the Babylonian
> numbers game. Better to accept whatever
> will be, whether Jove has allotted
> many winters, or this is the last, which now
> with opposing breakers wears out
> the Tyrrhenian sea. Be wise: Strain the wine
> and clip back long hope with our brief lifetime.
> Even as we speak, its envious course will have
> been spent. Seize the day, put scant trust in tomorrow. (Ode 1.11)

The girl, ironically named Leuconoe, Greek "Clear Mind," is obsessed with the future ("Where will it all end?"), which she attempts to discover by consulting astrologers (Babylonian numbers). Horace advises her to enjoy what is available in the present—wine and, we presume, love—not because love is for the young and youth is fleeting (as earlier lyric poets argued), but because life itself is. No one knows how long present opportunities will be available. Even the sea, though it seems eternal and unchanging, is exhausted by the ceaseless motion of the tide. Our time of life is so short that even as we are talking about it, it is already gone. Since we live within nature, we are (morally) obligated to accept what is appropriate to our mortal status: enjoyment of available pleasures.

Even as Horace espoused the countercultural tradition of praising pleasure, he also transformed *virtus*, dominant notions of virtue, achievement, and success into self-defined moral-philosophical and poetic values. In his hymn to a wine jar (Ode 3.21), a parody of a song of praise addressed to a god, he unites opposing attitudes and traditions—celebration of the here-and-now, the philosophical quest—and plays them off against one another. Enjoying himself at the home of his friend Messalla Corvinus, a nobleman with a philosophic bent, Horace invites the wine jar to join the party. Wine embodies the power of the god Dionysus-Bacchus, Releaser who frees men from the serious endeavors of culture, especially philosophy and politics: Corvinus's quest for wisdom through serious conversations; Cato's legendary moral rectitude; a hard(y) nature—a much-admired, old-fashioned Roman quality, which may, Horace slyly implies, also be inflexible and rigid; cares— private, public, and political—and the best-laid plans, all of which reflect excessive preoccupation with control; a poor man's fears of political and military force. All are subject to the formidable power of the jar and its contents, which very effectively performs the work of Dissolver of Boundaries. At the end of the poem, Horace imagines Venus and Bacchus will intervene to prolong the moment and the song that celebrates it until dawn, and perhaps also through the lasting darkness that comes to all. Art, playful as this poetic example is, is one of the most serious of all cultural endeavors, and may well, he suggests, outlast all the preoccupations listed in the poem that others take so seriously.

Horace goes so far as to disengage virtue from any kind of external power, redefining it as inner power or capability. His own virtues are poetic talent and independent moral judgment; moral virtues, private and public, ought to be valued more highly than achievement, success, and political, social, or economic standing. They alone truly deserve to be called achievements and to transcend death.[50] Caesar Augustus, first citizen (*princeps*) and de facto emperor of Rome, held the kinds of power Horace mistrusted. If Horace praised Caesar the man, he declined to praise the power. An attitude of philosophical detachment was a safe haven from political commitment. High stations were dangerous places, and Horace urged his readers to cultivate expectations and a lifestyle that were *humilis*, humble, lowly, literally close to or of the earth (*humus*). Human beings are earthbound, an attitude very consonant with Epicureanism. We should orient ourselves accordingly: not look beyond the present, what is available to us, our lifetime, except through art, moral reflection, and moral example.

Hesiod, the Stoic Seneca, and the Epicurean Lucretius all consider what it means to live in accordance with nature. Natural processes and patterns (Hesiod), *logos/ratio* (Stoics), and the material foundation of the universe (Epicureans) are guides to right attitudes and principles. While each implies an ethic derived from universal membership in the community of nature, only Epicureanism eschewed hierarchies of power. Lucretius suggested that basic human need is an economic value and that human status in nature should make us all equals in human society. But, paradoxically, his is an ethic for the private individual. Social norms and dominant cultural values ought to be avoided because they are likely to be sources of distraction and corruption. Epicureans stopped short of considering the wider implications of their views, a process that might have contributed to the development of public values which were different from those of the mainstream culture.

The ethics developed by Hellenistic philosophers and their Roman successors acknowledged each person's quest for happiness but remain focused on control: What is within our power? How can we maximize the range of what is voluntary in our lives and minimize the effects of what is involuntary? Men as individuals embark upon a philosophic quest, and their primary goal is the achievement of internal, self-control, strategies for governing their thoughts, affects, and actions. Although Hellenistic philosophies located the greatest virtue and value within life itself, all with the exception of Epicureanism made death and other natural limits central to their thought, placed a premium on reason, and manifested a preoccupation with control. These concerns connected them with traditional belief systems.

There were alternative, in some instances countercultural, attitudes to the achievement ethic in classical antiquity. For the Phaeacians, virtue is discrete from valor and not inherently in conflict with pleasure. Early Greek lyric celebrators of pleasure, including Sappho, defined their preferences against the dominant concept of virtue. Lucretius and Horace made a virtue of pleasure, but the philosopher imposed rather austere restrictions on pleasure as moral value. The Epicurean view, like the Stoic, elevated wisdom to the highest form of both but, unlike the Stoic, did not banish bodily experience, since everything we know comes from our physical existence. Horace held pleasure and virtue in equipoise: They were both complements and contradictions. In presenting a world view cheerfully constructed from oxymora, Horace characteristically resisted and subverted dualities and polarities in favor of a more open-ended, complex reading of human experience.

Our exploration of what the Greco-Roman legacy tells us about the identity of Others and definitions of Otherness has led us to consider close associations of earth and more generally nature, woman, the body, and the conditions of embodied existence. Definition is an act of separation; separation determines most relationships to Others. There is never any doubt, however, that Others have powers that men ignore at their peril; Others must be kept not just apart but under control, organized to serve men's power and their social and cultural values. Dionysiac myth and cult especially reveal how fundamental to Greek culture these ways of accommodating difference were. Aspects of nature provide guidelines useful to human activities—order, repetition and patterning, and, by inference, the principles of right season and appropriateness—and observation of likenesses that transcend categories of difference ensures that separation stops short of the extremity of isolation.

If they must, men may occasionally absent themselves from the pursuit of virtue/achievement and abandon control, but to engage with the involuntary more than absolutely necessary is risky behavior. In the classical legacy, pleasure, pain, and evil, all associated with woman, tend to be seen as the enemies of virtue and achievement, which are goods. Most of the time and under most circumstances, women must go where they're told—whether to stay at home or go to the mountains. Both Stoicism and Epicureanism offer women some hope of living the good life if they submit to male standards, the disciplines of philosophic studies and self-control.

In the next chapter, we consider how Greco-Roman views of social morality reflected and incorporated established constructions of gender difference and power arrangements, emphasizing male relationships and the proper division of power among men. We shall look at the ties that bind men in both the private and public spheres, in order to learn something about how relationships based on power evolved, and how the dichotomy between the domestic and the civil/political arose.

Notes

[1] Jean-Pierre Vernant, "The Masked Dionysus of Euripides, *Bacchae*," Chapter 14 in Vernant and Pierre Vidal-Naquet, *Myth and Tragedy*, trans. Janet Lloyd (Atlantic Highlands, NJ: Humanities Press, 1981), p.402.

[2] James Redfield, *Nature and Culture in the Iliad. The Tragedy of Hector* (Chicago: University of Chicago Press, 1995 [1975]), p.71.

[3] At *Iliad* 5.749 (also 8.393 and 433), Homer describes the Horai, goddesses named from *hora*, season. Keepers of the great cloud-gate which marks the entrance to the heavens and Olympus, home of the gods, they oversee the boundary between the temporal world of mortals and the timeless world of the gods. Mortals are "creatures of a day," *ephemeroi*.

[4] The Latin equivalent is *proprius*, adj., one's own, proper to one's self or a given time, place, set of circumstances.

[5] Laszlo Versenyi, *Man's Measure. A Study in the Greek Image of Man from Homer to Sophocles* (Albany: State University of New York Press, 1974), Chapter 2, "The *Erga*," pp. 43-69. esp. 57-60.

[6] Recent works on images women in the *Odyssey* include Nancy Felson-Rubin, *Regarding Penelope* (Princeton: Princeton University Press, 1994), and Beth Cohen, ed., *The Distaff Side. Reflections of the Female in Homer's Odyssey* (New York: Oxford University Press, 1995). Homer in general: Harold Bloom, ed., *Homer's Iliad* and *Homer's Odyssey* (New York: Chelsea House, 1996), and Seth L. Schein, *Reading the Odyssey* (Princeton: Princeton University Press, 1996).

[7] For an introduction to the oral epic tradition, see A.B. Lord, *The Singer of Tales* (New York: Atheneum, 1965 [Harvard University Press, 1960]).

[8] "In the perspective of the Homeric simile the human world receives its pattern from that already established in the natural world," Norman Austin, *Archery at the Dark of the Moon. Poetic Problems in Homer's Odyssey* (Berkeley and Los Angeles: University of California Press, 1975), p. 117. See also Martin Muller, "The Simile," in Harold Bloom, ed., *Homer. Modern Critical Views* (New York: Chelsea House, 1986), pp. 217-231; Carroll Moulton, *Similes in the Homeric Poems. Hypomnemata* 4 (Gottingen: Vanderholck and Ruprecht, 1977); Helene P. Foley, "'Reverse Similes' and Sex Roles in the *Odyssey*," *Arethusa* 11 (1978).

[9] At 4.791-793, Penelope is compared to a trapped lion, for she is besieged by suitors and prevented by social norms from taking action. The simile suggests both that she is like a warrior and that she is like Odysseus.

10 The cyclops violates the laws of hospitality even more flagrantly than the suitors. His bestiality—what he eats and how he eats it—is underscored by comparing him to a mountain lion: He crunches the bones of Odysseus's men (9.292).

11 Similes also bind the inanimate world with the animate: Odysseus hiding in his leaf-bed is like a farmer keeping fire alive by putting a brand in the embers (5.487-493). The sizzle of the cyclops' eyeball when stuck with the fiery stake is like a piece of white-hot metal plunged into cold water (9.392-396). (See also 12.230, 19.38-40 and 204-210, 20.24-30, 21.1-3 and 49f., 22.18ff. and 124. 24.168.)

12 On *homophrosyne*, likemindedness, see Norman Austin, *Archery at the Dark of the Moon* pp.188-189, 202-204; Nancy Felson-Rubin, *Regarding Penelope*, p.44 and n1.

13 Moulton, *Similes*, p. 133; Foley,"'Reverse Similes,'" p.7f.

14 When Odysseus plucks the bow to take fatal aim against the suitors, its string sounds like the voice of a swallow (21.404-411). Later, when Odysseus's little band and the suitors join in combat in the great hall, Athena assumes the likeness of a swallow and settles on a rafter to watch (22.240). Moulton, *Similes*, pp. 151f. See also Austin, *Archery*.

15 Walter Burkert, *Ancient Mystery Cults* (Cambridge: Harvard University Press, 1987), esp. Chapter 2, "Origins and Identities," pp. 30-53; and Marcel Detienne, *Dionysus at Large*, trans. Arthur Goldhammer (Cambridge: Harvard University Press, 1989).

16 Marcel Detienne, *Dionysus at Large*, pp.46ff. For dancing and the state of being filled with the god, *entheos*, see also E.R. Dodds, Introduction to Euripides, *Bacchae* (Oxford: Clarendon Press, 2d ed., 1960), pp.xi-xx.

17 "The constitution of an animal must be regarded as resembling that of a well-governed city-state. For when order is once established in a city there is no need of a special ruler with arbitrary powers to be present at every activity, but each individual performs his own task as he is ordered, and one act succeeds another because of custom. And in the animals the same process goes on [because of nature and because each part of them, since they are so constituted, is naturally suited to perform its own function; so that] there is no need of soul in each part, but since it is situated in a central origin of authority over the body, the other parts live by their structural attachment to it and perform their own functions in the course of nature." *Movement of Animals*, sect. 703a , = Aristotle, vol. xii, Loeb ed., trans. A. L. Peck and E. S. Foster (Cambridge, MA: Harvard University, 1968).

18 Froma I. Zeitlin, "Playing the Other: Theater, Theatricality, and the Feminine in Greek Drama," in Zeitlin and John Winkler, eds., *Nothing to Do*

with Dionysos? (Princeton: Princeton University Press, 1990), pp.63-96; Simon Goldhill, *Reading Greek Tragedy* (Cambridge: Cambridge University Press, 1986), pp.259-264, 265-286; Richard Seaford, *Reciprocity and Ritual. Homer and Tragedy in the Developing City State* (Oxford: Clarendon Press, 1994), Chapter 7, pp.235-280, and Chapter 8, pp.281-327.

[19] J.-P. Vernant, *Myth and Tragedy*, Chapter 14, "The Mask of Dionysus," suggests that Dionysus's mask signifies the god's presence and absence and his association with "the false solidity of the world of appearances," pp.384-403, esp. 393f.

[20] Vernant, pp. 398f. Seaford, *Reciprocity and Ritual*, in discussions of *Bacchae* and *Antigone*, points out that the *polis* cult of Dionysus "embodies the community of the *polis*" (pp. 252ff.) and "destroys the family to save the city" (pp.349ff.)

[21] Dionysus was the son of Zeus and Semele, daughter of Cadmus and princess of Thebes. Or so Semele claimed; her sisters Agave and Autonoe had their doubts. Semele asked Zeus to prove his divinity. He appeared to her as a bolt of lightning, which consumed her. Zeus rescued her seven-month fetus, Dionysus, and sewed him into his thigh until he was ready to be born. At the opening of Euripides' drama, Dionysus, who has grown up in Asia, returns to his native city Thebes. Pentheus, son of Agave, who succeeded Cadmus as king, and his mother refuse to acknowledge Dionysus's divinity.

[22] In the words of E. R. Dodds:

"We ignore at our peril the demand of the human spirit for Dionysiac experience. For those who do not close their minds against it such experience can be a deep source of spiritual power and *eudaimonia* [blessedness]. But for those who repress the demand in themselves or refuse its satisfaction to others transform it by their act into a power of disintegration and destruction, a blind natural force that sweeps away the innocent with the guilty. When that has happened, it is too late to reason or to plead; in man's justice there is room for pity, but there is none in the justice of Nature; to our 'Ought' its sufficient reply is the simple 'Must'; we have no choice but to accept that reply and to endure as we may." Euripides, *Bacchae*, Introduction, p.xiv.

[23] Froma Zeitlin,"Playing the Other."

[24] On the Demeter-Persephone myth, see Marilyn Arthur, "Politics and Pomegranates: An Interpretation of the Homeric Hymn to Demeter," *Arethusa* 10.1 (1977): 7-47; and Froma Zeitlin, "Cultic Models of the Female: Rites of Dionysus and Demeter," *Arethusa* 15 (1982): 129-157.

[25] According to the fifth-century A.D. scholar Proclus, quoted by Burkert, *Ancient Mystery Cults*, p.114, [the rites] "cause sympathy of the souls with the ritual in a way that is unintelligible to us, and divine, so that some of the ini-

tiands are stricken with panic, being filled with divine awe; others assimilate themselves to the holy symbols, leave their own identity, become at home with the gods, and experience divine possession."

[26] Burkert, *op. cit.*

[27] Froma Zeitlin, "Cultic Models of the Female."

[28] Seaford, *Reciprocity and Ritual*: The liminal savagery of girls, pp.384ff. A married woman maenad, because she reverts to that savagery as celebrant, may be required to sacrifice her own children, as Agave sacrifices Pentheus. The quotation is from p.364.

[29] Seaford, *Reciprocity and Ritual*, pp.383-385.

[30] While Dorothy Dinnerstein's focus in *The Mermaid and the Minotaur. Sexual Arrangements and Human Malaise* (New York: Harper and Row, 1976) is on the social and cultural consequences of assigning child-rearing exclusively to women, she also discusses the association of women and carnal pleasure (Chapter 7, "The Dirty Goddess," pp.124-159). See also Sara Ruddick, *Maternal Thinking. Toward a Politics of Peace* (Boston: Beacon Press, 1989), who points out the connection between birthing labor, embodiment, and carnality (Chapter 8, "Histories of the Human Flesh," pp.185-218).

[31] See K.J. Dover, *Greek Homosexuality*. Michel Foucault, *History of Sexuality*, vol. 2, *The Uses of Pleasure*, regards the proprieties of male homoerotic conduct as the most problematic area of Greek sexuality.

[32] On this poem, see Jane Snyder, *The Woman and the Lyre. Woman Writers in Classical Greece and Rome* (Carbondale: Southern Illinois Press, 1989), pp.22-24; Page duBois, "Sappho and Helen," John Peradotto and J.P. Sullivan, eds., *Women in the Ancient World. The Arethusa Papers* (Albany: State University of New York Press, 1984), pp.95-106.

[33] Julia Annas, *The Morality of Happiness* (New York: Oxford University Press, 1993), Chapter 7, "Rethinking What Is Natural," pp.188-200.

[34] On Lucretius's debt to Epicurus, see Diskin Clay, *Lucretius and Epicurus* (Baltimore: Johns Hopkins University Press, 1983).

[35] See, for example, Evelyn Fox Keller, *Reflections on Gender and Science* (New Haven: Yale University Press, 1985); Keller and Helen Longino, *Feminism and Science* (Oxford: Oxford University Press, 1996).

[36] On *ataraxia*, see Annas, *Morality of Happiness*, Part IV, "Revising Your Priorities", Chapter 16, "Epicurus: Virtue, Pleasure, and Time," pp.334-350.

[37] Quoted by Clay, *Lucretius and Epicurus*, p.178.

[38] Like Venus, Nature, too, is a governing power (*gubernans* 5.77; cf.1.19). The image has political associations and usually applies to Zeus/Jupiter and to kings. Unlike a deity, however, Nature is not responsive to human needs, susceptible to persuasion through prayer or sacrifice. Operating impersonally in

accordance with her own inexorable rules, just as atoms do, the force of Nature oversees everything in the universe and its atomic components.

[39] On Lucius Memmius and his clan, which traced its ancestry back to Aeneas, and on Memmius as generic Roman reader, see Clay, *Lucretius and Epicurus*, pp.212-220.

[40] For the interpretation expressed in the following paragraphs, I am indebted to Clay, *Lucretius and Epicurus*, Chap. 5, "*Paradosis* and Method."

[41] Life as possession for usufruct, Roman legal term.

[42] See Book 2.1-61.

[43] Recall Sappho's Anactoria poem, where the sight of military forces is rejected in favor of the pleasure of seeing the person one loves.

[44] Lucretius's description of atoms and space is pervaded by the notion of natural limit prominent in early Greek thought. All living things are subject to enclosure in the life cycle and its progressive stages leading to death, the ultimate limit. Lucretius reconstitutes this notion in terms of atomic science. The number of atomic particles is infinite, and space, too, is without boundary. Nature has set a limit to the divisibility of matter, however, in that there is a finite number of different kinds of atoms. By "laws" of nature, atoms combine in finite ways to form living species and fixed types of inanimate objects, and by "laws" of nature, each species follows a set pattern of development and possesses a distinct set of characteristics. Lucretius urges acceptance of limit, including the limit of human needs and the end of life, because it inheres in the material world of which we are a part. Neither reason, consciousness, achievement, nor memory authorizes exclusion from limit.

[45] Cicero, *De Finibus* 1.20.65; Seneca (Letter 6.6) says that the making of an Epicurean was not accomplished at school but through *conturbernium*, sharing a tent (as in an army encampment).

[46] Annas, *The Morality of Happiness*, Chap. 16; Nussbaum, *Therapy of Desire*, Chap. 4.

[47] Diogenes Laertius (*Lives of the Philosophers*, Book 10) relates that Epicurus corresponded with at least one woman and that several *hetairai* were associated with his Garden. He says in his will, however, that the daughter of a colleague should be provided for so long as she is obedient to her father's wishes.

[48] In more prevalent views, the father was the determinant of an embryo (the mother being merely its carrier and nurturer). Lucretius states that an embryo is formed from "seeds" of both the male and female. Thus both parents have a share in the genetic makeup of a new human being.

[49] The passage is modeled in part on Thucydides' description of the plague at Athens (Book 2.48ff.); see Clay, *Lucretius and Epicurus*, p.265f.

50 Horace's examples are diverse. They include the Republican heroes Regulus and Cato, both of whom took moral stances that ended illustrious public careers; cf. the unnamed hero described at the opening of Ode 3.3,1-8:

> The man of justice, integrity, and firm
> intent is not shaken by citizens'
> heated commands, nor an insistent
> tyrant's glare, nor South Wind sweeping
>
> the restless Adriatic, nor the terrible hand
> of thundering Jove: if the whole world
> should break apart and fall, its ruins
> will strike him unafraid.

[T]he feminized unity born from the ancient soil leaves the city whole, divided neither by political strife nor the competitive pursuit of glory.
Arlene Saxonhouse[1]

We find in consciousness itself a fundamental hostility toward every other consciousness; the subject can be posed only in being opposed—he sets himself up as the essential, as opposed to the other, the inessential, the object. But the other consciousness. the other ego, sets up a reciprocal claim . . .wars, festivals, trading, treaties, and contests among tribes, nations, and classes tend to deprive the concept *Other* of its absolute sense . . . individuals and groups are forced to realize the reciprocity of their relations. How is it, then, that this reciprocity has not been recognized between the sexes?
Simone de Beauvoir[2]

A moral philosophy is a particular rhetoric. . .[T]he rhetoric of universality has been entirely compatible . . .with the most complete (and often intentional) exclusion of women as moral agents from such loftily universal contructs as the social contract, pure practical rationality, or the good life for man, and with bypassing altogether in application whole areas of life that are the province of women (voluntarily or not), such as the rearing of children.
Margaret Urban Walker[3]

Chapter 6

Social Morality and Patriarchal Rule

In classical antiquity as today, morality, civility, and manners were considered to be the foundations of public order, harmony, and cohesion.[4] Norms of conduct, traditional social values of the dominant culture, incorporate the dualities and hierarchies of patriarchy, including assumptions about class, race, and gender. In Western culture, in both the Judeo-Christian and Greco-Roman traditions, assumptions about gender difference have informed power as moral authority. Moral authorities have been men who reflect and perpetuate patriarchal viewpoints by defining appropriate behavior for both men and women in separate public and private spheres. Others denied rule-making roles look to reconstituting both roles and rules. To question traditional morality challenges not only notions of male/female "natures," but the separation of private from public and the relationship of family to society. It also leads us to reconsider why the family was (and is) regarded as the bulwark of society.[5]

As we have seen, universal membership in nature did not make all men brothers nor all people kin because they belong to the human family. In Western culture, women have, for the most part, been assigned to the private/domestic realm, while men "belong" in public space.[6] Greek and Roman men were first and foremost members of a political state, citizens; to speak of citizenship in the natural world would have been oxymoronic. The Delphic maxim "Know yourself" reminded mortals of their human limits and deficiencies. It did not imply a positive universal bond created by life grounded in nature, much less imply viability itself as power. Norms and paradigms for social morality were man-made and male-centered: oriented to separation rather than connection and to control, honor, and respect among men. In order to provide a secure foundation for patriarchy and to ensure its perpetuation, men created lasting bonds among themselves: fathers and sons, brothers, fellow citizens, fellow members of communities of achievement. They considered these bonds, alternatives to unalloyed self-interest, to be regulated by principles of reciprocity.[7] What further insights do classical sources provide into the rationales for patriarchal social bonds? In this chapter, we look at works of Homer, Aristotle, Greek and Roman New Comedy, and two passages from ancient historians in order to explore the foundations and limits of Greco-Roman social morality, and to begin to consider by negative inference how relationships in postmodern society might be reconfigured.

In the pre-*polis* society of the Homeric poems, obligations, claims, and responsibilities are expressed in terms of relationships but by no means solely in terms of power. Characters often discuss with or among themselves how a particular person should act and why a particular act is right. They believe that certain rules apply to certain kinds of relationships, and they define appropriate conduct is terms of person, time, and circumstance, as well as gender, age, social, economic, or existential status. Rules reflect the particular seen as generic. Moreover, although obligations and proprieties in Homer are individual and contextual, the vocabulary of moral talk is or borders on the formulaic. It is impossible to say to what extent the unity of Homeric moral talk is a narrative strategy, and to what extent it reflects the *mores* of archaic Greek palace society (or a memory of them, to say nothing of how selective that memory might have been). Everyone speaks in the same terms and the same terms apply to all: god and mortal, noble and slave, male and female, young and old. Over time, some particularities of Homeric moral distinctions would become fixed in moral paradigms; we shall encounter them later as character types in New Comedy.

Relationships in Homer are governed by a principle of reciprocity, expressed by the adjective *philos*, dear, one's own, and related words (the noun *philia*, the verb *philein*). Linguist Emile Benveniste, philosopher Bernard Williams, and classicist Simon Goldhill have studied the meaning of these words.[8] *Philia* is closely connected with *aidos*, often translated 'shame,' but better understood in a broader sense, special regard or respect. One looks out for another, giving him/her/it the kind and amount of consideration due. Benveniste believes that the social sense of *philos* is prior to the familial and did not originally refer to personal emotional attachments; *philia* designated a relationship between fellow citizens and was therefore a public, social bond between men. In addition, *philia* also referred to the relationship with a *xenos*, stranger. A stranger who appeared at your home was a potential enemy, but once you received him with proper hospitality, you established mutual, ongoing ties of nonaggression and guest-friendship.

I want to talk about a verb which Homer frequently uses to convey moral meaning. Like *philos* words, *chre*, "it is right or fitting," applies to the evaluation of relationships. It carries nuances relating to human power, its limits and its potential, for the verb's first meaning is "it is determined by fate or necessity." *Chre* is also *the* word that reinforces the social hierarchy of the Homeric world, however—its privileges, prerogatives, and obligations. But how we should act in society often depends on how we should act as mortals; thus, expressions of social norms in Homer at least may have been experienced as conveying some kind or degree of religious sanction. Necessity is determined by fate, death, and divine will, but moral obligations, of course, also take human needs into consideration. For example, when toward the end of *Odyssey* 2 the old nurse Eurycleia learns that Telemachus plans to leave Ithaca in order to try to learn his father's fate, she fears the suitors will plot to harm him and pleads, "There is no need for you to leave home." But there is a "need," and it is multidetermined. The goddess Athena has suggested the plan to Telemachus, a son ought to search for his lost father, sons need their fathers, and now that Telemachus is no longer a child, he needs to make his debut in the outside world of heroes.

The moral force of divine dicta is evident in the first book of the

Iliad, too, when Achilles, enraged that the commander-in-chief has taken his war prize, the girl Briseis, is about to attack Agamemnon. Because the king has violated their mutual relationship, Achilles now regards him as an enemy. He is restrained, however, by Hera and Athena, who grabs him by the hair and tells him he will have "winnings three times as rich" in compensation for Agamemnon's arrogance. Achilles replies:

> Goddess, it is proper that I obey the word
> of both of you, even though my heart is very angry.
> It is better thus; if a man obeys the gods, they listen to him, too. (216-218)

It is not only proper, but necessary (*chre*) that Achilles obey the goddesses, who are more powerful than mortals, but he also reasons that the gods, too, honor the principle of reciprocity: Obey them, especially when they issue a direct command, and they are likely to be well disposed to you in the future.[9] Agamemnon also receives divine instruction early in the *Iliad*. Zeus sends Baleful Dream to him as he sleeps, which chides, "It is not right for a counsel-bearing man to sleep the whole night through" (24-25, 61-62). Now that Achilles has jeopardized the Greek position by refusing to fight, the commander-in-chief ought to be up and about, strategizing with the other chiefs.

Power relationships among men, measured in terms of honor and respect, are the most important human relationships in the *Iliad*, and they determine proper conduct in the public realm of the hero. After Achilles has withdrawn from battle, need, necessity, and propriety are at the center of discussions among the Greek commanders: damage control, and how to appease Achilles' anger so that he will resume fighting. Nestor advises sending Odysseus and Ajax to plead with him. He respectfully reminds Agamemnon, "It is proper for you to speak first, then listen to another who speaks for the common good (9.100-102). Nestor is old and venerable, but Agamemnon is the chief, the leader with the most *time*. He can only enhance the respect which is due to him anyway, the old man tactfully suggests, by accepting good advice and agreeing to the embassy. Achilles welcomes the emissaries: "Greetings. You have come as dear friends, and truly I have great need of you, even though I am angry, for you are dearest of the Achaeans to me" (197-198). Despite long-standing ties of *philia* with these men and despite his own need for emotional support, Achilles refuses their request. His insistence on receiving his rightful share of *time* is challenged by

Phoenix, his boyhood nurse-tutor, who, citing their own lifelong bond of *philia*, urges him to "tame his great spirit," to put the common good above private resentment: "It is not proper for you to have a pitiless heart." Even the gods, Phoenix points out, change their minds, and their virtue, honor, and power are greater than men's (496-498). Achilles reproaches him. A man ought to help his friends and harm his enemies;[10] Agamemnon is no longer any friend of his but Phoenix is, and should act like one.[11]

Only when Achilles is overcome by the need to avenge his dear friend Patroclus's death (Book 19) does he tell Agamemnon: "Now I put an end to my anger toward you, nor is it proper for me to rage unceasingly"(67-68). He values his relationship to Patroclus more than his relationship to Agamemnon. In his reply to Achilles, an apology of sorts, Agamemnon avoids admitting he treated Achilles disrespectfully and blames Zeus, who clouded his judgment by setting Ate (Delusion, personified and female) upon him. Zeus himself, Agamemnon recalls, was once overcome by Ate, victim of the machinations of his conniving wife Hera. The outcome was also a situation in which *time* was disregarded, one which was even more flagrant: Zeus's own son, the hero Heracles, came under Hera's power, and she made him subject to a mere mortal. Achilles is unmoved, either by the excuse or by Agamemnon's lavish gifts. His need of the moment is vengeance, which will be superseded only by the need for victory and by the necessity of death, Achilles' fatal day.

In the *Odyssey*, necessity and need, also expressed by *chre* and related words, apply to the rules and rituals of hospitality and to bonds of affection within the family, where emotional and psychological needs are recognized. Early in the first book, Athena, attentive as always to the fortunes of Odysseus and his family and disguised as Mentes, an old guest-friend, comes to the palace to play the role of mentor[12] to young Telemachus. The house of Odysseus labors under the greed of Penelope's 108 suitors, who, oblivious to any reciprocal obligation to their absent host, are devouring his goods. Telemachus welcomes the goddess properly: "Greetings, stranger. You shall be taken care of in our home. Later, after you have enjoyed a meal, you will tell us what you need" (123-124). Only after tending to a guest's immediate needs is it to polite to ask a him who he is, why he has come, and what he requires to continue his journey. When Athena-Mentes comments that by his looks, he must be Odysseus's son, Telemachus says he has his doubts. She invites his confidence by asking disingenuously, "What is your need?" a question which is not part of the ritual of guest-friendship but which sets the action of the poem, the homecoming of Odysseus, in motion. Athena advises Telemachus to seek news of his father from Nestor and Menelaus: "There is no need for you to endure [the present state of affairs at the palace] passively, since you are no longer a child," she tells him (296-297). She reinforces her advice when the two arrive at Pylos, Nestor's home: "There is no need to be diffident [toward these illustrious men], not even a little" (3.14). It is time for Telemachus to take his place in the world of heroes.

Meanwhile, Odysseus, too, has been a "guest," held against his will by the divine but demonized Calypso on her island. Although the goddess empathizes with his longing for home, regarding his need "as if it were my own" (5.189), nevertheless, she has used her greater power to gratify her own need for a desirable male companion, a rare instance of female subjectivity, as Margaret Miles points out.[13] Calypso does releases him, but only after Zeus orders her to do so. Odysseus next arrives as a stranger on the shores of Phaeacia and promptly finds himself in a situation that would test anyone's sense of decorum. Need is upon him (136)—for food, clothing, shelter, and passage home. Naked and bedraggled, he approaches Princess Nausicaa and her friends by the river where they have gone to wash clothes. Away from the palace, the startled young girl is not in a position to offer the usual amenities, but she responds to the unusual situation with sensitivity and poise: A man so down on his luck must be feeling very discouraged:

> Stranger, since you seem neither an evil nor witless
> man, Zeus himself distributes prosperity to mortals,
> the good and the bad, as he wishes to each of us.
> So, perhaps, he has given you these things, and you
> must endure them with firm heart. (6.187-190)

She tells her friends to treat him like a guest: "This unfortunate, homeless man, whoever he is, has come here, and it is our duty to take care of him, for all strangers and beggars are from Zeus" (206-208). Odysseus's reply is calculated to show the highest respect and honor to a very young woman who has only her girlfriends to protect her; he compares her to a palm tree he once saw on the sacred island of Delos, birthplace of the divinities Apollo and Artemis. Nausicaa need not be afraid; this man honors the laws of gods and men. As in the earlier scene between Athena and Telemachus, needs are mutually acknowledged and are also considered in terms of what the gods require.

After Odysseus arrives home in Ithaca, disguised as a beggar, and goes to the hut of his swineherd, Homer has Eumaeus, invoking right, *themis*, repeat Nausicaa's observation that all strangers and beggars come from Zeus verbatim (14.55ff.). Eumaeus, who was of noble birth but sold into slavery by his nurse, honors the same moral principle as Nausicaa: Even the poorest and most humble man deserves respect if he is decent. Eumaeus's present fortunes would be better, he tells the stranger, if Odysseus had come home and rewarded him with his own farm as promised, but the swineherd's loyalty is unshaken. When the "beggar" claims to know that Odysseus is on his way home, however, the swineherd rebukes him, for there is no way a mere beggar would have accurate information about a king.

Later, Odysseus, still in disguise (19.118-120), is granted a private interview with Penelope, who, inexplicably attracted to this man, invites him to tell his life story. He declines, pleading guest etiquette:

> I am very burdened with sorrow. But it is not right
> for me to sit groaning and weeping in another's house, since
> indiscriminate, ceaseless pain is rather base.

Odysseus is not, of course, in another's house. What more appropriate place to tell the story of his suffering and what more appropriate person to tell it to? But until he can figure out how to get rid of the suitors, he must maintain his disguise, and much as he relishes his expertise in lying, he cannot bring himself to deceive Penelope. Social convention has prevented Penelope from refusing the suitors' attentions and banishing them from her (that is, Odysseus's) household. These constraints, together with the emotional deprivation she has suffered in her husband's twenty-year absence, are her necessity and need; at long last, Odysseus is about to put an end to them, to renew the bonds of *philia* with his family and loyal members of his household, and to set things right in both the private and public spheres.[14]

While the story of the *Iliad* is concerned with relationships between and among men which are determined by respect and due honor, most relationships in the *Odyssey* fall within the private sphere—the family, the household, and ties of guest-friendship that bind one family to another. Frequently defined in affective and psychological terms, needs, necessities, and mutual regard often operate outside the hierarchy of male power and rule. Principles of reciprocity, however differently defined, apply in both the public and private spheres and in both poems.

In Western societies, bonds between men within the family and in society at large—father and son, brother and brother, host and stranger, citizen and citizen—have tended to be valued as the most important human relationships. Accordingly, definitions of reciprocity have been viewed in terms of *time*, honor or mutual respect due to each party from the other. Far less consideration has been given to what reciprocity might mean in other kinds of relationships, such as those which include women as well as men or take other kinds of power into account. Moreover, reciprocity was also associated with other abstract, male-defined values such as *arete, dike,* and *logos*, and with the notion that morality is derived from a social contract, one which elevated men out of the state of nature into civic and civilized life. The view that exchange or reciprocity should govern relationships between and among men, as seen in Homer and Hesiod, was translated to the social institutions of the *polis*.

In an essay addressed to his nephew Nicomachus, Aristotle discusses the kinds of public and private bonds which do, can, and should exist within a civic setting. Aristotle aruges that at the most abstract level, sociopolitical relationships must conform to a standard of justice (Book 5). Justice depends on judgment, the practice of reason, and a matrix of intellectual and moral virtues. Thus, the practice of *logos* and the application of various *aretai* must enter into definitions of these relationships (Books 6 and 7). Reciprocity (*philia*) within both the family and society at large must also be taken into account, and its connections to justice must be considered (Book 8). Aristotle concludes with reflections on the relationship between the individual citizen and his *polis*.

The chief virtue in the *polis* ought to be justice under the law; laws exist to benefit the community as a whole or those to whom power has been entrusted because they are the best qualified to hold it. Justice is the chief or perfect virtue: "the only virtue which is regarded as benefiting someone other than its possessor" (5.1129b). Everyone acts justly toward himself—man's "natural" orientation is to his own self-interest, separate from the interests of others and presumed to come into conflict with them often. While moral education and the law should see to it that everyone's interests receive equal consideration, justice is the distribution of honor or money or other goods among members of the community in proportion to their merit (*arete*; 5.1131a-b). This distribution will not be equal because the merits of the members will not be equal. Among equal members of society, under a politically just arrangement, there is a fair exchange of goods, services, and money. Within the family, however, there is another kind of justice. A man cannot really be unjust toward his slave or child because they are "his own" and a man does not harm himself or act against his own interest. Domestic justice arises in relationships between nonequals and the prime example is that of husband and wife, a subject Aristotle takes up at length in Book 8, after discussing connections among deliberative reason and other virtues (Books 6 and 7). Powers of deliberation and the process of deliberating were highly esteemed in the ideal and the practice of Athenian democracy, but *phronesis*, which Aristotle associates with both *logos* and citizenship, was an exclusively male quality.[15] Aristotle allows, however, that fellow-feeling (sympathy), emotional responses, and particularities of person, place, time, and circumstances can and, to some extent, should enter into acts of deliberation.

Reciprocity among equals exists only between and among men (Book 8). While male friendship may grow out of one of three things—mutual goodness, pleasure, or utility—the most noble foundation is mutual love that is grounded in goodness of character. Each "loves his own good, but makes the balance equal by wishing the good of the other." The good man, however, does not wish to be in a relationship of *philia* with a more powerful or a wealthier man unless that man is his superior in goodness. Examples of *philia* among unequals are relationships between father and son, older and younger people, people from different social or economic classes, and husband and wife. In these instances, mutual benefits and obligations are not equal, though a kind of equality as ratio or proportion is possible. Although most men might choose honor over love, it is morally preferable to be loved than to be honored, and *philia* should take goodness into account, whereas honor may disregard it. Further, it is nobler to give than to receive, though (again) most men may feel otherwise. Astonishingly, Aristotle's illustration of the ultimate in selfless love is a mother's love for her child—astonishingly, because other than the dominant husband's relationship to his subordinate wife, women are not mentioned at all in Aristotle's account. If a man gives affection that is proportional to his friend's deserts, differences in class and wealth may be minimized.

Both friendship and justice apply to both private and public relationships, but all associations are subsumed into the state, *politeia*. There are three basic forms of political constitutions, all analogous to patterns seen in family relationships: kingship, aristocracy, and timocracy. Both family structures and the constitutions that are their counterparts are defined by male roles. At best, each exhibits its own form of justice. The husband-father-king is head of the household. If he is good, he rules benevolently over all its members; if bad, he is a tyrant who looks out only for his own selfish interests. The husband-father-aristocrat is superior in merit (*arete*) to all members of his household, and, consequently, he deserves to rule them. Brothers in a family show due honor to one another and share power in accordance with such honor, as do comrades or male citizens in a timocracy. The political power which citizens share is equal and the *philia* among them is defined in terms of equality. This is the only instance Aristotle gives of what we would call equality; husband and wife benefit one other by performing different necessary tasks within the family, but they are not equal. Reciprocity can never be in any way equalized in our relations with our parents and the gods, for our debts to them cannot be repaid.

Reciprocity viewed as repayment of debts is carried over into the arguments of Book 9: How should diverse claims by individuals and groups within society be evaluated? We should compare "the fair claims of each group on the basis of their degree in kinship and their virtue or usefulness." Men in community are united by goodwill and similar views and goals, but self-love or self-interest is by far the more powerful motivation. Clearly, and Aristotle acknowledges that it may come as a surprise to many people, most men are capable of looking beyond their own interest. Why? True self-love is found in the good man, who loves the best part of himself: his intelligence (reason, *phronesis*). Such a man is concerned to act "to save his friends or his country," and "would prefer one crowded hour of glorious life . . . one great and dazzling achievement to many small successes." We seem to have come full circle, from Homeric *arete* with its aspirations to transcend death through victory in battle to the Aristotelian counterpart, the good man's quest for glorious moral achievement in the arena of civic life.

Aristotle defined social morality from a male cultural perspective. Male social relationships are primary, particularly those which bind men together through political or other ties outside the household. Male moral virtue, *arete* reformulated to describe the qualities and to suit the needs of civic man, is exercised through these ties wherever they exist. Men form ties so as (1) to assure appropriately reciprocal exchange with one another in accordance with each individual's merits; (2) to acknowledge and perpetuate the importance of the separateness and autonomy of the individual man within the community; and (3) to perpetuate collective male rule, from one generation to the next.

Relationships between and among women are not taken into Aristotle's account of social morality, nor is reciprocity at any point articulated in terms of women's experiences.

So-called New Comic dramas[16] enacted social theory, educating people into the responsibilities of private life and the family, the substructure on which the community of patriarchy depended.[17] New Comedy flourished at Athens during the fourth century (when Aristotle was teaching and writing) and continued to develop at Rome during the following two centuries. The plays of Menander, Plautus, Terence, and others were what we call domestic or situation comedies, models for Moliere, Shakespeare, and contemporary TV films and sitcoms. Because the domestic conflicts they enact are always somehow resolved (the world being a less-than-perfect place) so as to satisfy self-interest, the best interests of the family, and the requirements of common decency, T.B.L. Webster described them as "comedies of accommodation or reconciliation."[18] Despite, or perhaps because of, its premise that things will work out the way they're supposed to, New Comedy is grounded in the premise that private conduct must be regulated so as to preserve the integrity and continuity of the family and to perpetuate moral and social order. Two institutions, both subject to male oversight, were central to social and economic stability, respectively, rights of marriage and rights of property,[19] and they were also central to definitions of civility.

As in Homer, relationships are key, and propriety depends on gender, age, and social and economic class. But these are ordinary people, not heroes. Set in and around the home, these plays probe private relationships—between members of the family and household, a household and its near-neighbors, and families united through marriage—which were considered to be the foundations of community. They offer paradigms of how everybody can or should get along. Getting along, however, is hardly ever anyone's priority, for comedy tends to take a Hobbesian view of human nature: Every man is out for himself, yet most recognize that in order to get what they want, they have to make some compromises and adjustments. Choice in matters of the heart and hearth is, for the most part, a male prerogative, and comedy likes to capitalize on the subversion of that prerogative (Plautus) or, in less mischievous writers, the real challenges a man may face in trying to rule his own roost. Those most in need of oversight by the fathers, the senior patriarchs, are sons, the future patriarchs. The subordination of women and slaves is assumed, though wives and courtesans and even the rare maiden can be demanding or outspoken, and slaves in Plautus habitually coopt *patria potestas*, the authority which by rights belongs to the father-husband-master-head of household (at Rome, *patria potestas*). Marginal characters also appear in these plays, people who have neither a place in the community nor an investment in the established social order, such as mercenary soldiers and parasites (perpetually hungry men, without economic means and always trying to cadge a meal). Some senior patriarchs are themselves a threat—the miserly or misanthropic father who will not provide a dowry for his daughter or refuses permission for her marriage. The plots of these plays illustrate how socially acceptable and beneficial behavior has been conceived, what kinds of damage a member of the community whose character is flawed can wreak, and how that damage can be managed and minimized. They invite us to ask, Where have the lines of social morality been drawn, and who has drawn them?

Comic propriety is first and foremost a matter of sexual mores, which are supervised by male heads of families. To judge from its prominence in the themes and plots of New Comedy, controlling the sexuality of young men so as to ensure the perpetuation of patriarchy was a primary concern. The sexual conduct of future patriarchs must be overseen because the young are wayward, more committed to pleasure than to duty to family and society. But senior patriarchs, who ought to know better, also disrupt social order: by coveting (either as bride or mistress) a young girl who should be paired with a young man (preferably, if she is of suitable birth, in marriage), by obstructing the lawful marriage which will perpetuate their family line, or by choosing a self-indulgent single life instead of marriage. One way or another, the major threat to the integrity of the family comes from within the patriarchy. In Terence's *Woman of Andros*, for example, a young male citizen from a family of means falls in love with a poor, unconnected, foreign-born, but virtuous young woman. She becomes pregnant, and her only "speech" consists of the screams and groans of childbirth. The young man's father, at first ignorant of the affair, decides it is time for him to marry and suggests a suitable bride. Since Pamphilus loves both his father and his girl, he is assailed by conflicting loyalties. Fortunately, it is discovered that the girl, Glycerium (Sweetheart, a generic name), is the long-lost daughter of a well-to-do citizen and is therefore a suitable match. Simo permits the young couple to marry and accepts the newborn as a legitimate heir. All claims are satisfied: the father-son bond and Simo's concern that his son marry a woman of equal social and economic class and produce a legitimate heir, Pamphilus's love for his girl and his obligation to her and his child, society's interest in preserving continuity of the family.

Menander's *Dyskolos* (The Grouch), the only complete surviving example of a Greek New Comedy, combines the theme of perpetuating the family with a study of an antisocial personality. Cnemon, an uncouth and stingy old farmer, prototype of later comic characters such as Moliere's Harpagon and Shakespeare's Malvolio, is scarcely fit to live in human society. His wife left him when she could no longer tolerate his bad temper. He abuses everyone who comes near him, including his meek old womanservant and his high-minded stepson and neighbor Gorgias. He will not hear the suit of a well-born and deserving young Athenian, Sostratus, for the hand of his daughter Myrrhine. Cnemon— and this is essential to the definition of his antisocial nature—actually opposes his daughter's marriage, for, miser that he is, he would not spare a dowry, though he could afford one. Myrrhine's half-brother Gorgias is also a rustic, a rough, hard-working, no-nonsense fellow, but of a far better cast of mind. His initial suspicion of Sostratus—that he is a spoiled, well-to-do, urban sophisticate—is overcome when he learns the man honorably seeks his sister's hand in marriage and that he has no need of a dowry. By putting in a hard day's work in the field, Sostratus "proves" he is neither lazy nor decadent, and the young men become friends. In the postheroic and posttragic world of New Comedy, blood does not always tell, and moral goodness does not necessarily observe class boundaries. In the character of Cnemon, proverbial country thriftiness has degenerated into meanness and alienation from gods and men.[20] After a life-threatening accident, however, Cnemon experiences a partial change of heart, and in the event, his rotten disposition is upgraded to boorish.

Here is his transformation speech, a parody of the moment when a tragic hero recognizes his condition of error (*anagnoresis* of *hamartia*, Aristotle, *Poetics* 1452a-b6), spoken after Gorgias rescues him from drowning in the well (he fell in using an antique rope to rescue his antique pail and mattock):

> I think I've made just one mistake, in supposing
> I was completely self-sufficient and would need
> no one. But now I've learned the end of life is
> quick and unforeseen. I was wrong. You need someone
> to be there for you, standing by ready to help.
> By Hephaestus, I was dead wrong when I looked

at other people's lives and thought they calculated
everything in terms of their own gain. I imagined
nobody would have a good thought for anybody else.
That was my mistake. Just now, Gorgias, performing
the act of a most noble man, gave me proof.
I never allowed him near my door, never gave him
the slightest help, never spoke to him, never
exchanged pleasant small talk—and still he saved me.   (713-726)

Cnemon belatedly adopts Gorgias as his legal son, appoints him guardian of Myrrhine, and promises her half his property as dowry. Menander's moral is that men form alliances[21] with others through mutual need; they recognize they must sacrifice some degree of privacy and self-interest in order to survive, foster general good will, and ensure the continuity of their family line. Cnemon's meanness of spirit persists, nevertheless, and he refuses to take part in the wedding celebrations but is forcibly carried off to the festivities by a cook and a slave who are going to make him dance as punishment and cure for his bad temper. Despite male culture's persistent tendency to place a high value on separation and autonomy, *The Grouch*, like many other plays in this comic genre, seems to take an opposing view and to argue that there can be too much of a good thing and, for better or for worse, human bonds are here to stay. The most serious implication of Cnemon's initial refusal to let his daughter marry is that he would block the continuation of his family line and the formation of bonds between families on which the maintenance and growth of a society depends. Extreme self-sufficiency is not a virtue.[22]

New Comedy at Rome adopted many of the conventions of the Greek comic stage, but it had far less formal origins in native Italian farce.[23] Social order may be a necessity, but in the comedy of Plautus, it exists in order to be turned on its head. Not only does Plautus not identify with privilege conferred by power, he revels in depicting male authority figures, especially heads-of-household, in ridiculous postures. Slaves—who, since they are located at the bottom of the social heap, have nothing to lose—relish father-son misunderstandings and conflicts and routinely abate them, often apparently just for the fun of it. Subversiveness, practiced on a mock-heroic scale, is a virtue, and lying, trickery, and deception become noble enterprises. Although in the end slaves usually succumb to conventional morality and may even be pressed into enforcing it, their antics are powerful and entertaining arguments for an ethic of irreverence.[24] Given Plautus's great popularity,[25] Roman theatergoers enjoyed contemplating the subversion of social order from the safety of their seats, and keen as Plautus is on subverting Roman mores through farce, he also allows his characters to pause in the midst of the action to deliver thoughtful critiques of them.[26]

New comedies are preoccupied with putting and keeping people in their "rightful" places, in accordance with the social structures established by male rule. In many stories family members who have been lost are recovered, and identities (involving twins or look-alikes) which have been mistaken or confused are in the end sorted out. Rightful place defines membership in the community: Who belongs? Citizenship concerned Greek New Comedy's Athenian audience;[27] if the son's girl isn't a citizen, their children will not be considered citizens. The discovery that she is a citizen and from a "good" family comes about when she is discovered to be somebody's long-lost daughter, exposed at birth or kidnapped as a child.[28] Not only does a lover gain a wife (and legitimate offspring), but parent and child reclaim each other as well. Sons are also lost and recovered.[29] Moreover, people can't "know their place" if their identities are in question; your place depends on who you are, how you are different from everyone else, even if you look like them. Thus, the Menaechmi brothers are sorted out and restored to their correct identities and relationships, and Amphitryon, the "real" (or at least mortal) husband of Alcmena, is distinguished from his immortal phantom, Jove (*Amphitryon*).

In *Amphitryon* Plautus exploits the comic ramifications of existential as well as social order—the supposed difference between men and gods.[30] There are two sets of doubles: Jove and King Amphitryon of Thebes, and Mercury and the king's slave Sosia; the plot turns on the confusions of identity of both pairs. Jove, true to mythic form, has become enamored of a mortal woman, Alcmena, wife of Amphitryon, and at the opening of the play, disguised as the king, he is taking his pleasure with her. He is attended by his son Mercury, the god of trickery, who, in a reversal of highest and lowest, plays the stereotypical clever slave to Sosia's honorable straight man. The real Amphitryon and Sosia return victorious from a siege. Mercury convinces Sosia, sent ahead to the palace to tell Alcmena her husband has come home triumphant, that he is not himself, or else has been split in two. Jove-Amphitryon takes tender leave from the sweet and devoted Alcmena,[31] who is then astonished when he (the real Amphitryon) shows up again almost immediately. Amphitryon is less upset to discover that he has a double than he is to learn that his wife has apparently been unfaithful to him. Alcmena is devastated by the accusation of adultery. Although Jove feels a twinge of guilt at the misery his fling is causing, he pledges to make everything turn out fine after he has just a little more fun. In epic and tragedy, kings long to be gods; in this comedy, a god longs to be a king, and being a god, becomes one. Just when the permutations of confusion have peaked, Alcmena gives birth (without a single pain) to twin boys, Amphitryon's son and Jove's son Hercules, who (as in myth) shows himself a hero at birth by rising up from his cradle and strangling twin serpents with his bare hands. Jove announces the truth and Amphitryon is not at all perturbed that another has enjoyed his wife, being that he is a god (we aren't told how Alcmena reacted to the revelation). Restoring people to their rightful places in the family makes society as well as the family whole again. Plautus acknowledges these principles of social engineering, and the endings of his stories confirm them.

Terence, Plautus's younger contemporary, was brought to Rome from Africa as a slave and manumitted. More philosopher than social critic, Terence presents flexibility and balance, tolerance and self-control as the virtues on which social harmony depend. Cultivating them is the special responsibility of men of good social standing, but because men are born with different temperaments and outlooks, living up to that responsibility is not so easy: The major hindrances to social harmony are psychological, and conflicts arise because men can't help but disagree among themselves. Fortunately, conflicts can be resolved, mainly through education and self-reflection. Terence is often cited as an early Western exponent of *humanitas* (essential humanness, humanity, and humanism; see below on *The Self-Punisher*). The idea of humanism seems to point to what we all have in common and to further imply (though this is much more problematic) that human beings share similar needs, hopes, and psychological and emotional complexities. Terentian humanism operates primarily within familial bonds between men (brothers, fathers and sons). Althought many of his characterizations, including those of women, show empathy and compassion, *humanitas* is defined from within the context of patriarchal order and for the most part reflects male experiences.[32]

In *The Self-Punisher* and *The Brothers*, two sets of men, the older and younger generations, have different temperaments and views on how to live well and how to educate a boy so that he will grow up to be a good man (that is, fit to take his place within the system and presumably, in turn, to raise his own sons to do the same). The older men in both plays have the same opposing philosophies of parenting and education. One set advocates discipline, hard work, and strict rules, while the other is indulgent and permissive. In *The Brothers*, Demea, a poor Athenian farmer, could not afford to raise both his sons, Aeschinus and Ctesipho, so he allowed his brother Micio, a sophisticated urbanite, to adopt and raise Aeschinus. The boy becomes a carousing, whoring, hard-drinking young man who rapes and then falls in love with a dowerless girl.[33] He has promised to do the honorable thing, however, marry the girl and raise their child, who is being born as the play begins. But Aeschinus has somehow neglected to inform his father of the situation. Meanwhile, he has done his timid brother the favor of carrying off *his* girlfriend, a lute girl, to his own house, pretending that he wants her for himself. Demea's view seems to have been validated by the turn of events. He fulminates self-righteously about the evils of permissiveness while Micio waxes vague and philosophical but optimistic: Give the boy time; he'll straighten out. Demea is severely disillusioned, however, when he learns that his "model" son has fathered a child out of wedlock. He decides to take a leaf from Micio's book and swings to the other extreme; the girl can live with Ctesipho on the farm, but she has to work in the hot sun all day, and the young people have to sleep together whether they want to or not. Micio approves Aeschinus's marriage, but Demea has the last laugh. He makes his self-centered brother, a life-long bachelor, fulfill his obligation to society by taking a wife; moreover, he must cement the bond by giving some land to his new wife's needy relative. Everyone gets what he wants, sort of, maybe, but this is comedy, where there is no such thing as perfect bliss.

In *The Self-Tormentor*, Chremes and Menedemus are neighboring farmers and both have sons, Clitopho and Clinia. Clinia loves a poor young woman, Antiphila, but his father wises to thwart the relationship because young men who work hard enough shouldn't have time for love. The poor young guy takes his father's disapproval so much to heart that he runs away to join the army. Overcome with remorse, his father sells most of his property and sentences himself to hard physical labor. Chremes, observing his neighbor's distress, invites his confidence: *Homo sum; humani nil a me alienum puto*,"I am a human being; I consider nothing human foreign to me." Chremes will indeed be able to empathize with this specifically male problem, a troubled relationship between a father and his son. After Clinia returns and is staying at Clitopho's house, his wily slave contrives to import Clitopho's mistress

Bacchis and pass her off as Clinia's girl. A whore, she arrives with ten servants and countless trunkloads of clothes and jewels, a sure sign that she is no better than she should be. Bacchis is the opposite of Clinia's girl Antiphila, who, when someone goes to tell her Clinia is back, is discovered weaving, dressed in black, and wearing no makeup.[34] Bacchis is more than an example of the greed to which women are "naturally" prone, for Terence does allow her to speak, and she argues that desirable women have to make their money while they're young because men won't want them when they're older.

Antiphila is discovered to be wearing a ring that identifies her as none other than a daughter of Chremes and his wife Sostrata. Her father had ordered that she be exposed at birth because he could not afford to raise her.[35] But Sostrata rescued her child and gave her away in the hope that she would survive. Now Chremes acknowledges her and allows her to marry Clinia. As for Clitopho, he is ordered to stop squandering the family's resources on a whore and get married, and he obeys. Menedemus was too strict with his son, who was basically decent and loyal; Chremes was less strict, but his son was too weak to protect himself from an aggressive woman, and once he was in trouble, he concealed the situation from his father. In the end, both young men and their relationships with their fathers are put on the right track.

Terence's portraits of women, though they reflect cultural stereotypes, show some complexity. In *Her Husband's Mother*, a young wife leaves her husband and goes home to her mother. Suspicion falls on the mother-in-law, who is presumed to have driven the poor girl away out of stereotypical female jealousy. The truth, however, is that girl is very upset because she was raped by an unknown assailant before she was married and became pregnant. Fortunately (for whom, one might ask), the rapist turns out to be none other than her husband, so everyone is reconciled and satisfied with the outcome, and the mother-in-law is exonerated. A rape occurs in *The Eunuch*, also, where Pamphila, a young virgin, is under the protection of Thais, a professional prostitute, and the rapist, who is "in love" with Pamphila, pretends to be a eunuch and is supposedly guarding the girl. Thais, a shrewd businesswoman, is outraged; the girl is now "damaged goods," but as luck again would have it, Pamphila turns out to be the daughter of a well-to-do citizen, and she is given in marriage to her rapist. The young women of New Comedy, until or unless they are discovered to be daughters of respectable families, are forced to seek male protection through a sexual liaison, if not outright prostitution. Their economic dependence makes them very vulnerable, but the dramatic spotlight is not on their plight but on the keepers of the patriarchal system and their concerns. Rape is something that "just happens" and is subsumed by the comic plot. Women are depicted solely in relation to patriarchal values, one of a number of representations that makes us wonder to what extent women's alleged moral orientation to relationships[36] is a construct of patriarchal interests. The plots of New Comedy indicate that women in classical antiquity had few options other than to be "related."

In the social theory enacted in Greek New and Roman comedies, control of sexuality is the foundation of social morality. Control of female sexuality, especially women's childbearing capacity, is assumed and is not a source of conflict except as it impinges on patriarchal customs and institutions. Women as sexual objects outside of marriage are a danger to society. The virtuous and hapless young woman who gets pregnant by the son of a well-to-do family is an irresistible temptation, not a temptress. Young men must produce legitimate heirs within the bonds of marriage in order to perpetuate their bloodlines and preserve the family's goods. Aberrant—antisocial—behavior also undermines social harmony. "Good" behavior is by definition that which conforms to social norms, but the social theory evident in New Comedy offers a more complex view. Even though women are shown to be concerned with the well-being of their children and family, their desires receive limited recognition, and female characters remain, for the most part, even in Terence, daughters of Hesiod's race of generic woman.[37] Men, on the other hand, have different desires at different ages and stages of life. How can these varied needs be mediated when they conflict? Through empathy, understanding other people's feelings, and compromise. A father defending the integrity of his family was young once; it is only a matter of time before a son discovers he has become his father. But individual needs and self-interest, though viewed generically, must be satisfied, for a discontented person is a potential sociopath. Further, a family in which the father disowns his son because he seems to have turned out badly or the boy is estranged from an unsympathetic father is perceived as what we would call dysfunctional; for society's sake, such a family must be restored, refashioned into an integrated, harmonious unit.

Transgressions of sexual mores, though private acts, may have serious public consequences. The liaison of Paris and Helen was believed to have caused the fall of Troy, to recall classical antiquity's most notorious example.[38] Two stories from ancient historians illustrate the public and specifically political consequences of such private violations.[39] The story of Candaules and Gyges told by Herodotus (Book 1.8-14) and Livy's account of the rape of Lucretia (1.57-59) show the dire outcomes of abrogating (Herodotus) or violating (Livy) exclusive male private rights over women. Both stories illustrate the moral that order and the proper hierarchy of authority can be maintained only if those in positions of power uphold and enforce it. Herodotus begins his narrative of the conflicts between East and West that preceded the Greek-Persian wars with stories about woman-stealing on both sides of the Mediterranean, culminating in the Trojan War. After that war, the most prominent people in western Asia were the Lydians. Their king, Candaules, had an excessive passion for his beautiful queen, who, despite her critical role in changing the course of history, is nameless. Among the Lydians, it was shameful even for a man to be seen naked, and "a woman takes off her modesty with her clothes."[40] King Candaules' obsession led him to violate this custom. The king persuaded a trusted staff member, Gyges, to view his wife naked, so that he could see her beauty for himself. Gyges was aghast at this request but obeyed the king. He hid behind the door of the royal bedroom while the queen undressed. Unfortunately, as he slipped out of the room afterwards, the queen saw him. She said nothing to her husband but the next morning summoned Gyges and gaves him two choices: either kill the king, marry her, and assume the kingship (thus ending a 505-year dynasty), or kill himself. Gyges chooses to live and founds a new dynastic line.

Herodotus draws the following morals from this story. Though customs are relative to different peoples and cultures, they endure because they are tested over time by experience. Whereas in the largely private world of comedy, a man's departure from the code of sexual morality threaten the stability of his family, when a ruler violates the code, he loses his life as well as his power and fails to set a good example for his people. In Candaules' case, his fate is perhaps even more ignominious because he suffers it at the hands of a woman. The king violated both private and public morality and cannot be trusted with political power. The nameless queen assumes male authority in order to enforce the patriarchal code.

Livy's account of the rape of Lucretia, Roman paradigm of the virtuous wife, by Sextus Tarquinius, youngest son of the last king of Rome, is a variation on the same theme. Prototypes of corrupt and tyrannical power in the mythology of Roman history, the Tarquins brought about their own downfall, for the rape was the catalyst for the overthrow of their dynasty, the end of monarchy at Rome, and the founding of the republic. In Livy's story as in Herodotus's, violation of exclusive ownership of a woman brings about loss of ruling power. One evening a group of young noblemen decide to make surprise visits to their wives, in order to discover whose was the most virtuous. Other wives are having luxurious dinner-parties with friends; Lucretia is at home, making wool with her womenservants by lamplight.[41] Her chastity fires Sextus's lust, and the next day, while her husband is away, he returns. When Lucretia refuses him, Sextus first threatens to discredit her by killing a male slave and putting his nude body in her bed, then he rapes her. Afterwards, Lucretia summons her husband and father and tells them what happened. They assure her she is innocent. She replies, "Although I absolve myself of wrongdoing, I do not release myself from punishment; Lucretia's unchastity will not live on as an example to others." She takes out a knife concealed in her dress and stabs herself. Lucius Junius witnesses this horrible event. Scion of a noble family, he has hidden his indignation at past Tarquin transgressions and his own abilities so well that he has earned the nickname Brutus, Stupid. Withdrawing the knife from Lucretia's body, he and the others swear an oath to avenge Lucretia's death by overthrowing the monarchy. The Tarquins were already hated for oppressing the Roman people, disregarding civil rights, and bullying their neighbors, but it was this atrocious violation of private morality, rape of another man's woman, that impelled noble Romans to take political action.

* * * * *

In American society today, we also expect our public officials or candidates for public office to observe a code of sexual conduct. Customs are changing, for until recently the division between public and private (upheld especially by discreet wives) protected men in high places from the consequences of their private behavior. For us, a more important indication of social morality is civility. Civility, which begins at home and extends to all areas of social behavior, lies at the intersection of the public and the private. How people treat one another in everyday social relations is a measure of the quality of common life. If we do not share norms and values, or if we choose not to conform to them, what holds society together? Does democratic pluralism, which includes many traditions, undermine even a vision of social cohesion? Social morality in a pluralistic democracy must acknowledge diverse moral values, and diversity challenges a traditional unitarian view by maintaining that there is not just one truth, right, good, or virtue known to and made known by a single, higher male authority. "Civility" comes from Latin *civis,* citizen; the citizens who counted in the domain of action were men. Today, we are challenged to ask ourselves how we can have and hold a social morality not based on power relations, not imposed from the top down. Social morality has reflected long-standing practices of male authority, both within the public sphere, which is the exclusive arena of male activities, and the family, where a man should rule as head of the household. It has reflected male culture's orientation to separation, autonomy, and the protection of individual rights and self-interest. It has excluded women's moral experience, in part by favoring theory over practice, thereby disregarding varieties and gradations of moral experience. It also has tended to overlook issues that arise in contexts of personal relationships and caring activities, relegating them to the private sphere along with emotions and bonds of personal affection. Relationships, bonds of what the Greeks called *philia,* mean something different for men and for women. The important private bonds among men are paternal and fraternal, and these bonds, like earlier definitions of man in terms of mortality and human limits, adumbrate social constructions of "the human condition."

By defining relationships in male terms and by emphasizing control of *eros* as sexual desire and by transforming it into the desire for achievement, ancient thought deemphasized other kinds of human bonds, such as the mother-child relationship and ties between and among women.[42] The key function of traditional social morality has been to perpetuate the continuity of male power in both the private and public spheres. In the private sphere, connections among males were assigned positive value, and female conduct was deemed positive when it conformed to male needs and expectations; the best interests of women and children were assumed to be congruent or at least consonant with the requirements of male power. The family—the arena of sexuality, childbearing, and child raising—is subordinated to the public sphere, which is institutionalized, collective male power: the *polis,* encompassing both society and the State.

The family has long been the locus for the control of male sexuality and for the oppression of women.[43] There has never been such a thing as a sexual contract spelling out the rights and obligations of women in the family or in society at large analogous to a social contract, as Carole

Pateman has pointed out.[44] Women's place has been subsumed under the male social contract. "Humanism" itself incorporates gender bias, and "fellow feeling" is just that: men's empathy for other men. Neoconservative thinkers in present-day America are correct in believing that traditional "family values" are being challenged today as never before.

Notes

[1] Arlene Saxonhouse, *Fear of Diversity. The Birth of Political Science in Ancient Greek Thought* (Princeton: Princeton University Press, 1992), p.122.

[2] Simone deBeauvoir, *The Second Sex*, trans. and ed. H.M. Parshley (New York: Schocken, 1961 [1953]), p.xvii.

[3] Margaret Urban Walker, "Moral Understandings: Alternative 'Epistemology'for a Feminist Ethics," in Eve Browning Cole and Susan Coultrap-McQuin, eds., *Explorations in Feminist Ethics* (Bloomington: Indiana University Press, 1992), pp.165-175. The quotation is from p.174.

[4] "Morality" from Latin *mores*, customs or habits of an individual or a society. By derivation, the word "civility" refers to conduct becoming a *civis*, Latin equivalent of *polites*, citizen-member of a *polis*. See Emile Benveniste, *Indo-European Langauge and Society* (London: Routledge and Kegan Paul, 1973), p.273.

[5] The family is the place where children are brought up, and it is up to mothers and others who engage in what Sarah Ruddick calls maternal thinking to educate children into socially acceptable adulthood (*Maternal Thinking. Toward a Politics of Peace* [Boston: Beacon Press,1989]). Katherine Pyne Addelson, *Moral Passages. Toward a Collectivist Moral Theory* (New York: Routledge Press, 1994), argues that *eros* "must be tamed into civilized life" (p.53). The birth control movement in the U.S, the work of Margaret Sanger and later feminist initiatives, "expressed the common concern that was to be collectively enacted through the virtue of birth control *and* the virtue of industrial justice. Work that supplies the material needs of life is, after all, a procreational issue. At any rate, it seems to me that the envisioned syndicalist society would overcome the division of public and domestic. In the process, the selves of all participants were to grow in the freedom of creating collective possibilities" (p.89).

See further, her Chapter 6, pp.137-159, and below, my Chapter 8.

[6] Jean Elshtain, *Public Man, Private Woman. Women in Social and Political Thought* (Princeton: Princeton University Press, 1981); Susan Moller Okin, *Women in Western Political Thought* (Princeton: Princeton University Press, 1979).

[7] Not surprisingly, these rituals revolve around mortality. As Richard Seaford points out, in the *polis* death ritual is associated with hero-cult, which serves to perpetuate the life of the hero and to provide institutional expression of the quest for transcendence over death. It also mediates what Seaford calls hostile reciprocity, feelings of anger and aggression that would, unmediated, result in acts of violent revenge. *Reciprocity and Ritual. Homer and Tragedy in the Developing City State* (Oxford: Oxford University Press, 1994), Chapter 3, "Death Ritual and Reciprocal Violence in the *Polis*," and Chapter 4, "Collective Death Ritual."

[8] Emile Benveniste, *Indo-European Language and Society* (London: Routledge and Kegan Paul, 1973), pp.273-288; Bernard Williams, *Shame and Necessity* (Berkeley and Los Angeles, 1993), Chapter 4; and Simon Goldhill, *Reading Greek Tragedy* (Cambridge: Cambridge University Press, 1986), Chapter 4.

[9] It is interesting to contrast this incident with the meeting of Odysseus and Athena in *Od*.13, where similar qualities (such as craftiness), likemindedness, and affection, not power relations, create a bond between goddess and mortal. And in the encounters of Athena and Telemachus (*Od*.1) discussed below, the goddess asserts her authority to further Telemachus's maturation; in *Il*.1 she assuages Agamemnon's wounded pride.

[10] This view persists as a principle of Greek popular morality; Socrates-Plato challenges it in *Republic* 1; see esp. Simon Goldhill on *philia*, *Reading Greek Tragedy*, Chapter 4, "Relations and Relationships," pp.79-106.

[11] And it isn't proper for you to love him,
lest you become hateful to me, who loves you.
You should want to hurt any man who hurts me. (613-615)

[12] English "mentor" comes from Mentor, the name Athena assumes when she appears to Telemachus a second time in Book 2, now disguised as an older man, a citizen of Ithaca, and loyal to the king.

[13] Margaret Miles, *Carnal Knowing. Female Nakedness and Religious Meaning in the Christian West* (Boston: Beacon Press, 1989), p.4.

[14] John Winkler,"Penelope's Cunning—And Homer's" in *The Constraints of Desire. Sex and Gender in Ancient Greece* (New York: Routledge, 1990).

[15] In *The Fragility of Goodness. Luck and Ethics in Greek Tragedy and Philosophy* (Cambridge: Cambridge University Press, 1986), Martha Nussbaum

argues that moral goodness depends on rational self-sufficiency. The means to rational self-sufficiency is practical wisdom, *phronein*, which is discovered through deliberation. Aristotelianism (and its modern heirs, Sidgewick and Rawls, p.12) offers the best guide, in that it combines the emotional knowledge of the Greek tragedians with the "pure" intellectual knowledge of Plato (p.46). See also Nancy Sherman, *The Fabric of Character: Aristotle's Theory of Virtue* (Oxford: Clarendon Press, 1989). For a feminist critique of Aristotle, see Giulla Sissa, "The Sexual Philosophies of Plato and Aristotle," in Pauline Pantel, ed., *History of Women in the West* (Cambridge: Harvard University Press, 1992), vol. 1, pp.46-81. On Aristotle, see also Rosemary Tong, *Feminine and Feminist Ethics* (Belmont,CA: Wadsworth Press, 1993), pp.26-28, 182f.

[16] On New Comedy in general, see R.L. Hunter, *The New Comedy of Greece and Rome* (Cambridge: Cambridge University Press, 1985); and F.H. Sandbach, *The Comic Theatre of Greece and Rome* (New York: Norton, 1977).

[17] See Madeleine M. Henry, "*Ethos, Mythos, Praxis:* Women in Menander's Comedy," in Marilyn Skinner, ed., *Rescuing Creusa: New Methodological Approaches to Women in Antiquity,* special issue of *Helios* n.s. 13(2) (Lubbock: Texas Tech. University, 1987), pp.140-150.

[18] T.B.L. Webster, *Introduction to Menander* (Manchester: 1974).

[19] At Rome, the rights of marriage (*connubium*) and rights of property (*commercium*). See David Konstan, *Roman Comedy* (Ithaca: Cornell University Press, 1983), Introduction, pp.15-32, esp. "Taken together, the dramas of ancient comedy map out the ideology of city-state society and reveal to us the sensitive areas where the borders were vague, weak, or changing under the pressure of new historical circumstances" (p.21). The important borders are those relating to the sexual code and "protocols involving economic exchange, as well as varying degrees of civil and political rights" (p.20).

[20] He will not even loan a pot for the preparation of sacrifice at the near-by shrine of Pan and the Nymphs, through whose protection Myrrhine will make a fortunate marriage.

[21] Cf. Latin *societas*, the word the Romans used to describe a military or political alliance they formed with foreign peoples, from which we derive "society."

[22] In Plautus's *Pot of Gold*, the notorious pot belongs to the miser Euclio, who will not use the money to give his daughter a dowry. He will allow her to marry a man of his own age, Megadorus ("Big Giver" or "Big Gift") who will take her without a dowry. The match is inappropriate not only because of the age difference, but also because the girl and Megadorus's nephew are lovers and she has just given birth to his child.

[23] See Sander M. Goldberg, *Understanding Terence* (Princeton: Princeton

University Press, 1986), esp. Chapters 1 and 4; T.A. Dorey and D.R. Dudley, eds., *Roman Drama* (New York: Basic, 1965); and R.L. Hunter and F.H. Sandbach (above, note 16).

[24] See, for example, the role of Palaestrio in Plautus, *The Braggart Soldier*.

[25] Hunter, *The New Comedy of Greece and Rome*, pp.4-7; and Eric Segal, *Roman Laughter* (New York: Oxford University Press, 1987), passim.

[26] Segal, *Roman Laughter*, pp.15-41, points out that Plautus routinely overturns traditional Roman virtues, especially *pietas*, devotion between father and son, husband and wife. For Plautus's criticisms of Roman institutions, see *Amphitryon* 161ff. (slavery); *The Merchant* 817ff. (marriage); *The Persian Woman* 64ff. (the legal system); and the character of Pyrgopolynices in *The Braggart Soldier* (the warrior as hero); and lines 706ff. of the same play (the patronage system).

[27] Konstan, *Roman Comedy*, Introduction, p.18, and Chapters 1 and 4-6.

[28] Plautus, *Casina, The Rope*.

[29] Plautus, *The Captives, The Carthaginian*.

[30] In the Prologue (59-61) Mercury calls the play (probably with immortal tongue in divine cheek) a tragicomedy because you can't have a straight comedy with kings and gods as characters.

[31] She misses him as soon as "he" (= Jove) is gone, and loves him for his *virtus* (= *victoria)*: lines 632-653. See also 839-842, her definition of a woman's dowry: chastity, modesty, controlled desire, fear of the gods, love of parents, family affection, being a good wife to you (*morigera*, conduct in keeping with custom), generous to the good and helpful to the upright.

[32] This passage in Terence is the starting point for Monique Witting's "Homo Sum," in *The Straight Mind and Other Essays* (Boston: Beacon Press, 1992), pp.46-58.

[33] "Women in Canada Upset by Court Rulings on Drunkenness" by Clyde H. Farnsworth, *The New York Times*, November 10, 1994, p.A7, reports that "at recent criminal cases . . . drunkenness has been successfully used as a defense in assaults against women."

[34] For the "honest women wear rags" theme, see also *Phormio*, lines 93-110.

[35] For female infanticide in the Greek world, see Sarah Pomeroy, *Goddesses, whores, Wives, and Slaves* (New York: Schocken, 1975), pp.69-70 and 164-165. For the modern counterpart, see Roberta Steinbacher, "Sex Preselection: From Here to Fraternity," pp. 274-282 in Carol C. Gould, ed., *Beyond Domination: New Perspectives on Women and Philosophy* (Totowa, NJ: Rowman dn Allenheld, 1983).

[36] As Carol Gilligan, for example, argued in *In a Different Voice. Psychological Theory and Women's Development* (Cambridge: Harvard

University Press, 1982).

[37] Cf. Eve Cantarella, *Pandora's Daughters. The Role and Status of Women in Greek and Roman Antiquity*, trans. Maureen B. Fantham (Baltimore: Johns Hopkins University Press, 1987).

[38] See Herodotus's corrective at the opening of his *Histories:* Reciprocal incidents of woman stealing laid the foundation for deep antagonism between East and West, but no woman is raped and kidnapped without her consent; and H[ilda] D[oolittle]'s "Helen in Egypt."

[39] See Michel Foucault's discussion of the parallels between the virtues governing sexual conduct and those governing the exercise of political power: *History of Sexuality*, trans. Robert Hurley (New York: Pantheon, 1980), vol. 2, *The Uses of Pleasure*, pp.170ff.

[40] The Greek custom, which allowed men to exercise nude, was more enlightened; female nudity, however, was considered an aberration, that is, something customarily practiced at Sparta. Plato, *Republic* 5.457a-b, recommends that women guardians of the ideal state exercise naked, even though "people" may tend to laugh at them.

[41] R.M. Ogilvie, *Commentary on Livy, Books 1-5* (Oxford: Oxford University Press, 1965), calls the scene "pure New Comedy." It is also, we may add, highly stereotyped.

[42] Many feminist ethicists, among them Carol Gilligan, Nel Noddings, Sara Ruddick, Virginia Held, and Janice Raymond, have explored these bonds; see below, my Chapter 8, and Rosemarie Tong, *Feminine and Feminist Ethics* (Belmont, CA: Wadsworth Press, 1993), Chapters 5-9.

[43] For the family as the primary institution for the oppression of women, see Jane Flax, "The Family in Contemporary Feminist Thought: A Critical Review," in Jean Elshtain, ed., *The Family in Political Thought* (Amherst: University of Massachusetts Press, 1982), pp.223-253.

[44] Carole Pateman, *The Sexual Contract* (Stanford: Stanford University Press, 1988). See also Monique Wittig, "The Social Contract," in *The Straight Mind and Other Essays*, pp.33-45.

Both war and citizenship have, of course, been traditionally male preserves in Western culture. And the source of some of the complexities that are now surfacing is that the masculinity of citizenship and the masculinity of war have been conceptually connected in Western thought—and connected through some of the most central ideals of the philosophical tradition: individuality, selfhood, autonomy, the concern with "universal" moral principles, the transcending of "private interests."
Genevieve Lloyd[1]

The means available to us to conceptualize culture and the form of our culture itself make it very difficult to see beyond this choice: either respect for nature and woman's *difference* within it; or the desire to dominate or transcend nature to effect woman's *equality in culture* . . . The disjunctive difference/equality impasse reflects the problems involved in a dualistic understanding of the body and nature., on the one hand, and consciousness and culture on the other.
Moira Gatens[2]

Chapter 7

Rome: Synthesis, Codification, Expansion

By introducing the statesman and philosopher Cicero and the poet Vergil as synthesizers and codifiers of Greek social and cultural, intellectual and literary patriarchal traditions, I must hasten to forestall any impression—the lingering remains of a stubborn but ancient prejudice—that Romans were mere imitators of Greek achievements. Cicero and Vergil adapted their heritage in uniquely Roman ways to uniquely Roman circumstances. For reasons that will become apparent, we recognize their transformations of religious and philosophical, social and political values as our own. Or used to recognize. Rome was a conduit for the Greco-Roman legacy in Western Europe. Latin was the language of Christianity and its institutions in the West during the Middle Ages, and classical texts were preserved in its centers of learning. Reawakened interest in Greek and Latin texts and thought in the Renaissance created a community of learned men in both religious and secular spheres, and thereafter, a man's learning was defined not only by his knowledge of the Bible and other Christian texts but also by his knowledge of classical antiquity. A classical education was one of the cornerstones of universal public education in the United States, established in the late eighteenth century, and knowledge of "the classics"[3] continued to be considered necessary to the making of a well-educated man (sic). As long as Latin was a required subject in the public school curriculum, many children of ordinary citizens routinely read Cicero and Vergil. Today, we still hear echoes of Roman political thinking and rhetoric in the speeches of some of our public figures.[4]

Cicero's political and social philosophy informed early American ideas of community under a republican form of government and political leadership. He defined the nature of "human" society and how men should act in it. He considered social morality in terms of the experience of upper-class men and assumed that rule of the best men, the concentration of moral authority in the hands of the few, was in the interests of everyone. His republic, though democratic in some respects, was not inclusive. All of Cicero's writings, which were widely admired and emulated, reflect the primacy of the spoken word in classical antiquity and the influence of rhetoric on prose writing. Balance and antithesis, hallmarks of his style, are often expressed in terms of polar opposites—for example, both x and also its opposite y (at home and away, on land and sea); not x but its opposite y. It seems plausible that these stylistic features reinforced antithetical patterns of thought and language in the West. Two Vergilian conceptions, defining a man's quest as the pursuit of a god-given ideal and the historical destiny of a nation, shaped heroic visions of self and nationhood in subsequent centuries. Vergil, recalling the archaic Greek notion that Zeus has oversight over kings, conceived an alliance of divine and human ruling powers whose moral authority is underwritten by philosophic wisdom. He also constructed hierarchies of paired opposites aligned with good and evil which were integral to Greco-Roman conceptions of difference. While both Cicero and Vergil forged their ideas about the public good from within established traditions, each was also influenced by historical circumstances which he experienced and witnessed. Disregard for constitutional practices and procedures and the recurrent threat of autocratic rule, accompanied from time to time by civil violence, were facts of Roman public life in the last century of the Roman republic (first century B.C.). Cicero was impelled to see himself as guardian of legally elected government and as savior of his people.[5] Vergil, threatened with confiscation of his patrimony, recovered his lands through the intervention of Julius Caesar and secured the lasting favor of Julius's grandnephew Octavian, who became the emperor Augustus. Repeated severe crises called for rethinking the moral-ethical principles of public life as well as practical strategies to heal the *civitas*.[6] For Romans, tradition—philosophy and law, literature, religion and myth, legend and history—had become the accrued wisdom of the ages. Its authority was invoked to restore and to reconstitute Rome as sociopolitical entity and to regenerate its ideology.

From early legend to historical accounts, in both prose and poetry, Romans defined achievement as devotion to the ideal and the reality of the republic, skill in statescraft, and political and military honor. Here is Cicero's description of men's strivings:

> Since we are greatly impelled to augment the resources of the human race, are eager to make human life safer and richer by our considered plans and efforts, and are aroused to this desire by impulses from nature herself, let us hold to this striving, which has ever been the pursuit of all the best men.(*De Re Publica* 1.3)[7]

Membership in the sociopolitical community (Latin *civilitas*, from which English "civility" is derived), in any capacity or rank, was, in theory at least, a Roman's most cherished possession.[8] Defining it and public leadership and refining relationships between the public and private spheres, which in Roman social practice were often connected through intermarriage, were principal Roman contributions to the legacy. The republican form of government developed at Rome (as distinguished from Athenian democracy or other kinds of constitutions such as oligarchy or monarchy) served as a model for the United States constitution with its built-in system of checks and balances: a powerful legislative body, the Senate; popular assemblies, through which the voice of the people could be expressed; public officials elected to serve the State through performance of specified duties.[9] Power, especially social and political power, was concentrated in the hands of a small number of noble families, women and slaves were disenfranchised, men of common birth were excluded from holding the highest public offices, and the lowest socioeconomic class tended to be cut off from political influence. Membership did not come with equal privileges.[10]

Inclusiveness—how to create a more equitable society and facilitate greater participation in political affairs—was in fact a key issue in the civil unrest which disturbed Rome in the last century of the Republic, and reformers and thinkers of various persuasions addressed it. The Gracchi brothers, Tiberius and Gaius, though noble born, introduced programs for land reform and debt cancellation in the hope of redressing economic injustices and quelling social unrest among the Italian poor (129-123 B.C.). Political rights were also at issue in the decades which followed—the need to broaden access to voting privileges and political office, privileges of citizenship from which citizens who lived outside Rome were effectively excluded. Additional concerns were the financing of political campaigns and the obligations incurred by accepting financial support, the use of bribery to obtain political influence, and the use of intimidation and violence to gain or keep political power. The dictatorship of the conservative Sulla and the two triumvirates were extraconstitutional attempts to maintain civil order. As consul in 63 B.C., Cicero had the opportunity to expose a conspiracy against the government by a disgruntled senator, L. Sergius Catilina, before both the Senate and the Roman people, and in accordance with an emergency vote of the Senate, the conspirators were put to death. But it was through his public speaking that Cicero hoped to have the most influence, and he often stressed that civil order depended on a common purpose, the well-being of the republic. It followed that class conflicts such as strife between nobles and wealthy nonnobles (knights, *equites*) could be resolved harmoniously (*concordia ordinum*) and should be subordinated to the public good,[11] and that all men who loved their country, regardless of social, economic, or political rank, would be counted as "best men" (*optimates*).[12] Cicero's solutions to issues of inclusion were ideological rather than practical. Through his brilliant powers as a speaker, he was influential in the Senate, law courts, and the Forum, where public men spoke openly to the people. His philosophical writings became classics in moral and political philosophy.

In his dialogue-essay *De Re Publica* (The Republic), a Roman adaptation of Plato's work, Cicero considers the ideal and just distribution of power in the government of a well-ordered republic. The ideal republic, which was not very different from an idealized Roman Republic, enjoyed the leadership of men who combined idealized virtues of Roman heroes and the qualities of Platonic-Stoic philosopher-rulers. Inclusiveness as a value was subordinate to the superior wisdom of the best men, privileged in traditional ways by their cooptations of intellectual, political, and other forms of power. At moments Cicero sounds to us like a late-twentieth-century American neoconservative, for he believed that the best of human wisdom and experience and recollection of past Roman achievements would heal a battered *civitas*, re-create a sense of national identity and unity. Unfortunately, events did not justify his faith; autocracy won the struggle for leadership at Rome, and Cicero was hunted down and murdered on the orders of Mark Anthony, member of the Second Triumvirate, in 43 B.C.

The most noble arena of action for a man, Cicero claims, is service to the State, for *virtus* proves itself in use (an expression of quintessential Roman practicality). Nature herself (here as often invoked by men in the service of culture) is said to have implanted in man both a need to cultivate virtue and to contribute to the well-being of mankind in general (*RP* 1.1-2). The motivation to use the former in the service of the latter sets a man on the path to achievement, but ambition and self-cultivation are of limited worth without wisdom. How does a man become virtuous and wise? Above all, by understanding the acts of past exemplars and imitating their conduct. Cicero offers many historical paradigms drawn from the Roman community of illustrious, wise statesmen and their mutual admiration for one another. Most of these men were noble born. Cicero himself was not; he was a "new man,"[13] and it clearly was in his own interest to detach *virtus* and the ability to perform public service from accident of birth. The speakers of the dialogue, which Cicero places some eighty years in the past before the outbreak of Rome's civil disturbances, are learned noblemen who respect the constitution in theory and practice and who have given illustrious service to their country. The main speaker is Scipio Aemelianus Africanus the Younger, who had served as consul twice, held the higher office of censor, was conqueror of Carthage and Numantia, and friend of many distinguished men of letters. His friend Laelius, who had also been elected consul, shared his interest in philosophy. Other speakers were prominent men of their day known for their learning in the fields of law and jurisprudence.[14]

Though Cicero describes powerful men forging a political philosophy for all among themselves,[15] he nonetheless defines a republic (1.25) as "a coming together of a large number of people by common agreement based in law and an alliance based in the common good"; its most important public value is liberty. Men do not agree to equalize wealth and they are not equal in inborn abilities, but they should be equal under the law (1.32.49). The best political constitution is "mixed," combining the best features of monarchy, oligarchy, and democracy. A democratic republic such as Rome puts the freedom of the people first; "the best men, chosen by the people"[16] —not the richest or most noble born, but the wisest—are the best judges of what that freedom requires.

Unfortunately, few men know or possess virtue, yet "nature has provided not only that men who excel in the greatest virtue and courage (spirit) should rule over the weaker but that the weaker should also be willing to obey the best" (1.34.51). Thus, Cicero has no difficulty with the notion of "best men" or with their qualifications or right to leadership. The wisdom of most of Rome's kings, who ruled for 240 years after its founding, and of the early leaders of the republic laid the foundation for a great nation (Book 2). A virtuous ruler is the philosophically cultivated man; in him, reason rules over anger, greed, the desire for power and glory, and lust. As embodiment of the best qualities, he serves as a model to others, but he considers himself as much subject to the law as any other citizen. In fact, just as his mind-reason rules over the vices just listed, as well as over blood lust, cruelty, anxiety and grief, and fear and cowardice, so the virtuous ruler controls these bestial elements when they manifest themselves in the State (2.41.67-68).[17]

Civilized society operates on the principle of justice, which does not exist in nature but came into being and remains a guide because of men's inherent weakness. Justice is the rule of law, and "true law is right reason in agreement with nature, universal in its application, fixed, and eternal" (3.22.33),[18] a description that reflects male culture's recurrent fear of what is particular and changeful. Moreover,

> Don't we observe that domination is bestowed on the best to the advantage of the weak by nature herself? Why else does god rule over man, spirit over body, reason over lust and anger and other vicious parts of the same spirit?   (*Rep.* 3.25.37)[19]

Although he disclaims power and success, Cicero concludes the essay with a vision, membership in the immortal and eternal community of achievement—noble, virtuous spirits who dwell eternally in heaven, their reward for serving their country with devotion and wisdom. His vision takes the form of a dream experienced by Scipio, in which his father, Africanus the Elder, appears to him (Book 6.9-29). The elder Scipio has escaped the prison of his body and the earth to join this community of achievement, which Cicero conceives in both traditional and specifically Roman terms. Members of the community have demonstrated outstanding *virtus-arete* in the arts of civilization, military and athletic exploits, and political leadership. For Cicero, merit is defined through learning and philosophic wisdom, but especially through the political benefits men have conferred on their fatherland.[20] This is because the supreme god who rules the earth is pleased by "the assemblies and associations of men united by right" (6.13).

> The best concerns are those about the well-being of the fatherland, the spirit which is aroused by and involved in them will fly more swiftly to this resting place and home; it will travel even more rapidly if, while still trapped in the body, it looks beyond, and detaches itself as much as possible from the body. (6.26.29)

In a new vision of transcendence, immortality gained through public service, Cicero makes a claim for the value of practical moral philosophy. Against the more theoretical orientations of Platonic and Aristotelian philosophy, Cicero places the wise man squarely in the realm of public action, especially that which serves the State. Yet in considering the so-called common good, his philosophy fails to consider, Good for whom? and Good according to whom? Women and Others (including less-than-best men) are not part of his calculations.

In the *Laws (De Legibus)*, a sequel and supplement to the *Republic*, Cicero postulates that law is the highest reason (*ratio = logos*) and inheres in nature (1.6.18f., 2.7.16), a basic concept of Stoic philosophy. The law of reason, which is the counterpart of the divine mind in nature, tells us what to choose and what to avoid, and it is the foundation of social justice.[21] To obey the laws, then, is one way to live in accordance with nature as well as to live virtuously (rationally) (1.21.56). Natural virtue is susceptible to corruption both from without and within, but especially from within: pleasure (*voluptas*) is "the mother of all evils" (1.17.47). Cicero's metaphor reveals that although he places responsibility for resisting evil on the male philosopher, the association of pleasure with evil is traditional, as is the association of both with female power.[22] While in Books 2 and 3 Cicero does discuss many particulars of Roman religious and civil law, one is struck here, as with his earlier *Republic*, by how theoretical and abstract his discourse is and how extensively it evades the complexities of even men's life experience. Virtue, reason, and education as well as the inclination to moral self-cultivation are for men only and only "the best men" know what is best for everybody.

In *Moral Responsibilities (De Officiis)* Cicero presents a social morality suitable for the republic he has described in the two earlier essays. It is written as guide for his only son, a (reluctant, we suspect) philosophy student, who will (his father hopes) follow in his footsteps in service to his country. Although Cicero gives occasional nods to inclusiveness by acknowledging the scope and complexity of society, classicist Miriam T. Griffin comments, "We would not seriously misrepresent *De Officiis* to describe it as a handbook for members of the governing class on their duties to their peers in private life and to their fellow-citizens in public life."[23] Drawing on Stoic and Aristotelian principles of political philosophy, Cicero presents duties as absolute (1.8), universal (1.17), and abstract (passim) rules of conduct as if they applied to all members of the republic and, extended, in accordance with the Stoic view of the universal brotherhood of man, to all mankind.

> There is no part of life that can be separated from moral responsibility—neither in public nor private affairs, in the Forum nor at home, acting by yourself nor with others. You sow what is honorable in your life by cultivating it, what is dishonorable by neglecting it. (*Moral Responsibilities* 1.4)

The key to what makes Cicero's view inherently exclusive is his notion of honor. Latin *honestas* and *honestum* are related to *honor*, "high esteem or respect accorded to superior worth," as well as a particular mark of respect, honor, or privilege, including high public or political office.[24] While he defines what is honorable or worthy of a man in the context of Roman institutions, he reflects the long-established view that social stability depends on mutual recognition among men in the private and public spheres, an orientation that can be traced back to the Homeric code of honor among warrior heroes. Everything honorable arises from some one of these four parts:

> Either it involves perceiving the truth or cleverness; or preserving the bonds among men, giving each his due, and honoring contracts; or the greatness and strength of a noble and invincible spirit; or order and limit in everything we say and do, including modesty and moderation. (1.15)

Cicero names the "cardinal" male virtues designated by Plato and the Stoic philosophers, which arise from basic differences between men and other living creatures. While we share with other creatures an "instinct" for self-preservation and procreation, only man is associated with his fellow men through his powers of reason and speech, wisdom or the search for truth, justice and liberality, greatness of spirit, and a sense of appropriateness (decorum). Men value justice in order to avoid suffering injustice, (a definition; cf. Aristotle's definition of justice, above Chapter 6) and to protect private property, which included children and, in some cases, wives (1.20-41).

> While these obligations apply among "all humanity," within a given society,[25] Men's closest ties are those of race, nation, and language, but closest is that of city . . . men share not only markets, temples, porticoes and roads, but also laws, civil rights, law courts, and voting privileges . . . in addition, close friendships, and personal, business, and commercial relations. (1.53-54)

But since the desire to procreate is instinctual, private bonds, of both marriage and blood, are the most compelling human ties, the foundations of society. "Within the family, human society as a whole is compressed into a single unit"—bonds between husband and wife, parents and children, brother and brother, and among all members of the household. But even if emotional bonds among family members are the strongest of human ties, social bonds among men are the most worthy ("the alliance of the noblest men in a common purpose"). Devotion to country always comes first, parents second (1.54-57).

Observation of appropriateness, the fourth virtue (1.110-161), interests us[26] because it relies on particularity as a measure of value, and particularity assumes differences and takes them into account. But Cicero's general, abstract discussion acknowledges only differences among a select group of men. Latin *decorum*, an adjective, from which the English noun is taken, designated what is comely, seemly, fitting, proper.[27] It is difficult to define, Cicero admits, because it is inseparable from moral goodness and is therefore also associated with male honor. It is that "which gives rise to particular qualities such as behaving in accordance with reason and self-control combined with good breeding" (1.93-96). Since every man is born with a different character, what is right for him depends on his own nature. He may be reclusive or sociable, more or less ambitious, forthright or a good dissembler. But propriety also depends on one's station in life, age and stage of life, and career. It is determined by time, place, and circumstance. It should even determine how one appears to the world—dress, home furnishings, other aspects of life-style, and, not least, manners, the primary meaning of "decorum" today. Class and gender differences—the virtues of particular Others—are overlooked throughout the essay.[28]

Cicero also reformulated received concepts of the community of achievement and their ideologies to suit the sociopolitical community that was the Roman republic. The long-standing dichotomy between competitive and cooperative ethics is a recurrent theme in the second and last books of the essay, as Cicero wrestles with real and apparent conflicts between personal ambition and achievement defined as what is in the best interest of the republic. Recent events—his own exile, the murder of Julius Caesar—inform Cicero's wide-ranging thoughts on violence, anarchy, injustice, and greed. All men want the same thing, to be treated well and in a manner commensurate with their contributions; the welfare of society requires that justice prevail. Men are able to build cities and civilizations only through communal efforts and exchange of benefits. Ambitious men tend to be stubborn and self-willed, more likely to commit unjust acts in their pursuit of glory. In a just society, external rewards—honors, riches, political offices—tend to come to men who deserve them: those who act in accordance with justice and reciprocity.[29] Cicero lists six reasons (2.21) why men look out for the good of other men, a reflection of how Roman public life worked. The foundations of altruism, given in descending order of moral value, are 1) sheer kindness; 2) respect for the other man and a desire to see that he receives the rewards he deserves; 3) trust that the other man will reciprocate in kind; 4) fear of the other man; 5) hope that a more powerful man will reciprocate in kind but more generously, because he is able to give more generously; and 6) hope of (monetary) reward. These remarks reflect the common Roman practice of relying on *amicitia* or "friendship," a formal and informal exchange of favors, to get political business done. *Amicitia* is what we call political patronage.[30]

What does the scrupulous man do when self-interest (what is *utile*, expedient), his desire to be first and to advance himself, and social morality (the common good, *bonum*) conflict? Numerous examples drawn from Roman history illustrate that by honoring obligations to one another and to their country, men also act to their own greater advantage. What is expedient only appears to serve self-interest; the wise man recognizes that his own good and that of society are the same, and that to harm the one is to harm the other. Society is community among ruling men, and moral right the governing principle of relationships between and among them. It can never be advantageous to harm society by an act that also compromises the virtue of the individual.

The antitheses and generalities that characterize Cicero's thinking about public life to some extent also inform our own. Cicero shaped views on the nature of public life and community and on democratic leadership in the West, and he left an enduring mark on political discourse. In the third book of his *Republic,* of which we have only fragments, Cicero conceived what he called a *rector rei publicae,* a man who would serve as moral and political ruler of the republic, one who would keep the nation on the right and straight path.[31] He seems to have considered the possibility that even in a democratic republic, there might be a place for a benevolent autocrat, a possibility Vergil explores at length.

Vergil conjoined the ideal of *civitas* with cosmic order.[32] His vision of a timeless, universal hierarchy of power is best understood in its contemporary context, the collapse of the Republic and its constitution. Decades of uncertainty portending anarchy ended with the military and political triumph of Octavian Caesar, who established himself in the ambiguous role of *princeps,* first citizen. Though his power was by no means secure or unchallenged, within a few years the Senate named him Augustus, creating, in effect, a monarchy superimposed on traditional republican institutions. A ruling authority, working in concert with Jupiter and Fate, the poet imagines, had overseen Rome's founding; the same protective power has perpetuated its existence and promised empire without limit, *imperium sine fine* (1.279). Now, it was to be hoped, supreme authority vested in a ruler who respected Rome's heritage, Augustus, would restore the Roman *civitas* and refashion it into a more stable entity. Vergil's learned vision of a reconstituted past illuminating a glorious present and extending into an equally illustrious future is drawn from myth and religion, literature, legend and history, and philosophy.[33]

In the *Aeneid,* though men strive to maintain power and control by submitting to the greater though inscrutable wisdom of higher powers and though the Roman *civitas* reflects the order and justice of the universe, their very humanity makes them vulnerable to internal and external forces of evil.[34] Recent civil conflicts at Rome were prefigured on the very day Rome was founded, when the twin brothers Romulus and Remus quarreled and Romulus killed Remus. Vergil regards both conflicts as fratricide—brother against brother, citizen against citizen—the triumph of the baser part of human nature. The central panel of the shield which the god Vulcan made for Aeneas (Book 8) depicts the Battle of Actium, where Octavian defeated an army of Eastern barbarians led by Queen Cleopatra of Egypt and her lover, the renegade

Roman, Mark Anthony; all embody savagery, dissoluteness, and violence (*Aen*.8.675-713; Octavian celebrates his triumph at Rome,714-731). Vergil imagines Octavian, later Augustus, guided by Jupiter as Aeneas had been before him. There is even a supposed distant blood tie between the two leaders. Ascanius, also known as Iulus, was an ancestor of the Julian family (*gens*); Julius Caesar adopted his grandnephew Octavian. As the gods who are on the side of right protect and guide them, wise men struggle to make the forces of righteousness—political in the secular world, divine in the cosmic—win out over opposing forces: madness, evil, and chaos.[35] As in Greek tragedy and New Comedy, men feared sabotage from within the male community itself, forces that undermined men's best expectations of themselves. Vergil, like earlier writers, presents father-son relationships and the transmission of authority from one generation of men to the next within the family and State as the cornerstones of society; social order depends on the conservation of these relationships and the authority vested in them. Female powers, as we shall see shortly, are principal external threat to that wisdom.

The scheme of the *Aeneid* is grand, as befits an epic written in the Homeric tradition, and the configuration of opposing forces which it marshals is magnificent,[36] yet the poem can be read in microcosm, through the major themes introduced in the first book. *Arma virumque cano*, Arms and the man I sing. Everyone is familiar with Vergil's opening statement of his theme, which invokes the Homeric warrior-hero to be commemorated in song. The hero is not named, however, for almost one hundred lines; he is only described: the first to set out as a fugitive from Troy, driven by fate and destined to reach Italy, a man who suffered both in war and its aftermath in order to set in motion events that would lead to the founding of a city and to bring the gods to Latium. This warrior-hero is Trojan, not Greek, and he seeks not his homecoming but a vaguely defined place in a western land destined to become a new center of civilization. He will not live to see this destiny fulfilled. After his arrival in Hesperia, he must fight a war to establish the Trojan refugees in Italy, then marry and sire a new race, from which new founding fathers and the city of Rome will ultimately arise.

Though *insignis pietate*, exceptional in piety, this man is compelled to suffer unceasingly because of the wrath of the goddess Juno. *Pietas*, a distinctly Roman virtue which means more than "piety" or "pity," its English derivatives, names a key moral concept of the poem. It is *arete-virtus* defined as obedience to the will of Jupiter and Fate, devotion to the gods and respect for the difference between men and gods, and observance of established Roman religious practices. In Vergil's yoking of religion, morality, and politics, *pietas* is also devotion to Rome as ideal *civitas* and an idealized view of service to country and the obedience of citizen to the authority of the State and its ruler(s). In the area of personal relationships, it is the mutual devotion of parent and child, in particular father and son, brother and brother, friend and friend, husband and wife.

Since an outstandingly good man is the last person who should be tormented by the gods, why is Juno obsessed with destroying him, or at the very least obstructing his progress and causing him every imaginable kind of grief and anxiety? The goddess is irrational, *saeva*, ferocious as a wild animal, a creature at the opposite and opposing end of the hierarchy of being. The hero is tormented because of savage Juno's mindful wrath (*saevae memorem Iunonis ob iram*, line 4), which has many causes (lines 11-49): hopes and fears for the ascendancy of her favorite new city, Carthage, which she knows is destined to be conquered by the future Rome; her old partiality to the Greek city Argos, opposed to Troy in the recent war; the judgment of Paris; Jove's fondness for the boy Ganymede; fear that respect for her power and majesty is waning. Anger is a terrible force; we recall the opening words of the *Iliad*: "Sing, goddess, the wrath, and havoc wreaked by the anger of Achilles." *Tantaene animis caelestibus irae*, "Can such great wraths reside in heavenly spirits?" the poet asks.[37] It can and it does. Juno is also in the grip of grief (*quidve dolens* 9, *saevique dolores* 25) and nurses a perpetual wound (*aeternum . . . vulnus* 36). She voluntarily puts herself at the mercy of the basest parts of her divine soul and wallows in her own subjectivity, a generic female flaw.[38] She will emerge in Vergil's narrative as the antithesis of Jupiter, epitome of male rational control. Juno has already kept the Trojans from Italy for many years now; she will eventually admit defeat, but only after the Trojans have reached the promised land and fought and gained a foothold there: Such a massive endeavor[39] it was to found the Roman people, Vergil observes at the conclusion of the prologue (33).

Inflamed by past grudges and fearing that Jupiter and the Fates are bringing the Trojans closer to their Italian destiny, Juno plots immediate destruction. She seeks the aid of Aeolus, a small-time divinity who holds power to command *(imperium)* the winds. Obedient to Juno's order, he unleashes these unruly forces of nature. Aeneas, here named for the first time, quails with fear at the furious storm at sea and impending shipwreck. In his first brief speech, he wishes he had died at Troy. Although we are not expecting an exact replica of the Homeric warrior-hero, neither are we expecting the hero as coward.[40] But heroes, we recall from discussions of tragedy, exist at the extremities of action and suffering, and Aeneas is worn down by suffering and loss. Like Juno, he is "wounded," but unlike her, he will overcome his trauma through the guidance of Jupiter, the grand vision of Roman destiny his father will impart to him,[41] and his own moral development.[42]

Neptune, king of the sea, is livid at the disturbance Juno has caused and calms the storm:

> As often when among a great people rebellion arises,
> and the spirits of the common herd rage, torches and
> stones fly, madness ministers arms: then, if they happen
> to see a man distinguished in piety and deserved honors,
> they grow silent and stop in their tracks, ears pricked up.
> With words he rules their spirits and soothes their hearts.
> Thus did the crashing sea subside. (1.148-154)

This simile illustrates the correct use of *imperium*, by a divinity and a noble statesman. Power of command is the same in nature and culture, for just as nonrational forces of nature must be harnessed, compelled into an environment safe for man to live in, so, too, the common people, prone to unruly, unpredictable, irrational and animallike behavior,[43] must be tamed, made fit to live in civilized society.

While Aeneas and the Trojans safely make their way to Carthage on the coast of Africa and the nascent kingdom of Queen Dido, the goddess Venus, Aeneas's mother, alarmed by Juno's latest ploy, appeals to her father Jupiter. Aeneas's fate and fame are assured, he tells her, and he prophesies what destiny has decreed: the arrival of Aeneas in Italy and his apotheosis, the rule of Aeneas's son Ascanius, the three-hundred-year Trojan rule based at Alba Longa, the founding of the city Rome and Roman *imperium*, destined to extend to the ends of the earth under Julius Caesar, and finally, an era of unprecedented peace, symbolized by the imprisonment of impious Furor, madness and irrationality personified, within the gates of the temple of war (1.254-296). Roman rule, domestic and imperial, is the counterpart of the rule of reason, and an extension of the capability and authority of the best males, gods and men. These benevolent powers exercise dominion over chaos, disorder, and unruliness wherever these forces appear—in the natural world or in divine and human natures. Venus, female and the divine embodiment of yet another destructive, irrational force, sexuality, will shortly abandon her alignment with Jupiter and Rome's destiny. Intending to protect her son from proverbial Carthaginian treachery, she contrives to make Dido fall in love with Aeneas and later, in the fourth book, conspires with Juno to make the couple begin an affair. Thus, she temporarily deflects Aeneas from his goal, and he incurs yet another loss when he must leave Dido to resume his quest. Dido is, incidentally, destroyed in the process.

On his way to his fateful first meeting with Dido at Carthage, Aeneas visits the temple of Juno, where he beholds murals depicting scenes of the Trojan War and reflects on "human" endeavors, fame, and the commemorative power of art.

> What place,
> what region of the earth is not full of our labor?
> Behold Priam! Even here praise has its own rewards,
> there are tears for human events, and mortal affairs
> touch the mind. Let go your fears; this fame will bring
> some safety to you.   (1.459-463)

Aeneas is consoled to see that here, far from Troy, the valor and suffering of the war heroes are not forgotten. His response is self-congratulatory and narcissistic, yet he also senses an what is an epistemological truth for heroes: "We" empathize with "mortal affairs," which remind us of our own hopes and fears; they also touch our *mens*, the faculties (intelligence, reason, foresight, purpose) that affect man's understanding of his place in the universe and the meaning of his actions. Groaning and weeping, Aeneas feeds his eyes on the "empty representation" (*pictura . . . inani*).[44] The word *inanis* suggests that human perception and understanding are inherently deficient and insubstantial, that Aeneas "reads" the mural with limited, human understanding. Pain of loss clouds his power to evaluate the past and present, to plan for the future.[45] Vergil evokes the archaic Greek view of man as powerless— through lack of knowledge, through vulnerability to emotion—the major difference after mortality between gods and men,[46] yet his emphasis on suffering as something that disempowers men is distinctly his own. Even a man dedicated to a community guaranteed power of great scope and duration by destiny cannot completely understand the goal for which he sacrifices himself. Jupiter's guidance is the complement to his epistemological flaw.

The rest of *Aeneid* 1 focuses on Aeneas's meeting with Dido,[47] a woman of great energy and resourcefulness. Like Aeneas, she was forced to flee her homeland, but she fled for a personal reason, to escape the evil, power-hungry brother who murdered her husband. Though she is founding Carthage, destined to be a great power in the western Mediterranean, and is endowing the new city with all the arts of civilization, she is not—or shows no awareness of being—entrusted by destiny with a historical mission. A woman, Dido has credentials as *dux*—*dux femina facti*, a woman was the leader of the deed (Venus's description 1.364). The phrase, a virtual oxymoron, presents the queen as paradox, an anomaly in Roman and Vergilian political terms. Like Aeneas, she is dedicated to her people; she has assumed and is successfully exercising authority. She, too, exhibits exemplary *pietas*, but her virtue is the ability to feel empathy (*pietas* as pity). She welcomes the homeless Trojans with, *Non ignara mali miseris succurrere disco*, "Because of my own experience with misfortune, I am learning how to nurture fellow sufferers" (1.630). Her affair with Aeneas, however, will destroy her. Initially compared to the chaste hunter goddess Diana (1.496ff.), Dido becomes the hunted; she is compared with a wounded deer (4.65-79) and is later likened to a worshiper of Bacchus—ecstatic, out of control (4.296-302). *Amor (eros)*, like *ira* and the madness of civil war and other unsanctioned acts of violence, is a kind of *furor*. In succumbing to her sexual needs and her desire to have a child by Aeneas, Dido sacrifices her ability to function as ruler and nation builder. We recall a cultural prejudice which has survived almost up to the present time: A woman can have marriage and a family or a career (if she must) but not both. The paradigm of Dido illustrates that an exceptional woman may, under extraordinary circumstances, become a leader and wield authority, but ultimately she will subvert herself.[48] Though capable of pity, she lacks self-control, as well as the philosophic understanding which would impel her to obey a greater, wiser power. Because she lacks the more important component of *pietas*, submission to the will of Jupiter and Fate, she is fatally flawed.[49] Aeneas is temporarily deflected from his fated course by Venus and Juno[50] and by the weaknesses which inhere in embodied existence, in being human: These are the need for stability and security, the fulfillment of emotional and sexual desires. He recovers his better self, however, and sails for Italy when so ordered by Jupiter. Dido, all too human, is devastated by his departure and commits suicide.[51]

Aeneas's renunciation of Dido, the death of his father Anchises, and the prophecy Anchises makes to him in the underworld—the first Aeneas hears of Rome's destiny, to achieve world empire—move him farther toward a state of greater spiritual clarity and dedication, which becomes as unequivocal as merely mortal service can be. Once he arrives in Italy, however, he must fight "wars, gruesome wars" (6.86), the Sibyl tells him, in order to gain land and acceptance for his people in Italy. More important, he must marry Lavinia, daughter of King Latinus, eponymous founder of the Latin people, in order to father the new race which will become Roman.

Juno, intending to foil this union, visits Hades, where all spirits including powers of darkness dwell, and conjures the pestilential fury Allecto, "who holds mournful wars, rages, betrayals, and vile accusations dear" (7.325f.). Allecto maddens Amata, Latinus's queen, so that she rages against Aeneas's marriage to her daughter like a bacchant, acting as Dido did when crazed with love of Aeneas. A portent sent by Jupiter is interpreted by Latinus's father, the Italian god Faunus, to mean that his daughter is destined to marry a foreigner. Though Lavinia is already engaged to Turnus, an Italian prince, Latinus accepts Aeneas as future son-in-law; Amata does not. If men, even Aeneas, are unable fully to understand what must be, women willfully refuse to do so. Next, Allecto visits Turnus, a circumspect and honorable man, who now, inflamed and bereft of his reason and his promised bride, rushes out in the middle of the night to gather troops for war. Finally, she initiates fighting between Italians and Trojans, through one of those arbitrary events which have so often served as a catalyst for violence in the course of human history; she causes Ascanius, Aeneas's son, to kill a pet deer belonging to an Italian shepherd, whose angry friends seize arms and attack the Trojans. The war Allecto has instigated represents the triumph of forces of madness and destruction, not because it is war, but because it stems from Juno's opposition to fate. Female powers are destructive to others as well as self-destructive; women and goddesses—even Aeneas's divine mother—are untrustworthy and unstable, if not actually evil, unless subject to superior, male judgment and supervision:[52] Juno's savage wrath, the lapse of judgment that allows Venus to conspire with Juno, Dido's vulnerability, Allecto's inherent love of discord, Queen Amata's flight to irrationality.

In the second half of the epic, Books 7-12, the Trojans fight to make a place for themselves in Italy and win. The fluctuations of war are the setting for the development of a central theme, the devotion of fathers and sons, which Vergil shows to be a prerequisite for the continuity and well-being of the community. The importance of father-son bonds has already been established. In Book 2 (707-725) Aeneas's relationships with his father Anchises and his son Ascanius were fixed in an image of quintessential *pietas*: the three generations escaping from the flames of Troy. Aeneas carries his aged father on his shoulders (the old man clutches the household gods) and grips his young son by the hand. Aeneas's first action when he reaches Dido's court at Carthage is to summon Ascanius (1.643-646).[53] It is Ascanius who first recognizes the fulfillment of a prophecy, the sign that the Trojans have arrived at their destination.[54] Father Anchises often advises *pater* Aeneas in guiding the Trojans' progress, and when he dies (3.708ff.), Aeneas holds funeral games in his honor, as befits a hero and consort of Venus (5.42ff.). Vergil's heroes fight their *aristeiai* for their sons' survival and destiny— that of their bloodline and their people. Homeric honor included this notion; Vergil ties it to the patriarchal nation as well as to the patriarchal family. The future of the nation- and empire-to-be and their peoples is the future of every noble family: The fatherland (*patria* is an extension of the fathers, *patres*),[55] a critical point of intersection between private and public. Vergil does not completely overlook the contributions of mothers, however small by comparison; mothers and sons are also bound by ties of *pietas*.[56]

The continuity of Aeneas's bloodline is already guaranteed by Ascanius's known destiny: He will survive. Other father-son pairs figure prominently in Books 8-12. The exemplary devotion of King Evander and his son Pallas and the sacrifice they make in order to fulfill destiny are pivotal for Vergil's story. An exile from Arcadia in Greece, Evander has settled on the site of future Rome. He has become the founder and curator of what will become the city's heritage. Thus, when Aeneas arrives, Evander and Pallas are celebrating public rites in honor of the hero Hercules, a cult still practiced in Vergil's Rome which was associated with an important monument, the Ara Maxima (Greatest Altar).[57] Evander takes Aeneas on a tour, sharing his encyclopedic knowledge of religious sites, origins, and institutions with his guest.[58] This knowledge is something Evander would hope to pass on, along with ruling power, to his son, and he to his son, but it was not to be, for Pallas, whom his aging father entrusts to Aeneas's care, will be killed in battle by Turnus. At the climax and conclusion of both the war and the poem, Aeneas avenges Pallas's death by killing Turnus. Fathers suffer, and their collective grief is the suffering of the fatherland. Pallas's death, like Dido's, is a reminder that greatness comes at the price of many terrible losses.

Even among the demonized enemy—Turnus, his Rutulians, and their allies—fathers and sons are devoted to one another. Such are Mezentius and Lausus, whom Vergil places at the head of his catalogue of the opposing Italian forces (7.647-847). Mezentius is a man who scorns the gods (648; also 8.7), but Lausus is granted several heroic attributes—he is second in good looks only to Turnus, tamer of horses and conqueror of wild beasts; therefore, he deserved to be blessed with a better father and to inherit ruling power. Mezentius's only redeeming quality is his love for his son. A tyrant, he was exiled by his own people, the Etruscans—becoming a father without a fatherland—and took refuge with Turnus. Devoid of *pietas* toward gods and fatherland, Mezentius falls far short of Vergil's ideal of moral goodness, yet his devotion to his son, who reciprocates in kind, is exemplary. In narrating a succession of heroic encounters, Vergil highlights the poignancy of their relationship. But he also uses it to reemphasize, though in a different kind of context, the point he made earlier in the poem: Private emotions removed from public and religious contexts are insufficient. Both father and son must die, Lausus the victim of his father's impieties, but Vergil does not refuse to memorialize their suffering.

In the account of his *aristeia* in Book 10, mammoth Mezentius is compared to a wild boar (10.707) and to the giant Orion crashing across the sea or down a mountainside (10.763-767). He is finally stopped by *pius* Aeneas (783), who wounds him, and when Lausus rushes to his father's aid, Aeneas rushes against him. Vergil breaks his narrative to address Lausus directly (791-793): He "deserves to be remembered," and his loyalty will stand the test of time.[59] Aeneas tells Lausus that his piety is misplaced, and savage angers (*saevae irae*) rise in the breast of the Dardanian leader, recalling Juno and the dangers of all irrational passion. Mention of Dardanus, mythical founder of Troy and ancestor of Priam, places Aeneas in historical context, in the company of his ancestors and, by implication, his descendants. Unlike the impious Mezentius, father Aeneas gives due honor to the continuity of men's generations. After burying his sword in Lausus's body, the son of Anchises pities him, and recalling "fatherly" piety (824), vows to return the corpse for burial and, as an additional sign of respect, not to strip its arms. When Lausus's corpse is brought back, Mezentius embraces it, crying out that he cannot live now that his son is dead. He experiences the kind of recognition which often takes place in tragic (and sometimes comic) drama; he has learned too late the cost of his impiety:

> Now at last I come to a wretched end, now the wound is driven deep.
> I stained your name with my offense, my son, when, hated, I was driven
> from my fathers' throne and ruling power. I owed my fatherland
> and people the supreme penalty. I should have given up my guilty spirit
> to death from every side. (10.849-854)

Despite his wound, Mezentius rides out against Aeneas, who kills him. Mezentius, recalling one last time that he is a man without a country, asks only that he be buried with his son.

Earlier in Book 10 (439-507), Turnus killed young Pallas in battle, though Hercules had tried to save the boy by appealing to his own father, Jupiter. Something in Turnus, who is by no means a villain, is oblivious to the devotion of fathers and sons. "Tell Evander," he declares with shocking cruelty, "that I'm sending him the Pallas he deserves." Though he gives back the corpse for burial, he strips the arms, including a striking sword belt on which the story of the daughters of Danaus, a *nefas* (an evil act, forbidden by the gods), is engraved.

The story on the sword belt tells of male power conflicts and their sometimes homicidal consequences. Danaus, eponymous ancestor of one of the peoples of Greece, and his twin Aegyptus, ruler of Libya and Ethiopia, quarreled over who would succeed their father when he died. Aegyptus besieged Danaus's land and forced him to give his fifty daughters in marriage to his fifty sons, a strategy that would, presumably, unite the two ruling powers and end the strife. Danaus pretended to agree but ordered his daughters to kill their husbands on their wedding night; all but one complied. The murder of forty-nine young men by their wives, which obiterated the hope of family continuity, was evil, but fraternal conflict and the betrayal of brother by brother, its political legacy, civil war, and disruption of the continuity of male rule were greater evils. Turnus's marriage to Lavinia is also *nefas*, forbidden because she is destined to marry Aeneas, whom her father acknowledges as his rightful son-in-law. It is now inevitable that Aeneas kill Turnus. Turnus stands in the way of destiny, but he is a decent man, or was before Allecto inflamed his baser impulses. He is wearing the sword belt he stripped from Pallas's body, and at the sight of the boy's arms, "reminders of savage grief" (*saevi monimenta doloris* 12.945), Aeneas is maddened with rage ("inflamed by furies and terrible in his wrath," *furiis accensus et ira / terribilis* 946f.), which impels him to deliver the fatal blow.

Aeneas's rage at the death of Pallas, which fills the very last lines of the poem, counterbalances the rage of savage Juno with which the *Aeneid* began. Aeneas's motivation at this critical moment has been endlessly debated: When an exceptionally good man acts out of anger, has he been overwhelmed by an evil, irrational force in spite of himself, or are his action and motivation valid and necessary—sanctioned because the hero remains in control and, even thus aroused, serves an appointed end? Seen in this light, savage rage and grief are appropriate if aligned with destiny, commitment to rational self-control, righteous *imperium*. Aeneas kills Turnus in anger, but his passion and pain serve the right cause.[60] How many acts of violence has his legendary paradigm justified? On the other hand, though a man who is guided by religious and philosophical beliefs may greatly desire to live free from passion, he cannot because he is human. Only a god, Jupiter, has the capacity to be the perfect model of philosophical detachment and impartiality. Is there a place, then, for irrationality—*ira, furor,* and *amor*—in civilized society? There must be, because the irrational is part of the universe, thus part of human nature. But it must be subordinated, transformed, or sublimated, like the Erinyes in Aeschylus's *Oresteia*, like Erato in the invocation of *Aeneid* 7, where the muse of disruptive erotic love is reconstituted to celebrate the devotion of fathers and sons, of citizens and fatherland. Domination is a good when sanctioned and overseen by higher powers, when guided by reason, justice, and order, and Vergil, like others before him, presents it as the only alternative to chaos.[61]

In imagining an idealized *res publica,* Cicero and Vergil extended the moral ideologies of patriarchy. Both believed in the superior moral judgment of "superior" men, whose oversight of the common good would immortalize both community and individual. While Cicero's views grew out of practical experience and the realities of everyday political life, and while he believed in a republican constitution based on a division and balance of powers within the patriarchy, Vergil, writing his epic in the post-civil-war era, held that peace and civil order could be guaranteed only by the investiture of authority in a single leader who must answer to higher powers. By fixing human values into a fixed cosmic superstructure and order, Vergil elevated both private and public morality into the realm of the absolute and timeless. Jupiter, Aeneas, and his counterpart Augustus are supreme commanders, embodiments of ruling virtues. Rome as community and as empire, as well as the authority of Augustus, are aligned with moral good overseen by Jupiter and Fate.

In many respects, the story of Aeneas became, as Carol Gilligan has suggested,[62] the Western paradigm of an ideal male life pattern. A man's aim in life is his work, which is tied to the pursuit of a goal. Though he undertakes this work with the guidance of a mentor and carries it out with the support of a female helpmate, he is his own man, free and autonomous. Many a man may, in his own way, be a bit of a hero, if he fashions his self-image accordingly. His goal is, or he considers it to be, a kind of higher purpose for which he may be called upon to sacrifice personal attachments.[63] He must, however, meet his obligations to his son(s) and to other young men of the upcoming generation. Aeneas's quest, to initiate the dream that will become Rome, requires him to lose a wife at Troy[64] and to abandon Dido; he proceeds at the behest of Fate and Jupiter, his mentors, whose will is known to him only through prophecies and omens. His mother, Venus, is a powerful though far from reliable helpmate. But it is difficult to see Aeneas as a model of autonomy, and his actions do not fit the mold of Homeric achievement. Despite his heroic isolation, Aeneas is not in control of his fate any more than Achilles or Odysseus was, though, like them, he can and does choose to fulfill it. In pursuing (accepting?) the achievement that will win him immortality and by embracing his destiny, he becomes, paradoxically, a paradigm of male passivity. Submission to Fate and Jupiter is the better moral choice, yet to submit is to relinquish control and responsibility. Isn't such passivity a kind of moral abdication? Moreover, the *Aeneid* sets in clear relief the idea that victory and success come only at the inevitable price of violence, cruelty, loss, and suffering, but men should be willing to pay the price in order to fulfill their mission.

Foreshadowing the Church Father Augustine's two kingdoms, Vergil's outstanding man, a leader or ruler in the secular realm, is guided by divine authority. Of all pagan authors, Vergil was the most acceptable to Christian thinkers[65] because of his belief in the role of providence and divine guidance in human affairs and because he regarded superior wisdom and moral authority, vested in one (male) god, as the ultimate ruling power. This higher power worked to maintain order against forces of irrationality: the wildness of nature and of human nature, which is prone to the forces of love, rage, and madness, though female nature is the more susceptible to them. Female nature at worst is a seething cauldron of narcissistic malevolence, incapable of submitting to moral or any other social good. It is the cause of corruption in men, who are, however, also quite capable of corrupting themselves. In his *Confessions,* the Church Father Augustine describes his struggle to renounce the pleasures of embodied existence and the joys of reading pagan Cicero to embrace the true pleasure of loving God.[66] Catholic Christianity was to create new oppositions and to place a higher value on spiritual achievement and everlasting life in God than on the transient rewards of worldly success. The opposition between embodiment and mind/reason developed into a chasm between body and spirit, secular and sacred, and each was given a proper location: the City of Man and the City of God.

Tradition at Rome is the continuity of the male cultural community, an extension of the Homeric and Pindaric communities of achievement. It transcends the abilities and fortunes of noble individuals, family lines, and, in later times and other places, peoples and nations. More than any other Greek or Roman author, Vergil speaks for the power of tradition to infuse value and continuity into human affairs and to serve as guide for future generations. Values that inform tradition are today being questioned because they glorify and perpetuate the authority of ruling men and because they do not include the moral experiences of Others. Since antiquity we have assumed that tradition itself is authority; if we challenge this premise, what are we going to put in its place?

Notes

[1] Genevieve Lloyd, "Selfhood, war and masculinity," in Carole Pateman and Elizabeth Gross, eds., *Feminist Challenges. Social and Political Theory* (Sydney: Allyn and Unwin, 1986), p.64.

[2] Moira Gatens, *Feminism and Philosophy. Perspectives on Difference and Equality* (Bloomington: Indiana University Press, 1991), p.134.

[3] Latin *classis*, class, division, or rank (of citizens, students, or others); naval fleet (Oxford Latin Dictionary). Beginning in the 17th century,"classic" in English meant "of the highest rank"; "pertaining to Greek or Latin writers or works of literature"; and "a writer of the first rank and of acknowledged excellence" (Oxford English Dictionary).

⁴ If Cicero were alive today, he might have spoken thus:

> But this is the great danger America faces. That we will cease to be one nation and become instead a collection of interest groups: city against suburbs, region against region, individual against individual. Each seeking to satisfy private wants.
> If that happens, who then will speak for America?.What are those of us who are elected public officials supposed to do? I'll tell you this: we as public servants must set an example for the rest of the nation. It is hypocritical for the public official to admonish and exhort the people to uphold the common good if we are derelict in upholding the common good. More is required of public officials than slogans and handshakes and press releases. This is required: We must hold ourselves strictly accountable. We must provide the people with a vision of the future.

The speaker was Representative Barbara Jordan of Texas (a "new woman" in Congress, as Cicero was a "new man" in the Senate; see below) in her keynote address to the Democratic National Convention in 1976, quoted in her obituary, *The New York Times*, January 18, 1996, p.B10.

⁵ At the height of his career, Cicero delivered speeches in the Senate and before the Roman people as consul, second-highest elected post in the Roman *cursus honorum* (course of public offices), against Catiline, a disgruntled but impoverished nobleman whom he had defeated at the polls. Catiline formed a conspiracy against duly elected officials and the legitimate government, as Cicero tells it in his Catiline orations 1-4. See further, for example, Cambridge Ancient History, vols. 9 and 10; Ronald Syme, *The Roman Revolution* (London: Oxford University Press, 1960 [1939]), Chapter 10, "The Senior Statesman."

⁶ Alasdair MacIntyre reminds us of the adaptive powers of traditions in response to crises in Chapter 18, "The Rationality of Traditions," of *Whose Justice? Which Rationality?* (South Bend,IN: Notre Dame University Press, 1988), pp.349-369. Cicero and Vergil are apt illustrations of his observation.

⁷ There are always those, Cicero continues (1.4), who invoke danger and fear of death as disincentives, but the best men "think it worse to be used up by nature and old age than to seize the opportunity to give their life, which must in any case be given up to nature, to their country."

⁸ On *civilitas*, see the remarks of Miriam Griffin in *Seneca. A Philosopher in Politics* (Oxford: Clarendon, 1976), Chapter 3, pp.67-128. Emphasis on and articulation of this value is, arguably, characteristically Roman. Although women in Roman society fared better in terms of legal and economic rights than their Greek sisters and although they, too, were called upon to serve the religious well-being of the State, they had no place in Roman political institutions. See Yan Thomas, "The Division of the Sexes in Roman Law," in Pauline Pantel, ed., *A History of Women in the West*, vol. 1, *From Ancient Goddess to Christian*

Saints, trans. Arthur Goldhammer (Cambridge: Harvard University Press, 1992), pp. 83-138; Aline Rousselle, "Body Politics in Ancient Rome," in Pantel, pp.296-337; and Jane E. Gardner, *Women in Roman Law and Society* (Bloomington: Indiana University Press, 1986).

[9] So noted by Michael Grant in his introduction to Cicero, *On Government* (London: Penguin, 1993), p.7, n2: "This 'mixed' constitution, previously admired by the historian Polybius (to whom Cicero's debts were extensive), reappeared again and again in early discussions of the constitution of the United States of America, figuring prominently, for example in John Adams' *Defence of the Constitutions of Government of the United States* (1787)."

This is not the place for an essay on comparative government; a few points are relevant, however. The Roman Senate was composed of *senes*, older and presumable wiser men, and most of its members were elected from families whose ancestors had also served as senators. These men had risen through the ranks of public office (*cursus honorum*). There were three popular assemblies; in the most important of them, organized by tribe in groups of one hundred (centuries), voting took place by centuries (one century, one vote), but groups with more powerful members voted first, and lower-ranking centuries, made up of poorer citizens, might not get to vote at all.

[10] Michael Grant points out, "At all times during the Roman Republic, twenty or thirty men from a dozen familites almost held a monopoly of power [in the Senate]." Cicero, *On Government*, Introduction, p.5, n5.

[11] See, for example, the fourth oration against Catiline, 14-24, esp. 15.

[12] See, for example, his speech on behalf of Sestius, an elected official of the people (tribune), sections 96-102, esp. 97.

[13] A man who did not come from one of the dozen super-noble families or did not count a consul among his ancestors but nevertheless managed to get elected to higher public office was called a *novus homo*, new man. Cicero, though only an *eques* or knight by birth (originally men wealthy enough to own and keep a horse in the army; most knights in Cicero's time were businessmen or financiers) gained prominence through his rhetorical skills and was elected praetor in 66 and consul in 63 B.C. He was the first "new man" to become a member of the Senate as consul in 44 years.

[14] All success is evanescent, however. Even the most learned and devoted public servants are not always treated justly; Cicero, too staunch a traditional republican and too outspoken, was sent into exile (1.3-8), as Seneca would be after him. Wise men—those who have gained perspective on human affairs through study of philosophy and history—are aware that even the greatest earthly glory such as the Romans have achieved, most especially through world empire, is a small thing. This outlook gives a man perspective on his own endeavors. He has moral strength because he has some distance from the vicissitudes of public life (see esp. 1.17). It was a nice try, but Cicero in fact cared desperately what his contemporaries thought of him and what future genera-

tions would think.

[15] Cicero acknowledged that Roman law discriminated against women; at *Rep.* 3.10.17 he questions Voconian Law (169 B.C.), which limited women's right to inherit; the law which permitted Vestal Virgins (priestesses who served the cult of the goddess who protected public safety by guarding the symbolic public hearth) to have an heir but forbid their mothers to have one; and inequities in the laws stipulating how much property a woman may own.

[16] Cicero mistrusted the extreme political factions of his day—the democrats (*populares*), such as Julius Caesar, as well as the conservative dictator Sulla, for both threatened the republic with tyranny, something no wise and good man could contemplate.

[17] Vices are like wild animals, *belua*; cf. Vergil's description of the unruly common people (*Aen.* 1.148ff., discussed below).

[18] For justice, reason, and nature, see also Cicero, *Laws* 1.5.17.

[19] This and the fragment which follows are attributed to Cicero by Augustine. Speaking of different kinds of domination and subservience, Cicero says: "The mind is said to rule the body but also lust. It rules the body as a king rules his subjects or a parent children but it rules lust as a master rules his slaves, in order to coerce and break it. The power of command of kings, generals, public officers, senators, and public assemblies rules citizens and allies as the spirit rules bodies." He also says that parts of the body are ruled like sons because they readily obey (3.25.38).

[20] Both Scipios held the highest offices (consul, censor) and were outstanding generals in the wars against Carthage. In addition the Younger was a patron of the arts, associate of the playwright Terence, the historian Polybius, and the Stoic philosopher Panaetius. For further thoughts on happiness and fame, see *Laws* 1.11.31-32.

[21] *Lex*, law, is derived from the verb *lego*, choose (1.6.19). For justice, see 1.13.35ff. Cicero discusses the connection between reason and the divine mind at length in Book 2 passim.

[22] See also the story of Hercules' choice related in *De Officiis* 1.32.118. Two female forms appear to the hero as a young man. One offered him the Way of Pleasure, the other the Way of Virtue. The story comes from the Greek philosopher Xenophon, *Memorabilia* 2.1.21-34, who had it from Prodicus, a pre-Socratic philosopher. Xenophon describes how Pleasure, decked out as a whore, promises a life of ease, while Virtue, simple and modest, can show him only a hard and uphill path.

[23] Cicero, *De Officiis*, ed. and trans. M.T. Griffin and E.M. Atkins (Cambridge: Cambridge University Press, 1991), Introduction, p.xxv.

[24] Oxford Latin Dictionary, under *honor*.

[25] Cicero is describing degrees of *societas* among men (1.53).

26 We have encountered earlier expressions of this notion in chapters 3 (Hesiod) and 6 (Homer, New Comedy).

27 *Decorus,-a,-um*, from the noun *decus*, ornament, honor, also gives us English "decoration." By Cicero's time Aristotle's *to prepon* (*Rhetoric* 3.7ff.), had become a familiar aesthetic standard. A character in a drama should speak and act in a fitting manner, for example (see 1.97); similarly, the style and diction of a public speech or any literary work should fit the subject matter, audience, etc; see further Cicero, *De Oratore* (The Orator). Ciceronian decorum was tied to appearance and conduct, which should reflect the inner man.

28 For Cicero's class biases, see M.T. Griffin, Introduction, pp.xxiiiff. of Griffin and Atkins, ed., Cicero, *De Officiis*.

29 Cicero's own ambitious career and hopes for immortality belied his idealism; for his life, see Elizabeth Rawson, *Cicero. A Portrait* (London: Lane, 1975).

30 The Romans also had a system of social patronage which crossed class lines. A prominent man might serve as patron to the less fortunate, exchanging, for example, getting out (the right) votes in return for economic aid.

31 Latin *rectus,-a,-um*, meant, paradoxically, right and therefore straight. See also the straightness of *dike* and straight and crooked *logos* in Hesiod: Pietro Pucci, *Hesiod and the Language of Poetry* (Baltimore: The Johns Hopkins University Press, 1977), pp.45-50 and 67-71 and passim.

32 For additional reflections on the relationships between Cicero and Vergil, see John R.C. Montague, ed., *Cicero and Virgil: Studies in Honour of Harold Hunt* (Amsterdam: Adolf M. Hakkert, 1972).

33 Anchises' account of the transmigration of souls in *Aen.* 6 is Platonic, and Vergil's emphasis on moral responsibility to one's people and fatherland is Stoic. The epic reflects less Epicurean influence. According to the *Life* which has come down to us from the fourth-century A.D. scholar Donatus, Vergil was a serious student of philosophy and, after finishing his epic, intended to spend the rest of his life studying it.

34 See, for example, Jasper Griffin, *Virgil* (Oxford: Oxford University Press, 1986), Chapter 4, "The *Aeneid* and the Myth of Rome," pp. 58-196, and Francis Cairns, *Virgil's Augustan Epic* (Cambridge: Cambridge University Press, 1989), Chapter 1, "Divine and Human Kingship," pp. 1-28. For themes and structure of the *Aeneid*, see, for example, Phillip Hardie,*Virgil's Aeneid. Cosmos and Imperium* (Oxford: Oxford University Press, 1986); Susan Ford Wiltshire, *Public and Private in Virgil's Aeneid* (Amherst: University of Massachusetts Press, 1989).

35 For the evolution of Vergil's response to his own changing times, see Gary B. Miles and Archibald W. Allen, "Vergil and the Augustan Experience," in John D. Bernard, ed., *Vergil at 2000. Commemorative Essays on the Poet and*

His Influence (New York: AMS Press, 1986), pp.13-41. For Vergil's development of the analogies between universal and sociopolitical order, see Hardie, *Vergil's Aeneid: Cosmos and Imperium*.

36 The oppositions of the *Aeneid* are similar to those of those of Aeschylus, *Oresteia*, discussed by Froma Zeitlin, "The Dynamics of Misogyny: Myth and Mythmaking in the *Oresteia*," in John Peradotto and J.P. Sullivan, eds., *Women in the Ancient World. The Arethusa Papers* (Albany: State University of New York Press, 1984), pp.159-191, esp. 181f. For philosophical legacies of these oppositions, see Sheila Ruth, "Bodies and Souls/Sex, Sin and the Senses in Patriarchy: A Study in Applied Dualism," *Hypatia* 2.1 (winter 1987): 149-163.

37 Recall, too, the Stoic philosopher Seneca's special condemnation of anger as one of the basest and most destructive of human emotions.

38 As in Plato and other philosophic traditions, Vergil associates moral virtue with a rational, "objective" power. In his Introduction to *Virgil, The Aeneid. Modern Critical Interpretations* (New York: Chelsea House, 1987), Harold Bloom describes Juno as "the male dread that origin and end will turn out to be one" (p.2).

39 The literal meaning of *moles*, here used figuratively and translated "massive endeavor," means great mass or weight. The unruly winds are imprisoned underneath a mountainous mass; only thus can they be kept under control (1.61 and 134).

40 Jason, protagonist of the Hellenistic epic poet Apollonius of Rhodes's *Argonautica*, has been called an antihero because of his introspective and indecisive temperament.

41 Book 6.756-892.

42 Did Aeneas succeed in fulfilling his destiny through moral grit, becoming, perhaps, a kind of Stoic wise man-king? Or is he a mere puppet in Jupiter's and Vergil's hands? For differing views of his character, see, e.g., Victor Poeschl, "Aeneas," in Bloom, ed., *Virgil's The Aeneid. Modern Critical Interpretations*, pp.9-30. (Reprinted from Victor Poeschl, *The Art of Vergil. Image and Symbol in the Aeneid* (Ann Arbor: University of Michigan Press, 1962.).

43 Although the Oxford Latin Dictionary gives the first meaning of *vulgus* as "the common people," the second meaning is "a (particular) multitude of ordinary or undifferentiated people, (usually with some derogatory implication." The ears of members of the crowd prick up like animals' when they are attentive.

44 Vergil recalls the Platonic view that art is twice removed from truth: reality is the world of ideas, mental images, of which the physical world is only a copy, and art, in turn, is a copy of the physical world, Plato, *Republic* 10.595a-608b.

45 This way of looking at the division between the private and public in the *Aeneid* (personal needs, desires, interests vs. present and future common good, Roman destiny) was expressed by Adam Parry, "The Two Voices of Virgil's *Aeneid"* in Bloom, ed.,Virgil's Aeneid. Modern Critical Interpretations, pp.57-74. See also Wiltshire, *Public and Private in Virgil's Aeneid.*

46 So also at the end of Book 8, Aeneas gazes at the scenes depicted on the shield, gift of his mother, which shows the triumphs of Roman civilization and order over barbarians, the most recent of which is the victory of Augustus Caesar over Mark Anthony and Cleopatra in the battle of Actium. "Not knowing" (*ignarus*), he lifts the weapon. He does not fully understand what it means for civilization to win out over barbarians. It hasn't happened yet.

47 For a reading of Dido in relation to the dominant values of the *Aeneid*, see Christine G. Perkell, "On Creusa, Dido, and the quality of victory in Virgil's *Aeneid*," in Helene P. Foley, ed., *Reflections of Women in Antiquity* (New York: Gordon and Breach Science Publishers, 1981), pp.355-378; and Cairns, *Virgil's Augustan Epic*, Chapter 2, "Kingship and the Love Affair of Aeneas and Dido," pp.29-57.

48 The warrior woman Camilla, an ally of Turnus, is a gifted fighter but is killed in battle when, momentarily distracted by the glitter of a handsome sword belt, she is overcome with greed (11.782 "She burned with a female love of booty and spoils"; see 768-835).

49 One may certainly object that she can hardly submit when no higher power has troubled to clue her in on its agenda.

50 Robert Coleman finds that the gods in the *Aeneid*, modeled on Homeric divinities, are too frail to bear the moral weight which Vergil puts on them. "The Gods in the Aeneid," in Ian McAuslan and Peter Walcot, eds., *Virgil*. Greek and Roman Studies (Oxford: Oxford University Press, 1990), pp.39-64.

51 See Kenneth McLeish, "Dido, Aeneas, and the Concept of Pietas," in McAuslan and Walcot, eds. *Virgil*, pp.134-141.

52 In Book 5, Juno incites the Trojan women, exhausted by many years of wandering, to burn the ships so that they may end their journey and stay in Sicily. The women cannot subordinate their individual needs to destiny.

53 In a misguided effort to protect Aeneas, Venus sends her other son Cupid, Aeneas's half-brother, to court, in the guise of Ascanius, and wisks Ascanius off for a long nap on a mountainside. Cupid is instructed to do what he does best. See 1.656ff.

54 At 7.116ff., the Trojans eat their "tables," the bread they are using as plates to hold their food. See also Ascanius's anxiety for the safe return of his father, who has gone to seek aid. (9.252ff.)

55 The adjective *patrius*, of the father or fatherland, expresses this link, and Vergil affixes *pater* to Aeneas's name several times in the poem. At 1.580, when

he reveals himself at the court of Dido, the designation *pater* stresses his role as father of *his* people, perhaps anticipating Dido's offer to join the Trojans to her own Tyrians; it also anticipates Aeneas's concern for Ascanius, whom he has left behind on the ship. See also 8.28f. (his anxious concern for the future of his people, concern which the spirit of the River Tibur allays) and 8.115 (Aeneas announcing himself and his Trojan-born companions to Pallas when they arrive at the site of future Rome).

[56] When Aeneas kills Lausus, for example, the blade of his sword penetrates the golden tunic his mother wove for him (10.818); and when the brave young Trojan Euryalus is about to leave with his friend Nisus on a dangerous reconnoitering foray, he begs Ascanius to take care of his mother, and Ascanius, touched by this display of parental devotion (*patriae . . . pietatis* 294), promises to tend to her as if she were his own mother (9.280ff.). See Wiltshire, *Public and Private in Vergil's Aeneid*, Chapter 2, "Grieving Mothers and the Costs of Attachment," pp.38-55.

[57] The altar stood in front of the temple of Hercules Victor (the Conqueror); according to the historian Livy (1.7), worship of the hero was instituted by Rome's founder, Romulus, in accordance with the practice established by Evander.

[58] Book 8.306-368.

[59] So also at 9.446-449, Vergil breaks the narrative with an apostrophe to the Trojan Nisus and Euryalus, devoted friends and brave warriors.

[60] Miles and Allen, "Vergil and the Augustan Experience," in Bernard, ed., *Vergil at 2000*, pp.36-38, argue that Vergil sees human nature as fundamentally ambivalent; even Aeneas is overcome by anger at the moment when he thrusts his sword into Turnus's body—an indication that every man is vulnerable to passion. Jasper Griffin comments, "Romans were aware . . . that war should not be conducted in an irrational spirit of violence . . .But Virgil perhaps saw more deeply when he created this scene. Killing has its own logic, and war is not in truth compatible with calm rationality." Besides, he adds, "Turnus had it coming to him." *Virgil*, p.101.

[61] On the ending of the *Aeneid*, see Johnson, *Darkness Visible* (Berkeley and Los Angeles: University of California Press, 1976) pp.114-134. See also his reading of the moral structure of Vergil's universe, Part III.

[62] Carol Gilligan, *In a Different Voice. Psychological Theory and Women's Development* (Cambridge: Harvard University Press, 1982), pp.151, 152, 155.

[63] Adam Parry, "The Two Voices of Virgil's *Aeneid*," in Bloom, ed., *Virgil's The Aeneid. Modern Critical Interpretations*, pp.57-73, hears "a public voice of triumph" and "a private voice of regret" in the poem (p.72).

[64] Aeneas lost his wife Creusa in the chaotic moments of fleeing Troy (though he managed to escape with his father and son), and he renounced Dido. He does sometimes long for attachment, however. When his mother, Venus,

appears to him in the first book disguised as a Tyrian huntress, he recognizes her and, as she vanishes, complains that he is never allowed to embrace her.

[65] Domenico Comparetti, *Vergil in the Middle Ages*, trans. E.F.M. Benecke (New York: Macmillan and Co., 1895), on the use of Vergil's text as a source of prophetic guidance (*sortes virgilianae*; the text was opened at random and a pointer or *virga* placed on a line of verse).

[66] The work of Cicero that mesmerized Augustine was the lost rhetorical essay, *Hortensius*. See Margaret Miles, *Desire and Delight. A New Reading of Augustine's Confessions* (New York: Crossroad Publishing Co., 1992), pp.30, 41. Saint Jerome also found Cicero irresistible; see Elizabeth Rawson, *Cicero. A Portrait* (London: Allen Lane, 1975), p.300.

For each aspect of *eros*, the centrality of hostility, the wish to do harm, marks a fascination with death—the death of the other as a separate being, the denial of one's own body in order to deny one's mortality, and the recasting of even reproduction as death. These, then, are the outlines of the community structured by a masculine *eros*, a community that expresses the life activity and experience not of the ruling class but the ruling gender.

Nancy Hartsock[1]

[P]art of the privilege accorded to members of a political body is that their needs, desires and powers are converted into rights and virtues. The alleged equity of universalizing ethical principles that were developed from a particular historical and political perspective is one of many indications of the arrogance of Western moral philosophy.

Moira Gatens[2]

The option of transcendence, of a religious indifference or a philosophical detachment, may be less available to women because women are more likely to be possessed by the spirits and stories of others. The strength of women's moral perception lies in the refusal of detachment and depersonalization, and insistence on making connections that can lead to seeing the person killed in war or living in poverty as someone's son or father or brother or sister, or mother, or daughter, or friend . . . [T]he promise of joining women and moral theory lies in the fact that human survival, in the late twentieth century, may depend less on formal agreement than on human connection.

Carol Gilligan[3]

Chapter 8

Other Voices, Other Values

At the beginning of this book, I made the following argument: Rethinking the influence of the Greco-Roman legacy in America is necessary in order to resolve our present conflict between pluralism and multiculturalism, on the one hand, and "traditional values" on the other. I have presented Greco-Roman attitudes to difference as a primary source of that conflict, an intrinsic obstacle to accommodating diversity in America. Greco-Roman understandings of difference are oriented to male power and control—differences between men and gods and the principal difference among mortals, that of gender, which is seen in terms of negation, opposition, deficiency, and deviance. These perceptions of difference have informed the dominant North American culture from its beginnings, accepted by early American as well as present-day admirers of the Greco-Roman legacy. Today, however, many people are unfamiliar with the classic tradition or indifferent or hostile to it. Uncritical admiration, ignorance, and indifference are obstacles to changing our society's attitudes to difference and looking beyond that goal, to transforming broader social and cultural attitudes so as to make them more useful to our own and future times and more consonant with American democratic ideals.

In America, the belief that everyone has a fixed place in a social hierarchy is anathema. This tenet pertains to hierarchies derived from place of national origin, race, or class; it took the nineteenth-century women's movement to even begin to suggest that it might also pertain to gender. Despite the homogenization of mass, consumer-driven culture, every person in America is supposed to be unique. Because we glorify individuality at the expense of community, as Alasdair MacIntyre and others have pointed out,[4] a sense of national unity and social cohesion are at risk. We persist in believing that society should not impose preset limits to our potential, ambitions, or achievements—though in fact both patriarchy and capitalism do just that. For many centuries, the Greco-Roman legacy served as a cultural touchstone in the West, yet the paradigms, norms, patterns of thought, beliefs, and values which it transmitted are informed by antithetical, hierarchically ranked dualisms; in each of these, gender difference is a defining point of reference. If we prize diversity and opportunity, then all difference, including gender difference, must be regarded as multiple, complex, and open-ended— not reducible to antithetic binary terms. Because of pressure to create and sustain a single society out of many heterogeneous parts, no one— not even the most conservative or reactionary among us—can deny or avoid challenges to traditional attitudes to difference. As Moira Gatens puts it, "The great diversity, characteristic of contemporary urban life in terms of race, values and beliefs, can be seen as conducive to a radical reassessment of how we live in socio-political communities."[5] The best outcome of such reassessment, Gatens suggests, would be a new ethic, open to many voices, values, and lines of reasoning.[6]

One of the principal aims of contemporary feminist thinking is to go beyond the gender-linked dualisms that inform our heritage[7] in order to reconfigure the relationship between power and difference. Tradition is the foundation of social morality and bears the weight of authority. As Hannah Arendt pointed out, authority (Latin *augere*, increase, create, make grow), or those with authority, are those empowered to augment founding traditions, which she traces to the ancient city-state.[8] Women's long-standing lack of authority, as Kathleen B. Jones[9] further notes, reflects their actual lack of power. Those who hold authority enforce a system of rules designed by men to govern a hierarchic social order; they rule, the rest obey.[10] Herein lies women's challenge to the authority of tradition in America, and in this chapter we listen to some of their voices.

Women, always the principal outsiders in relation to patriarchal values, have expressed a heightened awareness of their location in the twentieth century.[11] They have recognized "woman" as the creation of male imagination and needs, made-to-order and moulded (the Pandora syndrome) to suit men's image of perfect beauty (the Helen syndrome) and perfect fidelity (the Penelope syndrome). Women whose appearance or behavior does not conform to the pattern are made invisible, silent, or otherwise nonexistent. Twentieth-century women have recognized women's lack of both visibility and authority in almost every area of serious endeavor. They have recognized the association of women with evil, treachery, and deception among the compendium of female stereotypes—the adultress, the wicked stepmother, the meddlesome mother-in-law, the woman scorned, the temptress, the agente provocatrice. Women have expressed their awareness in many different ways, by social and political activism, with the particular aim of changing public policy and law now detrimental or indifferent to women; by challenging the assumptions and practices of traditionally all-male jobs and professions; by calling attention to the fact that male viewpoints dominate language,[12] social and cultural assumptions and attitudes, ideas, and values. Susan Bordo has critiqued the modern notion of intellectual, rational, and scientific objectivity which she traces to Descartes. The challenge to objectivity—which, Bordo argues, should be seen as male subjectivity on which men have bestowed a kind of impersonal and absolute validation—has touched many areas of knowledge, from those which obviously involve value judgments to scientific inquiry.[13] These are transformations few of even our most radical foremothers envisioned.[14]

Feminist philosophers are talking about women's perception of what is real, what is and can be known, how it is known (most notoriously, the history of male appropriation of reason),[15] how and by whom values should be decided and prioritized. They envision changes in many areas—politics, religion, ecology, education, the arts and sciences, and more—that will reflect women's knowledge and experiences in all their diversities. They claim for women the power to express and interpret them, changes proposed against traditional limits imposed by patriarchal culture. In what ways are women striving, as I am, not just to include women in definitions of what it is to be human, but to recast basic concepts of what it is to be human and by so doing, remake values that may transform the future?

There is no single accepted theory, dogma, or orthodoxy in feminist theory; ideally at least, there are many feminisms in order to reflect diversity among women arising from such differences as color, class, race, life experience, and moral orientation. Although some feminist thinkers share what Nancy Hartsock has called a feminist standpoint,[16] others, like Jane Flax, Elizabeth Spelman, and Maria Lugones, draw attention to differences among women—of class and color. The very notion that there is a single way of looking at things, one vision of Reality or Truth, as Flax and others have pointed out, is itself a male construct, derived from Platonic metaphysics and refashioned for modern times by the seventeenth-century Enlightenment. Although postmodern philosophers such as Lyotard, Derrida, and Foucault have deconstructed Enlightenment orthodoxies—in particular, orientation to what Flax calls "an archimedes point"—their arguments for thinking in fragments overlook gender relations and issues of gender and power.[17] Too often theories, products of abstract and allegedly objective thinking, have often been used to control Others and to disregard or deny their experiences.[18] Feminist ethicists tend to require that a moral theory be grounded in what is particular, concrete, and appropriate,[19] that it consider context or situation and relate to actual decision making and experience, *praxis*. As Virginia Held puts it, "Practice is involved both in understanding what we ought to do and in carrying out the norms of morality."[20]

Attempts to map the limitations of male culture and conceive alternatives to it entail some pitfalls. Male culture defined woman generically and in binary terms: the not-male, she-who-is-lacking; women defining themselves risk perpetuating the oppositions they are trying to avoid by making virtues of supposedly "essentially female" qualities:

orientation to connection, relationships and relatedness; a predisposition to care for others, especially to nurture the young, support men in their endeavors, and tend the vulnerable; valuation of cooperation over competition and peaceful over violent conflict resolution; willingness to put the well-being of others first or at least to take everyone's interests into account; an openness to emotional feelings, embodied existence, and natural processes. Essentialism may tend to overcompensate, to valorize traits men have belittled, whereas we need to regard difference not as monolith, *the* Other, but as an inclusion of many alterities and complexities.

Presumption of a feminist standpoint does implicitly acknowledge a community of experience among women: How do biological experiences unique to women and their psychological and emotional components (menstruation, pregnancy, childbirth, nursing, menopause, as well as their social roles as primary care givers in a variety of capacities, affect women's knowledge and experience of the world and the kinds of moral judgments and choices they make?[21] What will "the human condition" look like once it takes women's shared and individual experiences into account? How will the map of human moral experience change? How can ethics and social morality be reoriented to more and different varieties of experience? How can they incorporate the complexities and subtleties of process and change?

Greco-Roman perceptions of difference involve issues of narcissism, self identity, separation and connection, the very issues that psychoanalysts in Western culture see as marking the growth and development of each human being in his/her progression to adulthood. Early Greek thoughts about the differences between human and divine are preoccupied with power: a poignant awareness of man's powerlessness, together with an overriding desire to overcome what he saw as his inherent limitation. This view was narcissistic—oriented to self-reflection and self-reference. These psychic and religious orientations devalued temporal life, embodied existence, and life in nature and relegated generic woman, defined by her sex, to these devalued locations. They placed a premium on separation: escape from life's inherent limits (transcendence), and within a man's life span, maximization of his freedom to make choices and take action. The drive to primacy, the achievement ethic, and the quest for transcendence expressed men's attempts to defend themselves against feelings of powerlessness. The Greek and Roman male need for separation reflected men's fears of the unknown, irrational, embodied, changeful, and perishable. Men projected these qualities onto women apotropaically: in order to get away from, to be rid of what was dangerous and evil. There was safety in separation, and keeping women separate has been an ongoing source of women's oppression, as Jane Flax has argued,[22] Separation and avoidance of connection also defined men's relationships to Otherness and Others; these relationships, too, were oriented to power and self. Greek and Roman men had ambivalent feelings about connecting with any being(s) other than the immortal gods, with whom they craved association. Western culture embraced and enacted the belief that the desire for separation is male, for connection female.[23] Women have been the designated beings-in-relation, and feminists are divided as to whether they are so "by nature," or have become so through repeated social norms and practices. In either case, they consider male culture deficient because it strives to deny connections and relationships, aspects of human experience that must be included and given voice and value if culture is to be made whole and complete.

A notion of selfhood derived from psychoanalytic theory assumes the centrality of narcissism and conflicts between separation and connection. In the views of Sigmund Freud and Jacques Lacan, man is born into narcissism; the helpless infant driven to ensure his survival and completely powerless to do so alone becomes the man driven to promote his own good. A newborn, in Freud's view, because he is utterly dependent on others, exists in a state of "primary narcissism," though it is far from clear why a helpless infant's state—getting what he needs to survive: food, a safe environment, loving nurturance—should qualify as narcissistic. The will to survive, surely, is the essence of health, while narcissism may prevent, disrupt, or distort a person's ability to relate to others or to function within society.[24] Greek Narcissus was not, of course, an infant, but a self-fixated young man with a (presumably) abnormal lack of interest in the beautiful young nymph Echo. The alleged self-interest of an infant is entirely appropriate, and s/he must relate to caretakers and do so with a modicum of charm in order to survive. Man's beginning in narcissism, Freud also claims, not only colors his entire life experience but also in some essential way defines the human condition. Human beings form ties with others only to satisfy their narcissistic needs.[25] Remembering his infantile dependency on his mother, man, paradigm of what is human, loathes women[26] and any state of dependency or vulnerability. He is alone and that is the way he wants it. He sacrifices absolute autonomy, however, in order to enter into the life of culture. Not incidentally, he also relinquishes polymorphous perversity (any and all forms of expressing his sexual drive) to heterosexuality, the price of civilization.

According to Lacan, a grim narcissism pervades the human condition from birth to death. What is not self or identical with self is not only other but alien, and self wants "its complete capitulation—or annihilation."[27] An infant fantasizes that he is completely omnipotent (recall Greek aspirations to divinity), but when others fail him or when he realizes that he is dependent on others, he feels betrayed and alone. Once past the preoedipal state, he must enter into the realm of the phallus—language and culture, the Law of the Father (alien to men because they are not self-created, and thus doubly alienating to women). From the Greeks onward, women have been allowed to exist as objects within that order but not as subjects, that is, as makers of symbols from an independent or interdependent position of creativity.[28]

Because female identity has been located in connection, girls and women have been denied separate and equal selfhood. "Recognition" means acknowledging another person, including the Other, as a separate subject with needs, feelings, and thoughts equal in value and importance to one's own. Psychoanalyst Jessica Benjamin observes that failure of recognition begins at home, within the patriarchal family: how a girl is perceived and treated, how she perceives herself, what kinds of roles her mother plays.[29] The construction of gender difference in psychoanalytic theory, Benjamin points out, entails domination because it ensures that difference will fail to be recognized. The patriarchal family initiates each new human being into his or her gender identity, laying the foundation for socially and culturally determined gender roles an individual will play (or is expected to play) later in life, as Jane Flax, Nancy Chodorow, and Dorothy Dinnerstein have argued.[30] Chodorow and Dinnerstein believe that the subordination of women in patriarchal societies can be altered only by changing family arrangements, by making men and women equal partners in parenting.

Within the traditional family, a child learns gender-appropriate attitudes and behavior regarding separation and connection. The intense mother-child bond formed at birth (the preoedipal phase) changes as young children enter a phase of separation (the oedipal phase). At this point boy must "give up" his mother in order to assume male gender identity, which will require separation from the family. He is being prepared, as Chodorow has pointed out,[31] to enter the public domain, the adult male world of "work" and "action," while a girl sustains a lifelong gender bond with her mother and therefore locates her identity in relationships. In today's economy since many mothers work outside the home and fathers are increasingly expected to assume more responsibility for child care and maintaining the home, paradigms have become somewhat less rigid. Nevertheless, women continue to bear primary responsibility for child care, and it remains to be seen how gender roles and areas of responsibility would be more radically modified if mothers' work outside the home and fathers' participation in nurturing gained greater social acceptance and value. What Chodorow calls "the reproduction of mothering" as institutionalized under patriarchy has perpetuated the dichotomy between public and private. The family thus constituted is the training ground for that separation, a difference that probably cannot be modified unless family structure changes. That, in turn, may depend on new theories of psychological development which do not support patriarachal rationales.

Yet how could both separation and connection not be central to the development of every human being from a state of helpless infancy to competent adulthood? Although separation and connection are associated with gender difference in Western culture—with the greater need for separation and individuation designated male, the need for connection female (if only by default) —all children experience both needs, which should be viewed as complementary rather than unalterably opposed or mutually exclusive. The object-relations theory of D.W. Winnicott and others, which has particularly interested feminists, posits a universal human need for relationships with others (objects). It emphasizes the positive influence of the early mother-child bond. As an infant learns to distinguish between him- or herself and (m)other, he is learning difference and separation but also recognition of the other. If nurtured by a "good enough" mother, he achieves individuation, "independence," but the primary goals of maturation are not separation and individuation, but reciprocity—mutual recognition.[32] The appearing-disappearing game almost universally played by babies and young children, which Freud called "fort-da" (away-here),[33] is an enactment of the need to exercise control over separation, connection, and reconnection. The late psychoanalyst Louise Kaplan suggested that it is one expression of the human desire to create, enjoy, and sustain connection, emotional discourse.[34] In the game, which children and parents or other adults of both genders play, the baby separates herself from another person by hiding (her eyes, by pretending to be invisible) and then "comes back"; the other person, in turn, does the same thing. Not only does everyone need both connection and separation, but, Kaplan further suggests, both needs persist throughout a person's lifetime and vary and find different forms of expression at different life stages. It seems likely, though, that since both are informed by socially determined gender identities, men and women are expected to deny the "opposite" need and because these identities are so determined, they are less free to respond to and mediate among the demands of each.

Narcissism, separation and connection, and powerlessness are central to worldviews and constructions of gender that feminist thinkers are currently challenging. Seen in the broadest possible light, the worldview now being challenged defines reality in terms of separation and autonomy rather than connection and interdependence. It assumes that self-centeredness and self-interest motivate most "human" behavior." It accepts a fundamental psychic opposition between self and other(s). In liberal political theory, it champions individual rights and autonomy. Reacting against plurality and complexity as negative and disruptive outcomes of modern and postmodern times, it seeks to recover a unitary system of values.

In the remainder of this chapter, we shall look at these challenges as they relate to my reading of the Greco-Roman legacy: (1) The drive to primacy. The legacy of the achievement ethic is our cultural predisposition to value competition over its alleged antithesis, cooperation, and to pursue (individual, corporate, national) success. In glorifying war (and, not incidentally, other forms of violence—among men, against Others), the heroic ethic devalues the particularities of existence and affiliations other than those among men that are defined in terms of power. (2) The relationship between the public and private spheres. Modern political theories—like most psychoanalytic theories—have tended to assume the inevitability of conflicts involving separation and connection and the necessity of mediating them in ways which do not sacrifice autonomy and self-interest, an outlook indebted to Enlightenment views. Feminist political and moral philosophers are questioning the separation of spheres on the basis of gender difference (public/male-private/female) and are exploring relations among public and private values. (3) The separation of nature from culture and society. Even if most people could agree that traditional woman/nature, men/society/State/culture dichotomies are simplistic and outmoded, even if we could agree that the claims and responsibilities associated with each domain are not intrinsically opposed to one another, how do we go about constructing different realities and relationships among them? Treating nature like a woman, the outcome of the persistent cultural identification of the two, has led to current ecological and environmental issues, including public welfare and safety, distribution and conservation of resources, the preservation of biodiversity—all are perceived as conflicting, to a greater or lesser degree, with the agenda of the late capitalist economy—profit and other business-related interests. Many scholars and activists take a holistic approach to these issues, linking the integration of women and nature within culture and society, protection of resources, and spirituality. Rethinking these relationships, as well as connections between public and private, holds a promise of more inclusive definitions of community.

(4) Ethics. How have traditional attitudes to separation and autonomy, affiliation and connection informed public and private values? Thinking differently will require radical revision of patriarchal definitions of gender and, consequently, the formulation of different values. Many paradigms for human relationships have been drawn from the patriarchal family. They have focused on bonds between and among men, while women in relationships were perceived only in terms of male needs. Feminist thinkers, having grown suspicious of models based in binary oppositions, look to multiple structures more complex and multifaceted than dyads (with the sometime exception of the mother-child bond). The difference between feminist and dominant ethics has been expressed recently in terms of (male) justice and (female) care. Are men's and women's values essentially different? If so, do differences in values arise solely or mainly from involvement in different spheres of activities? Do men and women engaged in the same spheres of activity experience the same kinds of involvement with them? Lastly, feminist moral thinkers have challenged male cooptation and valorization of reason, mind, knowledge, and such abstract and ideal values as justice (the supreme social value since Plato and Aristotle) and the exclusion of emotions and other human faculties, sensations, and experiences from moral thinking.[35] How can we conceive and construct our individual and shared, private and public, lives differently? How do we begin to change cultural values in the context of the rampant, unconsidered competition generated under late capitalism?

* * * * *

In earlier chapters, we discussed the drive to primacy through achievement—military, athletic, political, cultural—as a strategy for transcending death. Mary Daly has also traced Western culture's preoccupation with mortality and power as control to classical antiquity. In *Gyn/Ecology. The Metaethics of Radical Feminism*,[36] Daly calls the Judeo-Christian and Greco-Roman origins of patriarchal culture "necrophilic," and connects obsession with death to envy of female power to give birth.[37] Men, by coopting women's support and nurturance for themselves and for patriarchal culture, by making mothers solely responsible for care of the young, have robbed women of their own creativity and autonomy.[38] Defining women as deficient, defective, and derivative (Eve is Daly's example; we think also of Pandora, who is, like Eve, an embodiment of evil)[39] is a projection of male feelings of powerlessness and inadequacy. Here is Sheila Ruth's description of this posture and the dualisms it assumes, body/spirit in particular:

> The equation of woman and death is the key to understanding this mindset, since dualism is a strategy in patriarchy for avoiding death. It begins in a primary terror: Death is bad, the worst thing conceivable; nothing is more awful. At all costs, it must be conquered, negated. It proceeds: bodies are the things that die, visibly, right before our eyes, displaying to us in painfully vivid terms our own mortality. Our bodies, which betray us to death, are therefore bad. In that case, if we wish not to die, we must separate from our bodies. We must instead posit a different part of ourselves, one that is detachable, which does not die and which may connect us with all that is eternally pleasant, good, and unending. That would be spirit, not body, that is the opposite of body and bad, hence good.[40]

As Elaine Scarry and Sara Ruddick point out, from the perspective of male culture, denial of death and the body are prerequisites, negative corollaries, to the endurance of civilization, for mortality and embodiment consign men to change and impermanence. Both suggest that war and violence have key functions in this equation. War (exclusively) and civilization (primarily) are designated (by men for men) male spheres of activity; the exclusion of women from the community of achievement—that aspect of civilization which men value most—is associated with the impulse to deny, reject, or minimize bodily existence. War and violence are strategies for acknowledging the power of the body; they make a virtue of necessity:

> This history [of the human flesh] stands against the militaristic concep-

tions of a body whose fate is excused by heroic death, a body that is counted but doesn't count, a body whose vulnerability is not an occasion of protection and welcome, but of conquest.[41]

Patriarchal culture espouses what Ruddick calls "a legend of heroically violent manliness" and "the masculinity of war . . . sustains both women and men in their support for violence."[42]

Further, patriarchal culture's valuation of "mind, objectivity, detachment, culture, impersonal concern, public order, and agreement" over "subjectivity, passion, nature, particular affections, domestic confinement, parochial prejudice, and irresolvable difference," with which the body is associated, is perhaps best understood as a defense against birthing labor.[43] Scarry[44] argues that physical vulnerability—the power to inflict and to suffer pain—is at the very root of "the making and unmaking of our world" (the subtitle of her book). Destructiveness ("deconstruction") is an essential facet of Western culture. Weapons are not just instruments of injury, but tools of power. Creative acts are the result of defensive imaging (imagining) against "human" vulnerability, products of those acts are the artifacts of civilization. Without the experience of pain, we would have neither civilization nor acts of mass violence.[45] Moreover, war carries the power of enactment, that is, people behave "as though war carried the power of its own enforcement."

> The dispute that leads to the war involves a process by which each side calls into question the legitimacy and thereby erodes the reality of the other country's issues, beliefs, ideas, self-conception. Dispute . . . is a correction and reversal of [war]. That is, the injuring not only provides a means of choosing between disputants but also *provides, by its massive opening of bodies, a way of reconnecting the derealized and disembodied beliefs with the force and power of the material world*.[46]

Scarry links war and the peacetime ethic of competition in that war is a kind of contest, and the aim of all contests is to establish winners and losers,[47] to determine who is to have power over whom. Cultural concepts of masculinity are traditionally associated with military or competitive thinking, a connection that is currently both strongly attacked and strongly defended in this New Age as a model of a more nurturing and "sensitive" man struggles to emerge.[48] So-called maternal thinking (what Ruddick calls "attentive love"[49]) focuses on nurturing and education, on the best interests of the child; it is based on an ethic of caring.[50]

Competition for primacy establishes a hierarchy of dominion, and predominance confers power of dominance. The association of excellence and power expressed by Greek *arete* was extended to power of another sort. Recognized merit both validated and was validated by social and moral authority based in dominance: over those allegedly without *arete*; within the hierarchy, dominance over those with allegedly less *arete*. As the Pericles-Thucydides funeral speech argues, those who are (or designate themselves) superior in *arete* are entitled to hold power, including political power.

War and competition are the necessary underpinnings of Western culture, Nancy Hartsock points out, and she is particularly interested in how they have shaped ideas of community. Current Western political communities are characterized by what she calls a "warrior barracks culture," which is derived from the agonistic orientation of ancient Athens.[51] Under modern capitalism, a new kind of community has emerged, the market economy operating via commodity exchange; like the old, however, this new community is also driven by competition.

> A community that bases itself on the self-interested passing back and forth of objects can only be an instrumental community in which exchange and competition lead directly to relations of domination.[52]

What Hartsock calls the agonal model of community (from Greek *agon*, contest) is all male and informed by a destructive, disembodied, and depersonalized concept of *eros*, which drives men to strive for mastery over those worth mastering, a perpetual quest for power.[53] We saw in earlier chapters how Pindar and Vergil coopted sexual *eros*, transforming it into a drive toward achievement deserving of the ultimate power, immortality. *Eros* as sexuality, pleasure, and life force are thus brought under male control—redirected and sublimated as Freud said it should be—in order to assuage men's feelings of existential powerlessness and to serve the cause of civilization.[54] Helene Cixous's and Catherine Clement's characterization of "society," while placing greater emphasis on narcissism, is similar:

> At first what *he* [traditional man] wants, whether on the level of cultural or of personal exchanges, whether it is a question of capital or of affectivity (or of love, of *jouissance*)—is that he gain more masculinity: plus-value of virility, authority, power, money, or pleasure, all of which rein-

force his phallocentric narcissism at the same time. Moreover, that is what society is made for—how it is made; and men can hardly get out of it.[55]

By no means do all feminists distance themselves from male culture's attitudes to conflict and competition and its focus on transcendence, as the views of Simone de Beauvoir show. Andrea Nye reminds us that in existentialist philosophy, conflict is the essence of human relations and manifests itself as a struggle for dominance. Such a view derives, Nye suggests, from "the terrifying separation and aloneness of the Cartesian ego."[56] According to de Beauvoir, transcendence presents a terrible dilemma to women. Throughout history men have oppressed women by confining them to what she calls immanence: endless daily chores, care of the body, childbearing, narcissistic play-acting, frustrated eroticism. Men took transcendence unto themselves, the struggle of a sovereign and free spirit to break out of the confines of nature. Her description of this struggle recalls the imagery of Plato's *Phaedrus*, where the soul of the wise man is imagined as breaking free from its earth-bound prison, the body, and soaring heavenward, to the real world of Ideas:

> Culture must be apprehended through the free action of a transcendence; that is, the free spirit with all its riches must project itself toward an empty heaven that it is to populate; but if a thousand persistent bonds hold it to earth, its surge is broken.[57]

Imagining the triumph of patriarchy over matriarchy in prehistoric times, she writes:

> Spirit has prevailed over Life, transcendence over immanence, technique over magic, and reason over superstition. The devaluation of woman represents a necessary stage in the history of humanity, for it is not upon her positive value but upon man's weakness that her prestige is founded.[58]

But women, too, ought to be free to avoid "mere repetition," the prime example of which is reproduction. *Human* reproduction, however, in Virginia Held's critique of de Beauvoir, is transcendental, because each human being is unique, and acts of mothering may be culturally transformative.[59] It is not evident that feminists seeking to reevaluate patriarchal values wish to become "free and sovereign spirits" (subjects) on the male model. Sara Ruddick commonsensibly questions the dichotomy between immanence and transcendence and their gender-specific, stereotypical associations:

> [It is not] surprising, given the work women have done, that they should be associated with affectionate ties to individuals and domestic practices—though it is not at all clear why these should be opposed to, rather than, say, made a requirement for public responsibility and transcendental reflection. On the other hand, no possible biological difference between males and females could make one sex more 'bodily' than the other.[60]

As society changes, male/transcendence, female/immanence dualities are breaking down. More women are undertaking work which has in the past lead to achievement and transcendence, and more men are assuming everyday responsibilities for home and children. It remains to be seen how cultural attitudes to transcendence and immanence will change once women are not denied the former and men do not seek to escape the latter—when, in other words, both genders are thought of as "belonging" in both domains. Correction of these views of gender difference will entail recognizing that both men and women potentially possess a wide variety of physical, mental, and spiritual attributes in combinations that may be neither preordained nor predictable.

In our own as in Greco-Roman societies, the drive to primacy coopts definitions of work, resulting in a conflation of work and achievement. Expressed in comparative judgments which aim to identify the superlative, we see it in today's terms as being and being recognized as #1. Excellence and merit have generally been prerogatives of gender, class, and race,[61] and for a woman to gain recognition for her excellence and merit has been (among women) proverbially difficult, for male culture dictates that women are passive, not active by nature, and the only actions it acknowledges are those that lead to achievement. Such things as women do—childbearing, child care, nurturance—fall outside the domain of recognition.

Moreover, in a market economy, both achievement and success, another long-standing conflation, are measured in terms of profit. While the achievement ethic held that only productive work has value and that some kinds of productive work have more value than others, the most valued work in a market economy is work which generates capital. Accordingly, members of the work force who generate capital have value. This ethic dismiss values outside the domain of consumer economics,[62] for example, artistic and intellectual work that doesn't sell, or doesn't sell to a large enough market to make a profit; labor that merely contributes to everyday maintenance, which women have routinely performed, has been routinely discounted.[63] This work has by long tradition been performed in the household (we think of Isocrates' fifth-century B.C. essay on household management, advice to a new husband on how to train his 14-year-old bride), but women in the twentieth-century labor force have tended until very recently, at least, to be hired only into lower-paying jobs where they provide supporting or caretaking kinds of services. The traditions of patriarchy and the more recent demands of capitalism conspire, as Rosemary Radford Ruether points out, to put women at double risk in the domain of work.[64] Women's reproductive labor, although it combines a bodily activity and a creative act par excellence,[65] is also discounted.

Definitions of work, excellence, and achievement and the modes of domination inherent in productive endeavors assume competitive and adversarial relationships.[66] Excellence is thought to be attained through competition, which is also a necessary condition for the emergence of new work and for human progress in general. Our assumptions and beliefs about the conditions under which outstanding work is produced, the pool of potential producers, and the avenues for bestowing and receiving recognition are even today modeled largely on these traditional readings of "reality." Discoveries, inventions, and innovations often emerge, however, from a matrix of fortuitous and fortunate ideas or circumstances, and frontiers of knowledge are expanded through the cumulative process of cooperative investigation. Nonetheless, new work must meet the standards of an elite group, which has the power to name achievement and bestow success, a condition that tends to reinforce an established point of view and given set of values.

Feminist thinkers wonder whether values will change as women enter and participate in the community of achievement, and if so, how. Are women allowed to be present only if they validate the established values of the community, allowed to participate only to the degree that the community permits or in ways which the community recognizes? Must women learn to compete because that has been the male practice, and if so, must that competition be waged in accordance with male models? Helen Longino notes, "Our conceptual linking of competition with domination, hierarchy, and scarcity prevents us from appreciating the value of competitive challenge in developing skills and talents and ultimately undermines our potential to change ourselves and our worlds."[67] Victoria Davion has also suggested that the greatest value of competition is the opportunity it affords to develop a strong sense of self, a quality men are likely to have too much of and women too little. She points out that competition has been associated with autonomy, self-definition, and creativity, powers and possibilities denied to women.[68] Our reflections suggest that the difficulty is not with competition *per se*, but with cooptation of value to work and to activities traditionally available only to men and denial of the fact that those who do such work generally receive a tremendous amount of guidance from male mentors and support from women in order to achieve their goals. There is an additional dichotomy in that nurturance, reciprocity, mutuality, and compassion are traditional feminine virtues believed to belong in the private sphere, whereas competition and achievement are the dominant values of the public.

Maria Lugones and Elizabeth Spelman point out that scarcity is implicit in the competition ethic, because in traditional thinking only one can be best, and that one is separate from the rest, all of whom become secondary.[69] The desire to excel is not in and of itself "definitive of competition," which requires a context of opposition. The person who desires to excel and the work she achieves exist "in community," in a social context; "excelling" does not necessarily mean "excelling over." They discuss compassion as a feminist ethic, complementary to competition, but warn that because it is other-directed, it presents a pitfall for women. We can conceive of a kind of complex balance if we try to imagine women as both subjects and objects of both competition and compassion. In their essay "Competition: A Problem for Academic Women," Evelyn Fox Keller and Helene Moglen consider issues affecting women pursuing intellectual and artistic work, whether inside the academy or not. Although women are often reluctant to compete with one another, they cite the need to adapt to the "real world," where values of the male academic world dominate:

> What does it mean to be a good feminist in a real world, where real power, real issues of professional survival, and real opportunities to exert influence are at stake, where the need for some standards of excellence—however drastically they must be revised—survives as a necessary source of motivation; where neither power, excellence, nor the capacity or the ability to influence is ever distributed equally?

Women must come to terms with certain "basic realities":

"Resources are not infinite" (that is, equal support cannot be given to all who deserve it), and "it is neither possible nor advantageous for women to avoid the dilemmas of power, be it power in the interests of another or power over others."[70] It is not clear whether they regard traditional hierarchic power structures as fixed and inevitable, or whether these structures might be modified if we were to give up "the bifurcation between these two modes of interaction [competition and cooperation]."

Are there other paradigms? Perhaps we can look to nature for guidance. Does the often-cited Darwinian principle, survival of the fittest, give biological validation to the Greek love of competition, or does it also simply reflect a long-ingrained cultural bias? The necessity of competition and scarcity as operative forces in biology, however, are questioned by Michael Gross and Mary Beth Averill. In "Evolution and Patriarchal Myths of Scarcity and Competition,"[71] they challenge the Darwinian notion that competition among and within species explains adaptation, evolutionary change, or other natural phenomena. Gross and Averill, suggesting that Malthus's theory of the role of scarcity in economic behavior may have influenced Darwin's thinking,[72] propose that natural abundance explains survival as well as or better than scarcity and competition. Similarly, Frans de Waal, considering biological bases for moral behavior among primates, finds diversity and complexity which cannot be reduced to "natural" selfishness.[73]

Both the economic and the biological-evolutionary views are ingrained in our attitudes to competition and scarcity in productive endeavors today: The best will win out, the fittest will survive by competing successfully for limited resources (wealth, praise, rewards, recognition). Are these assumptions indeed as "necessary" as male culture seems to believe? This issue has implications for the well-being of everyone, but especially for families with minor children; ultimately, it is about accommodating productive and reproductive labor in terms other than the traditional male/female division. Women, though present in the work force in great numbers, earn less than men and have great difficulty finding adequate and affordable child care. Women who want to stay home with their children may not be able to afford to do so, and if they are single heads of households and do so, they have no income. A glass ceiling may prevent them from rising to higher-income, decision-making positions in the public sphere—business, industry, and government. Men, too, however, may find themselves at odds with the achievement ethic, on temperamental or philosophical grounds. And although men traditionally have access to achievement in ways that women do not, many are excluded through poverty, lack of access to education, class, and race.

The drive to primacy—the achievement ethic—has traditionally separated men from women, assigning men to the public sphere (community, society, State, corporation) and confining women to the private (family, household). Feminists designate this confinement of women—the practice of Greco-Roman societies reflected in literature and philosophy—as the locus of women's oppression.[74] In classical antiquity, we recall, separation was extreme. Women, were confined to the *oikos* and had no political and at best very restricted economic and legal rights; had social value through citizenship and economic value through efficient management of their individual households; made significant contributions to the religious well-being of the *polis* but only in ways defined by patriarchal authority; and were rarely allowed to contribute to the cultural or intellectual well-being of the *polis*, except as mother-teachers. The family in ancient literature, as we saw, was the locus for control of sexuality, both women's and men's, for insuring legitimacy of issue (especially sons), and for the transmission of patriarchal power. The key relationships were paternal and fraternal; both served as paradigms for relationships between and among men outside the family.[75]

The classical city-state has been recognized as the context from which the private/public dichotomy in the West is derived. For Hannah Arendt, who viewed the Athenian *polis* as a vehicle for collective transcendence,[76] "if there was a relationship between these two spheres [private and public], it was a matter of course that the mastering of the necessities of life in the household was the condition for freedom of the *polis*."[77] One must differentiate oneself from the world of nature, a condition Arendt sees as inevitable within the world of work. The construction of the public sphere represents an opportunity for a "second birth," one controlled by the individual himself, and this second birth, unlike the first, carries an invaluable potential reward, immortality. The *polis* is "a system that operates both as an equalizing institution and as a meaning-creating and immortality-ensuring human construction . . . [It] operates not only to make immortality possible for the many but to give more permanence to the evanescence of human action and speech by providing witnesses to tell the story." Thus the *polis* is "a guarantee against the futility of individual life, an arena reserved for relative (though not eternal) permanence." The existence of the public realm, then, means that everything that appears in public can be seen and heard by everybody; "the point of achieving preeminence is not simply to savor victory and the defeat of another but to create meaning and establish relations." Nancy Hartsock, citing also Dorothy Emmet, Hanna Pitkin, and Bernice Carroll, is critical of Arendt's view on power and her failure to acknowledge its ambiguities. She prefers to regard power "as energy and competence rather than dominance."[78] The Greco-Roman tradition split "power to" along gender lines by assigning all positive capacities other than the ability to give birth to men and most negative capacities (for evil, corruption, changeability, among others) to women. Though such a view may strike us as simplistic and extreme today, there is still considerable debate about who has the natural capacity do what, and to what extent abilities are determined by biology, heredity, or social norms and expectations.

We look next at the political aspect of the public sphere. The United States constitution and government is modeled on the Roman republic, and our political ideology, like Rome's emphasizes the rights of citizens and individual autonomy, a view which facilitates the quest for primacy. The modern emphasis on the individual is indebted, however, to nineteenth and twentieth century liberal thought. Carolyn Whitbeck, Susan Bordo, Alison Jaggar, Andrea Nye, and Lynn Arnault offer various challenges to the model of the individual as the hero of nineteenth- and twentieth-century liberal thought, as well as to the model of the autonomous thinker.[79] Whitbeck regards both patriarchy and individualism as manifestations of the most fundamental dualism of Western thought, the distinction between self and other. Both outlooks assume that self and other are eternally in conflict, hence the need for a "rights" ethic, based on contracts among men of equal standing which "keep competition within bounds." Although the first separation, the differentiation of (male) self from (m)other takes place in private, within the family, it is extended—in every sense—into the public sphere. The model of the autonomous individual is the modern counterpart of the warrior-hero fighting in single combat, the outstanding man who wins membership in the community of achievement.

The principal fallacy of liberal thought and the communities that embody it, Alison Jaggar points out, is blindness to the actual subordination of women while assuming that the rights of the free, male individual must be protected from encroachment on the part of the State or society.[80] Until the passage of the Nineteenth Amendment in 1920, the only individuals empowered in the United States, an exemplar of a liberal political community, were, of course, exclusively male.

Relationships between private and public are at the heart of many issues affecting the lives of women today: equal pay for equal work, access to positions of authority, availability and affordability of child care, and most personally, the struggle to balance responsibilities to work and family. Women who pursue both career or job and family must marshall exceptional psychic and physical stamina. They seldom receive sufficient support from society or sometimes even from their own families. Women's assumption of responsibilities in the work world and in many other places of privilege (rather than service) in the public domain has not earned rewards commensurate with their contributions except after long legal and judicial struggles. Within the family, women are expected or expect themselves to do most of the work women have performed or overseen in the past. Finding adequate child care (a family member, a facility, a nanny) is a private problem—theirs, mother's work, not a matter for public concern despite political lip-service to "our nation's future" and "the citizens of tomorrow." On the one hand, we look to government powers and agencies, enforcement arms of public social policy, however, for protection and justice; on the other, we are protective of our "right" to make individual decisions in areas that are (and should be?) "private." Despite demands of the workplace in a heavily competitive market economy, we also want employers to be responsive to personal life circumstances: the birth or adoption of a child, serious family illness, elder care.[81]

Thus, while sexual conduct and reproduction in American society, as in Greek and Roman city states, is mainly a private, family matter, its regulation has come under the purview of law and the State. In both private and public spheres, control has reflected men's interests and values. Today, women are asking to be recognized as human beings no less capable of making moral judgments and decisions than men and as full members of society; they are attempting to make social practices, legal codes, and public policy reflect their points of view, interests, and concerns. Many aspects of sexual conduct—homosexuality, premarital sexual relations, adultery, prostitution, rape, abortion, and pornography—have been subject to legal oversight, American law, yet laws to protect women against domestic abuse and violence are often ineffective: "She must have been asking for it," some think, the way they think a woman who has been raped must have done something to provoke it. Two of the most passionately argued current issues which touch on the boundary between private and public are abortion and pornography. Whether seen as involving a woman's right to privacy, self-determination (control of her own body), or both, freedom of choice, with all its libertarian echoes, challenges public male authority as well as private, paternal rights. (Some women philosophers hesitate, it should be noted, to speak of rights at all, on the grounds that it is a flawed construct of male liberal political theory.[82]) Women object to pornography on the grounds that it encourages violence against women and perpetuates male attitudes which reify women and strip them of human dignity.[83]

Philosopher Kathryn Pyne Addelson addresses Americans' uncertainty about the boundaries between public and private. Arguing for what she calls a collectivist moral theory, she suggests that moral issues which affect everyone but have been kept in the closet of the private life—such as birth control, homosexuality, the valuation of different kinds of labor—should be brought out into the public arena, where they can be addressed by all, not just members of a hypothetical community privileged by gender and class. "The point for a collectivist moral theory is to investigate the processes through which the social order is generated and regenerated, and through which the normal and the deviant are enacted." Moreover,

> the ability to define (or redefine) a moral problem grants the power to disable an opposition and define the solution to the problem—thus to some degree, the future of the group. The ability to make a moral problem public, and so to define it, is an ability to definethe way "we" should live. It is a way of defining the common good. The battle for the twentieth century has been, in its crucial aspects,a battle waged by making moral problems public and so defining public morality.[84]

A collectivist/syndicalist approach to social morality aims to unify public and private by avoiding the monopoly of public patriarchy and the limitations of the private family, held together by the erotic bond, Addelson argues. It can do so by extending the bond of *eros* beyond the family to a broader concept, the creation of brotherhood and sisterhood in society and "the empowerment in the relationships created in the collective action, empowerment of the person as well as the working class." Addelson reconfigures public relationships, and her approach also intends to counteract marketplace values which, many feminists agree, have displaced moral values in our society.

The Greco-Roman legacy both reflects and perpetuates man's longing to separate from nature by ensconcing himself in a society and culture of his own making—a longing to escape dependence on the Earth, the processes and finitude of the body, the immanence which he projected onto woman. Within civil society, from city-state to nation-state, public institutions and norms are designed to live on in a communal life. Culture is transmitted through successive generations of men and transcends geographical boundaries as well as time. These are contexts in which men can manipulate and control process and change, which they have coopted from nature. Rethinking these issues offers the opportunity to formulate new definitions of community; in the past, most definitions of community have assumed a male membership, and most have unquestioningly incorporated traditional, male values. The dominant classic tradition confined women to nature and assimilated both to disorder, chaos, absence or dissolution of boundaries, fluidity, impermanence, and change. It declared men exempt from nature, time, and change, or, at the very least, entitled to try to claim exemption. The Christian dichotomy between body and mind, flesh and spirit, reaffirmed and extended the classical view.

The Greco-Roman woman/Earth/nature, men/society/State/culture dichotomies inform perceptions of reality and cultural traditions in the West. Assimilation of the generative and nurturing powers of woman and Earth, the tendency to define the identify of each solely or mainly by these powers, the dichotomy between (male) production and (female) reproduction, and men's assumed right to hegemony over both have been challenged by feminists and others in the late twentieth century. As Catherine Roach has put it, "the nature-culture dualism . . . is in need of being biodegraded for the sake of environmental soundness.[85] Male culture claimed hegemony over nature, Susan Griffin and Carolyn Merchant have pointed out, on the grounds that man, unlike other animals, has intelligence and was created in God's image. Griffin collated many corresponding negative images of women and nature and has shown how the emergence of what is called reason in modern science served to validate male control over a natural world imagined as female.[86] Looking at the history of scientific worldviews, Merchant traced the idea of man's right to dominate nature to the classical writers Aristotle, Cicero, and Pliny.[87] Roman and Renaissance thinkers imagined nature as a living organism, one properly ruled by its "head" (man). With the advent of the scientific and Industrial revolutions, however, nature was reimagined as machine, to be "run" by human intelligence. If nature is not a living thing, then it is safe to think that it exists solely to serve men's needs; we have no ethical responsibility for its welfare, nor does it make any ethical demands on us. "Mechanism and its ethic of domination legitimates the use of nature as commodity, a central tenet of industrial capitalism."[88] Irene Diamond has shown how late-twentieth-century technology exercises control and exploits the fertility and reproductive powers of the earth and women alike: the earth by the practices of agribusiness at the expense of sound uses of soil and human labor, the overuse of energy and other resources by First World countries; women by development of reproductive technologies. Commodification, characterized by narcissistic (unscrupulous self-interest) and instrumental rationales, sanctions the reign of unchecked greed we are currently witnessing. Living out this worldview could be dangerous to ourselves and to the planet.[89]

Today, many scholars and activists alike see human beings and the natural world as interconnected and interdependent on both local and global levels; they are concerned therefore with the uses of land and human labor, worldwide availability and distribution of food and other necessities, and the development, management, and conservation of natural resources, including human fertility. Some biologists—James Lovelock, Lynn Margulis, and others—have proposed what they call the Gaia hypothesis (from the Greek goddess Earth): Interconnection among all living things is both a key principle of evolution and a requirement for sustained viability within nature. All living and nonliving things exist within a web of complex and interdependent relationships. Connection, rather than separation, informs the thoughts of those who are rethinking relationships between women and nature and between nonhuman and human nature.[90] From recycling to prevention or clean up of toxic waste to the spirituality movement,[91] many seek an alternative to a worldview in which man exists in a kind of "existential isolation,"[92] as Stephanie Lehar puts it—a condition recalling the separation of (essential difference between) men and gods in Greco-Roman thought.

Ynestra King, a cultural-socialist ecofeminist, sees woman as bridging the gap between culture and nature by virtue of her primary role in raising a helpless infant into the life of society and culture. However, "the western male bourgeois subject extracts himself from the realm of the organic to become a public citizen, as if born from the head of Zeus." Activities women engage in, such as "mothering, cooking, healing . . . and foraging," are "as social as they are natural."[93] King makes a plea for "rational reenchantment" through reconnecting classic dualisms and being free *in* nature, that is, by using our understanding of the natural world of which we are a part in a noninstrumental way."[94]

Dorothy Dinnerstein traces the nature-culture dichotomy to an infant's fundamental psychic ambivalence toward his mother: "[T]he early mother, monolithic representation of nature, is the source, like nature, of ultimate distress as well as ultimate joy."[95] Ambivalence to nature is also evident in Greek and Roman thought, we recall. On the one hand, nature is a paradigm for decorum; the wise man strives to live in accordance with nature. But because nature brings death as well as life, unpredictable and uncontrollable change as well as the orderly succession of the seasons, it is also fearsome and threatening—like woman. What we don't find in classical sources is a view of woman as paradigm, for she represents powers which, men fear, cannot be controlled. An instrumental approach to nature and woman (sliding easily into exploitation) is the modus operandi of man who has created and recreated himself in the image of the autonomous hero. It is a stance he deems necessary if he is to come up against the world in order to compete successfully and to make his mark.[96]

Connection, relationships, and often (but not always) an attitude of caring are at the core of feminist ethics and moral theories, which seek to change social and cultural attitudes to human and nonhuman nature. In recent years the work of Carol Gilligan has informed many discussions of feminist moral theory. In "Toward an Ecological Ethic of Care," Deane Curtin describes how Gilligan's voice differs from that of traditional male moral philosophers:

> Whereas the rights approach [to moral thinking] tends to emphasize identity of moral interests, formalistic decision procedures, an adversarial understanding of moral discourse, personhood as autonomous, and a valorization of the nonbodily, Gilligan's research indicates that women's moral experiences are better understood in terms of recognition of a plurality of moral interests, contextual decision making, nonadversarial accommodation of diverse interests, personhood as relational, and the body as moral agent.[97]

In research on attitudes to abortion, Gilligan found that girls and women tend to make moral decisions based on particular circumstances and relationships. By trying to take into account what is best for everyone concerned, not just what is best for themselves, they hold themselves accountable to an ethic of care. Challenging Lawrence Kohlberg's study of moral thinking, which took men's thinking as the norm, Gilligan found that women's moral reasoning was different from that of men, who tended to rely on self-interest and abstract moral principles, in particular a notion of justice.[98] Care seemed to be an ethic of the personal and private, justice of the public spheres. Thus, there is one set of values for the women's world constructed to serve male needs, another for the world of male public and political action. The drawback of perceiving these positions as opposed and characteristically female and male is that such a view perpetuates both the dualisms we seek to dissolve and the essentialist fallacy. Care as an ethic has also been explored by philosopher Nel Noddings, who defines it in terms of responsiveness or receptivity.[99] But in the caring relationship Noddings takes as her principal example, that of mother and child, responsiveness and receptivity are mutual but cannot be fully reciprocal.[100]

The idea of an ethic of care is rather too limited to describe accurately the range of quests feminist moral thinkers have recently undertaken. One shared aspect of these quests is a belief that relationships rather than the separate, autonomous and independent individual—the hero, the noble Roman stateman, citizen of the liberal State, the patriarchal head of household—must hold an important place in moral theory. Val Plumwood has proposed that relationships to others and to nature should be considered essential to and incorporated into definitions of self.[101] Similarly, Karen Warren and Jim Cheney speak of "defining relationships," that is "relationships understood as essential to a definition of who one is.[102] Emphasis on relationships further implies that paternal and fraternal bonds, both private and public, are no longer to be taken as the measure of human ties and as privileged over other human ties. Other relationships ought to figure in the making of different theories which assume a bridge between private and public and which therefore must also, by implication, challenge the subordination of private to public. Yet if we are going to give greater value and emphasis to relationships, which ones should be considered primary, worthy of being elevated to the status of paradigm? Maternal-child or specifically mother-daughter relationships,[103] friendship or specifically female and/or lesbian friendship[104] have been put forth as models which rely on connection and emotional bonding rather than on separation and power. If we are going to reject paternal and fraternal relationships as *the* or the primary paradigms of both private and public relationships, however, why perpetuate the exclusions of the traditional paradigm scheme? In order to realize diversity and inclusiveness, we need a matrix of paradigms that are not hierarchically ordered. Whatever paradigms we may envision for the future, however, it seems overwhelmingly likely that patterns established by family relationships in infancy and childhood will be reflected in adult behavior and in social and cultural norms.

When we discussed Greek notions of justice in earlier chapters, we saw that justice was associated with reciprocity. Once justice became a civic—political and social—value, however, it was divorced from both woman and nature and was inscribed in the book of dualisms. Traditional definitions of justice are drawn from notions of male honor and due respect. Reciprocity in contemporary feminist thought assumes recognition of another as subject and as a person who deserves respect comparable to what oneself deserves. As Robin S. Dillon points out, the etymological meaning of "respect" is "to look back at " or "to look at again," suggesting "both that we re/spect things that are worth looking at again, and also that in respecting something we pay careful attention to it."[105] This kind of respect has not been accorded to women, who have, typically, been either reflections of men's gaze or altogether invisible.[106]

We conclude this chapter with Virginia Held's reflections on the processes of what she calls "moral experience."[107] Held considers relationships between parents and children, friends, the individual and society/State in the light of both men's and women's experience—the rational and public male domains of society and culture together with the emotional, embodied, private female domains of the family. She concludes that both "reflective choice" (men's reliance on rules and reason) and "caring action" ("women's work") are "needed for the development of adequate moralities."[108] She is critical of "contractual thinking," the predominant Western mode of thinking indebted to Thomas Hobbes, because it excludes personal ties from moral decision making.[109] Held proposes that the household, rather than the marketplace, the cornerstone of most Western capitalist societies, might serve as new model for society. She means not the traditional patriarchal family but what she calls the postpatriarchal family, where "every member of a family is worthy of equal respect and consideration."[110]

To understand how radical this notion is, it is useful to compare Plato's utopian approach to what he apparently perceived as a conflict between the family and society. Expressing men's recurrent fear that family bonds were stronger than public commitments and were therefore a threat to loyalty to society and the State, he proposed (*Republic*, Book 5) that newborns be taken from their mothers at birth and that all adults who had been allowed to mate nine months earlier by the rulers, philosophers-kings, were to regard all children subsequently born as their own. Whole generations were to relate to one another as parent and child. The translation of personal ties to the public realm was designed to eliminate conflict of interest between public and private. In Held's view, the way to eliminate any such conflict is to extend the primary relationship between mothering persons and child outward into the public sphere. "The proper care and development of all children" should be at the center of society's concerns and that focus should carry over to "trusting and mutually supportive" relations between individuals within communities and societies as well.

> When we explore the implications of these speculations we may come to realize that instead of seeing the family as an anomalous island in asea of rational contracts making up economic and political and social life, perhaps it is instead economic man who belongs on a relatively small island surrounded by social ties of a less hostile, cold, and precarious kind.[111]

Carol Gould imagines the reformulation of boundaries between private and public and the amalgamation of these spheres thus. She has been speaking of "the full development of both individuality and community":

> Specifically, the concern with community, which in modern times has been principally a woman's concern in regard to private life, needs to be brought more fully into the public sphere. The values of cooperativeness, reciprocity, and mutuality need to be introduced more fully into the social relations of the public sphere of work and politics and should be among the criteria for changes in the forms of social organization. Conversely, the values of individual achievements and self-esteem, which traditionally have been primarily male concerns in the context of public life, need to be more fully introduced into personal relations in the private sphere.[112]

* * * * *

Is a new social morality possible? Where can its foundations best be located? How can we disentangle the conflation of power, excellence and merit, and moral virtue? Definitions of power, virtue, merit, and achievement were coopted long ago by patriarchal culture; the conflation of all these has obscured important differences that feminists, preceded by countercultural thinkers, ancient and modern, are now attempting to reclaim. The heritage of the community of achievement is exclusionary, a primary source for ideas of difference in our culture today.

How can we overcome the moral and intellectual fragmentation characteristic of modern/postmodern times? I believe, along with others such as Virgina Held and Jane Flax, that we may have to live with it for a while in order to work our way through it. In earlier chapters, I presented what I see as the salient features of Greco-Roman culture, the qualities that are at the core of our legacy to these peoples and their cultures. I have presented these qualities in the form of a kind of argument, as a way of looking at how the Greco-Roman roots of Western culture developed. These features are death-centeredness, orientation to transcending mortality rather than integration into life; fear and denigration of nature, the body, and woman because they are seen as implicated in process, change, and impermanence; concomitant feelings of powerlessness, which provide the foundation for a narcissistic world view; the drive to be different by being first; the heroic ethic and the cultural necessity of war; translation of these values into the *polis*, forerunner of Western political institutions, where they inform ideas of citizenship, community, and civilization; the theory and practice of educating members of the patriarchal community—the family; definitions of virtues, social morality, ontology, and epistemology made by men and defined narcissistically, to express their point of view and to serve what they perceived as their interests; in general, rejection of connection and relationship in favor of separation and autonomy. Women's critiques of Western culture, with and without explicit reference to classical antiquity, focus on issues that can often be traced to our Greco-Roman legacy and its exclusions.

Women's view from outside that heritage has created a desire to alter mainstream cultural worldviews, to focus on different locations where power is multifaceted, oriented to gradations of appropriateness, and therefore better constituted so as to serve a greater variety of human needs. This late-twentieth-century view encompasses social action as well as both pragmatic and utopian visions of an integrated society. Understanding the psychological, religious, and social forces that shaped Greco-Roman ideas of difference may contribute toward narrowing the distance between dream and reality.

Notes

[1] Nancy Hartsock, *Money, Sex, and Power. Toward a Feminist Historical Materialism* (Boston: Northeastern University Press, 1983), p.177.

[2] Moira Gatens, *Feminism and Philosophy. Perspectives on Difference and Equality* (Bloomington: Indiana University Press, 1991), p.138.

[3] Carol Gilligan, "Moral Orientation and Moral Development," in Eva Feder Kittay and Diana T. Meyers, eds., *Women and Moral Theory* (Savage, MD: Roman and Littlefield, 1987), pp.19-33.

[4] See, for example, Alasdair MacIntyre, *After Virtue* (South Bend, IN: Notre Dame University Press, 1981).

[5] Gatens, *Feminism and Philosophy*, p.136.

[6] Gatens, *Feminism and Philosophy*, p.139.

[7] See esp. Caroline Whitbeck, "A Different Reality: Feminist Ontology," in Carol C. Gould, ed., *Beyond Domination. New Perspectives on Women and Philosophy* (Totowa, N.J.: Rowman and Allenheld, 1984), pp.64-88; reprinted in Ann Garry and Marilyn Pearsall, eds., *Women, Knowledge, and Reality. Explorations in Feminist Philosophy* (Boston: Unwin Hyman, 1989), pp.51-76.

[8] "What Is Authority?" in Hannah Arendt, *Between Past and Future* (Cleveland: Meridien, 1961), pp.121f.

[9] Kathleen B. Jones, "On Authority," in Irene Diamond and Lee Quinby, eds., *Feminism and Foucault* (Boston: New England University Press, 1988), pp.119-133.

[10] Authority protects individual rights, a community of autonomous selves. Jones proposes a redefined authority "expressing and enabling political action in community—interaction among equals," which would reinforce "communal connectedness" and incorporate compassion as a commonly recognized value. Jones, "On Authority," pp.126f.

[11] Virginia Woolf, *A Room of One's Own* and also *Three Guineas*, esp. "The public and private worlds are inseparably connected; the tyrannies and servilities of one are the tyrannies and servilities of the other." For women as outsiders in relation to male culture, see Mary Lynn Broe and Angela Ingram, eds., *Women's Writing in Exile* (Chapel Hill: University of North Carolina Press, 1989); and Adrienne Rich, "Disloyal to Civilization: Feminism, Racism, Gynephobia," in *On Lies, Secrets, and Silence. Selected Prose 1966-1978* (New York: Norton, 1979), pp.275-310.

For women as outsiders in philosophy, see Genevieve Lloyd, *The Man of Reason. 'Male' and 'Female' in Western Philosophy* (London: Methuen, 1984); Judith Hughes, "The Philosopher's Child," in Morwenna Griffiths and Margaret

Whitford, eds., *Feminist Perspectives in Philosophy* (Bloomington: Indiana University Press, 1988), pp.72-89; Morwenna Griffiths, "Feminism, Feelings and Philosophy," Ibid., pp.131-151; Joanna Hodge, "Subject, Body and the Exclusion of Women from Philosophy," Ibid., pp.152-168; Paula Ruth Boddington, "The Issue of Women's Philosophy," Ibid., pp.205-223; and Ann Garry and Marilyn Pearsall, eds., *Women, Knowledge, and Reality* (Boston: Unwin Hyman, 1989), esp. essays in Part 1 Methodology, pp.1-46, Part 2 Metaphysics, pp.47-108, and Part 3, pp.109-172; and Susan Bordo, "Feminist Skepticism and the ''Maleness'' of Philosophy," in Elizabeth D. Harvey and Kathleen Okruhlik, eds., *Women and Reason* (Ann Arbor: University of Michigan Press, 1992), pp.143-162. See also Sandra Harding, "Why Has the Sex/Gender System Become Visible Only Now?" in Sandra Harding and Merrill B. Hintikka, eds. *Discovering Reality. Feminist Perspectives on Epistemology, Metaphysics, Methodology, and Philosophy of Science* (Dordrecht: D. Reidel, 1983), pp.311-324.

[12] So Alicia Ostriker's *Stealing the Language: The Emergence of Women's Poetry in America* (Boston: Beacon Press, 1986). In the view of French feminist Julia Kristeva, language cannot be stolen, because there is only one symbolic order. Women can, however, achieve subjectivity within that order; see Toril Moi, ed., *The Kristeva Reader* (Oxford: Basil Blackwell, 1986), and *Sexual/Textual Politics* (London: Methuen, 1985). Alternatively, language must be embodied and made to express female experience—"writing the body," in the *ecriture feminine* of Helene Cixous and Luce Irigaray. For discussion of feminist approaches to language, see Andrea Nye, *Feminist Theory and the Philosophies of Man* (New York: Routledge, 1989), Chapter 6, "A Woman's Language," and essays by Janice Moulton and Andrea Nye (Part V, The Philosophy of Language) in *Women, Knowledge, and Reality*, pp.217-249.

[13] Evelyn Fox Keller, *Reflections on Gender and Science* (New Haven: Yale University Press, 1985), and Evelyn Fox Keller and Helen Longino, eds., *Feminism and Science* (Oxford: Oxford University Press, 1996).

[14] Among homages to feminist foremothers are those of Rosemary Tong, *Feminine and Feminist Ethics* (Belmont, CA: Wadsworth, 1993), Chapter 3, "Women's Morality: Precursory Feminine and Feminist Approaches to Ethics," pp.25-48; Kathryn Pyne Addelson, *Moral Passages. Toward a Collectivist Moral Theory* (New York: Routledge, 1994) (on Margaret Sanger); and Sara Ruddick, *Maternal Thinking. Toward a Politics of Peace* (Boston: Beacon Press, 1989) (on Jane Addams and Olive Schreiner).

[15] Genevieve Lloyd, *The Man of Reason,* begins her survey of the male cooptation of reason with Plato and Aristotle. Additional reflections on reason: Lydia Lange, "Woman Is Not a Rational Animal: On Aristotle's Biology of Reproduction," in Harding and Hintikka, eds., *Discovering Reality*, pp.1-17; Margaret Whitford in Griffiths and Whitford, eds., *Feminist Perspectives*, pp.109-130; Part III of Garry and Pearsall, eds., *Women, Knowledge, and*

Reality, pp.109-172; Harvey and Okruhlik, eds., *Women and Reason*; and Margaret Urban Walker, "Moral Understandings: Alternative 'Epistemology' for a Feminist Ethics," in Eve Browning Cole and Susan Coultrap-McQuin, eds., *Explorations in Feminist Ethics. Theory and Practice* (Bloomington: Indiana University Press, 1992), pp.165-175.

[16] Nancy Hartsock, *Money, Sex, and Power*, Chapter 10, "The Feminist Standpoint: Toward a Specifically Feminist Historical Materialism," pp.231-251, and her essay in *Discovering Reality*, pp.283-310; Sandra Harding, "Why Has the Sex/Gender System Become Visible Only Now?" in *Discovering Reality*, pp.311-324. For recognition of white, middle- and upper-class bias in the women's movement, see Elizabeth V. Spelman, *Inessential Woman. Problems of Exclusion in Feminist Thought* (Boston: Beacon Press, 1988); Addelson, *Moral Passages*, Chapter 5; and bel hooks, *Ain't I a woman: Black women and feminism* (Boston: South End Press, 1981).

[17] Jane Flax, *Thinking Fragments. Psychoanalysis, Feminism, and Postmodernism in the Contemporary West* (Berkeley and Los Angeles: University of California Press, 1990), Chapter 6, "Postmodernism."

[18] An observation made by many, among them: Page du Bois, *Sowing the Body. Psychoanalysis and Ancient Representations of Women* (Chicago: University of Chicago Press, 1988), Chapter 1; Jane Flax, "Political Philosophy and the Patriarchal Unconscious: A Psychoanalytic Perspective on Epistemology and Metaphysics," in *Discovering Reality*, pp.245-281; Jean Grimshaw, *Philosophy and Feminist Thinking* (Minneapolis: University of Minnesotta Press, 1986), pp.82-83, 90-95; Jane Miller, *Seductions. Studies in Reading and Culture* (London: Virago, 1990); Mary Field Belenky et al, eds., *Women's Ways of Knowing. The Development of Self, Voice, and Mind* (New York: Basic Books, 1986); Susan Sherwin, "Philosophical Methodology and Feminist Methodology: Are They Compatible?" in *Women, Knowledge, and Reality*, pp.21-36, and other essays on methodology, metaphysics, theory of knowledge, and philosophies of language and mind in the same collection. For a discussion of the psychological repression of the feminine in Irigaray and Cixous, see Gatens, *Feminism and Philosophy*, Chapter 6, "Psychology and French Feminism," pp.100-121.

[19] Seyla Benhabib, "The Generalized and the Concrete Other: The Kohlberg-Gilligan Controversy and Feminist Theory," in Seyla Benhabib and Drucilla Cornell, eds., *Feminism as Critique. Essays in the Politics of Gender in Late Capitalist Societies* (Cambridge: Polity Press, 1987, pp.77-95, and also in Eva Feder Kittay and Diana T. Meyers, eds., *Women and Moral Theory* (Rowman and Littlefield, 1987), pp.154-177.

[20] Virginia Held, *Feminist Morality. Transforming Culture, Society, and Politics* (Chicago and London: University of Chicago Press, 1993), p.22.

[21] For reflections of women's experiences of embodiment, see Elizabeth

Grosz, *Volatile Bodies. Toward a Corporeal Feminism* (Bloomington: Indiana University Press, 1994).

[22] Jane Flax, "Political Philosophy and the Patriarchal Unconscious: A Psychoanalytic Perspective on Epistemology and Metaphysics," in Harding and Hintikka, eds., *Discovering Reality*, pp.245-281. See also Sandra Bartky, *Femininity and Domination. Studies in the Phenomenology of Oppression* (New York: Routledge, 1990).

[23] Judith V. Jordan, Alexandra G. Kaplan, et al., eds., *Women's Growth in Connection. Studies from the Stone Center* (New York and London: The Guilford Press, 1991).

[24] See esp. Elisabeth Young-Bruehl, *The Anatomy of Prejudices* (Cambridge: Harvard University Press, 1996), pp.230-238.

[25] Flax, *Thinking Fragments*, Chapter 3, "Freud: Initiation and Omission in Psychoanalysis."

[26] Jane Flax states that boys' separation from their m/others "involves contempt and hostility which carries over into adult life." *Thinking Fragments*, pp.122f.

[27] For a summary and critique of Lacan's views, see Flax, *Thinking Fragments*, pp.93-107, 126-132. The quotation is from p.94. For additional criticisms of Lacan, see also Drucilla Cornell, *Beyond Accommodation. Ethical Feminism, Deconstruction, and the Law* (New York: Routledge, 1991).

[28] For a scathing indictment of the narcissism of male culture, see Helene Cixous and Catherine Clement, "Sorties," pp.86-100, in *The Newly Born Woman*, trans. Betsy Wing (Minneapolis: University of Minnesota Press, 1986).

[29] "At the heart of psychoanalytic theory lies an unacknowledged paradox: the creation of difference distorts, rather than fosters, the recognition of the other. Difference turns out to be governed by the code of domination." Jessica Benjamin, *The Bonds of Love. Psychoanalysis, Feminism, and the Problem of Domination* (New York: Pantheon, 1988), p.135.

[30] Jane Flax, *Thinking Fragments*, pp.159-168; Dorothy Dinnerstein, *The Mermaid and the Minotaur. Sexual Arrangements and Human Malaise* (New York: Harper and Row, 1975); Nancy Chodorow, *The Reproduction of Mothering. Psychoanalysis and the Sociology of Gender* (Berkeley and Los Angeles: University of California Press, 1978). On the "domestication of women," see Gerda Lerner, *The Creation of Patriarchy* (Oxford: Oxford University Press, 1986); and Gayle Rubin, "The Traffic in Women: Notes on the 'Political Economy' of Sex," in Rayna Rapp Reiter, ed., *Toward an Anthropology of Women* (New York: Monthly Review Press, 1975).

[31] Chodorow and Dinnerstein argue that as long as child care remains primarily a mother's responsibility and fathers do not take responsibility for nurturance, opposite gender identities will be perpetuated and women will not be

free to participate as full members of society. For critiques of both (but mostly Chodorow), see Iris Marion Young, "Is Male Gender Identity the Cause of Male Domination?" in Young, *Throwing Like a Girl and Other Essays in Feminist Philosophy and Social Theory* (Bloomington: Indiana University Press, 1990), pp.36-61. See also Mitchell Aboulafia, "From Domination to Recognition," *Beyond Domination*, pp.175-185.

32 For feminist views of the object-relations theory, see Chodorow, *Reproduction of Mothering*, Part II, Chapter 7 and passim, and *Femininities, Masculinities, Sexualities: Freud and Beyond* (Lexington: University of Kentucky Press, 1994). Carol Gilligan, "Moral Orientation and Moral Development," in Kittay and Meyers, *Women and Moral Theory*, pp.28-29, criticizes Chodorow's use of object-relations theory:

> Object relations theory ties the formation of the self to the experience of separation, joining separation with individuation and thus counterposing the experience of self to the experience of connection with others. This is the line that Chodorow traces in explicating male development. Within this framework, girls' connections with their mothers can only be seen as problematic. Connection with others or the capacity to feel and think *with* others is, by definition, in tension with self-development when self-development is linked to separation. Thus, object-relations theory sustains a series of oppositions that have been central to Western thought and moral theory, including the opposition between thought and feelings, self and relationship, reason and compassion, justice and love.

See also Alison M. Jaggar, *Feminist Politics and Human Nature* (Sussex, Eng.: Rowman and Allanheld, The Harvester Press, 1983), pp.374ff. Flax, *Thinking Fragments,* pp.107-132, criticizes D.W. Winnicott for taking very little account of sexuality and gender and for failing to acknowledge the complexity of the woman who is the mother. Associations of power and gender difference also seem to be ignored.

33 Sigmund Freud, "Beyond the Pleasure Principle," "On Narcissism," and *Totem and Taboo* in *Collected Papers* (New York: Basic Books, 1959).

34 Louise Kaplan, *No Voice Is Ever Wholly Lost* (New York: Simon and Schuster, 1995); and Susan Bordo, *The Flight to Objectivity. Essays on Cartesianism and Culture* (Albany: State University of New York Press 1987), pp.105ff.

35 As a number of feminist thinkers suggest; see, for example, Virginia Held, *Feminist Morality*, p. 29; and Morwenna Griffiths, "Feminism, Feelings, and Philosophy," in Griffiths and Whitford, eds., *Feminist Perspectives in Philosophy*, pp.131-151; Alison M. Jaggar, "Love and Knowledge in Feminist Epistemology," in Harvey and Okruhlik, eds., *Women and Reason*, pp.115-142.

36 Mary Daly, *Gyn/Ecology. The Metaethics of Radical Feminism* (Boston:

Beacon Press, 1978).

[37] Mary Daly, *Gyn/Ecology*, pp.57-64. On "womb envy," see Eva Kittay, "Womb Envy: An Explanatory Concept," in Joyce Treblicot, ed., *Mothering. Essays in Feminist Theory.* (Totowa, NJ: Rowman and Allenheld, 1984); and Virginia Held, "Feminism and Moral Theory," in Kittay and Meyers, eds., *Women and Moral Theory*, p.122.

[38] See Dorothy E. Smith, "A Sociology of Women," in Julia A. Sherman and Evelyn Torton Beck, eds., *The Prism of Sex. Essays in the Sociology of Knowledge* (Madison: University of Wisconsin Press, 1979), pp.135-187.

[39] On Eve, see also Margaret Miles, *Carnal Knowing. Female Nakedness and Religious Meaning in the Christian West* (Boston: Beacon Press, 1989), pp.84, 119, 152-3, 162 ("Eve" as the basis of a fictional figure of 'woman'"), and 115-6, 125-38 and passim. On Pandora, see Page duBois, *Sowing the Body. Psychoanalysis and Ancient Representations of Women* (Chicago: University of Chicago Press, 1988), pp.43-49, esp. 46f. She points out that according to the myth told by the eighth-century poet Hesiod, this first woman was formed by the gods from clay—like a vase—and given to mankind. The generic woman of Greek myth is the creation of patriarchal divinities. On the association of women and evil in Western thought (with references to Aristotle and Homer), see Nel Noddings, *Women and Evil* (Berkeley: University of California Press, 1989).

[40] Sheila Ruth, "Bodies and Souls/Sex, Sin and the Senses in Patriarchy: A Study in Applied Dualism," *Hypatia* 2.1 (winter 1987): 149-163. See also Rosemary Reuther, "Spirit and Matter, Private and Public: The Challenge of Feminism to Traditional Dualism," in Paula M. Cooey, Sharon A. Farmer, and Mary Ellen Ross, eds., *Embodied Love. Sensuality and Relationship as Feminist Values* (San Francisco: Harper and Row, 1987); Jane Flax, *Thinking Fragments*, pp.36f.

[41] Ruddick, *Maternal Thinking. Toward a Politics of Peace*, p.216. On men's need for war under patriarchy, see Jo-Ann Pilardi, "On the War Path and Beyond. Hegel, Freud and Feminist Theory," in Azizah Y. al-Hibri and Margaret A. Simons, eds., *Hypatia Reborn. Essays in Feminist Philosophy* (Bloomington: Indiana University Press, 1990), pp.5-17. In *Ordinary Heroines. Transforming the Male Myth* (New York: Continuum, 1994), Nadya Aisenberg explores the bankruptcy of the male heroic ethic.

[42] Ruddick, pp.151f.

[43] Ruddick, pp.193ff.

[44] Elaine Scarry, *The Body in Pain. The Making and Unmaking of the World* (Oxford: Oxford University Press, 1985).

[45] Scarry observes that war is a contest, a predicate which both contradicts and obscures another, that war is injuring. The juxtaposition is, in her view, a virtual obscenity, for a contest is a kind of play or a game, while "the activity of

war is, viewed within this opposition [between play and work], the most unceasingly radical and rigorous form of work." *The Body in Pain*, Chapter 2, section I, pp.63-81.

[46] Scarry, *The Body in Pain*, p.128. The italics are hers.

[47] Ibid., section II, pp.81-91.

[48] For Ruddick's observations on masculinity and war, see *Maternal Thinking*, pp.151f. She comments, "As Elaine Scarry has shown in some detail, military thinking provides identifiable techniques of description and evasion that focus the mind on strategy rather than suffering, sacrifice rather than killing, and the cause rather than the bodies torn apart in its name."

[49] Ibid., p.123.

[50] For an overview of maternal ethics, see Tong, *Feminine and Feminist Ethics*, Chapter 7, "Maternal Ethics," pp.135-157; discussion of Ruddick, pp.136-142.

[51] Nancy Hartsock, *Money, Sex, and Power*, and "The Barracks Community in Western Political Thought" in Judith Stiehm, ed., *Women and Men's Wars* (New York: Pergamum, 1983); Hartsock's concept is discussed by Virginia Held, *Feminist Morality*, pp.143f.

[52] Hartsock, *Money, Sex, and Power*, p.50. See also Virginia Held, "Feminism and Moral Theory," in Kittay and Meyers, eds., in *Women and Moral Theory,* pp.114-117 ("Mothering and Markets").

[53] Ibid., Part II, Chapter 7, "Gender and Power," pp.155-185, and Chapter 8, "The Erotic Dimension and the Homeric Ideal," pp.186-209.

[54] Hartsock, pp.166-169, briefly discusses Freud, Marx, Marceuse, and Battaille on *eros* and points out "the variety of ways our society puts *eros* in the service of violence and even death" (p.168). In her conclusion (pp.255f.), she quotes Audre Lourde, who described the mythic force of Eros, "personifying creative power and harmony" and spoke of "the possible empowering erotic nature of work" (Hartsock's words). Hartsock suggests, "[W]e can begin to see some of the outlines of an understanding of power which stresses both its dimensions of competence, ability, and creativity, and does not lose sight of the importance of effective action in the world, action at least in part defined by its sensuality and its variety of connections and relations with others in the community."

French feminists Helene Cixous anad Julia Kristeva affirm women's limitless life energy, power, and joy: *jouissance*. One might say that they are reclaiming for women the life force which the Greeks appropriated to the male god Dionysus.

[55] Cixous and Clement, *The Newly Born Woman*, trans. Betsy Wing, p.87.

[56] Andrea Nye, "Preparing the Way for a Feminine Praxis," *Hypatia* 1.1 (spring 1986): 101-116. The quotations is from p.110. This view of conflict

recalls the philosophy of Heraclitus. For the Cartesian view of subjectivity, see Bordo, *The Flight to Objectivity. Essays on Cartesianism and Culture*. On existentialism and feminism, see Gatens, *Feminism and Philosophy. Perspectives on Difference and Equality*: "It is undeniable that she [de Beauvoir] was one of the first, if not the first, to make a viable distinction between woman's biological sex and the way that sex is lived in culture. . . The existentialist perspective . . .was a crucial factor in the successful completion of this task. However, this distinction can be made without assuming the masculine perspective along with its denigration of the female body and femininity" (p.58). And "The female body is other to her [woman's] humanity, her subjectivity, in short to her transcendence, which can be asserted only on condition that she escapes the grip of the female body" (p.59).

[57] *The Second Sex*, trans. and ed. H.M. Parshley (New York: Bantam, 1961 [1949]), p.670.

[58] *The Second Sex*, p.69.

[59] Beauvoir cites Levi-Strauss, the conclusion of *Les Structures elementaires de la parente*: "Passage from the state of Nature to the state of Culture is marked by man's ability to view biological relations as a series of contrasts; duality, alternation, opposition, and symmetry, whether under definite or vague forms, constitute not so much phenomena to be explained as fundamental and immediately given data of social reality" (*The Second Sex*, Introduction, p.xvii). Virginia Held, *Feminist Morality*, pp.125-127, also discussed the views of Hannah Arendt and Sherry Ortner on reproduction and the female/male, nature/culture dichotomies, respectively.

[60] Ruddick, *Maternal Thinking*, p.194. For additional discussion of Beauvoir, see also Part III, "Beauvoir and Feminist Philosophy," in a-Hebri and Simon, eds., *Hypatia Reborn. Essays in Feminist Philosophy*, pp.233ff.; and Spelman, *Inessential Woman*, Chapter 3.

[61] In classical antiquity, the significant racial distinction was the difference between Greek-speaking and non-Greek-speaking (barbarian) peoples.

[62] See Hartsock, *Money, Sex, and Power*, Part I (pp.1-144).

[63] Olive Schreiner, *Women and Labour* (London: Virago, 1978); Dorothy Smith, "A Sociology of Women," in Sherman and Beck, eds., *The Prism of Sex*.

[64] Rosemary Radford Ruether, "Spirit and Matter, Public and Private: The Challenge of Feminism to Traditional Dualism," in Paula M. Cooey, Sharon A. Farmer, and Mary Ellen Ross, eds., *Embodied Love. Sensuality and Relationships as Feminist Values* (San Francisco: Harper & Row, 1987), pp.65-76. "[W]e are forced to consider . . .the difference between women's role as childbearer and nurturer and the male economic and political sphere that has been defined over and against it. . . [T]his entails a shift in what we view to be normative and central to human society, namely, a focus upon the creation and sustaining of human life and the reintegration of an alienated work world into

it" (p.75). "The issue of the liberation of women restores to center stage the basic questions about the meaning of an unalienated, humanized life in postindustrial society" (p.76).

[65] Women's special "excellence" in the Aristotelian sense was her reproductive capacity, and women's work was reproductive labor.

[66] Janice Moulton, "A Paradigm of Philosophy: The Adversary Method," in Garry and Pearsall, eds., *Women, Knowledge, and Reality*, pp.5-20; Sandra Lee Bartky, *Feminism and Domination. Studies in the Phenomenology of Oppression* (Boston and London: Routledge, 1990); and Part IV, "The Analysis of Domination" in *Beyond Domination*. Many, including Jane Martin, *Reclaiming a Conversation. The Ideal of the Educated Woman* (New Haven: Yale University Press, 1985), pp.6-7, 14-15, and passim, use the terms productive and reproductive labor to differentiate between men's and women's work.

[67] Helen E. Longino, "The Ideology of Competition" in Valerie Miner and Helen E. Longino, eds., *Competition. A Feminist Taboo?* (New York: Feminist Press, 1987), pp.248-258. The quotation is from p.256.

[68] Victoria Davion, "Do Good Feminists Compete?" *Hypatia* 2.2 (summer 1987): 55-63; the Comment/Reply by Linda Timmel Duchamp, "Desperately Seeking Approval: The Importance of Distinguishing between Approval and Recognition," *Hypatia* 3.2 (summer 1988): 163f.; and Davion's Comment/Reply, "Competition, Recognition, and Approval-Seeking," *Hypatia* 3.2 (summer 1988): 165f.

[69] Maria C. Lugones and Elizabeth V. Spelman, "Competition, Compassion, and Community: Models for a Feminist Ethos," in Miner and Longino, eds., *Competition. A Feminist Taboo?*, pp.234-247. The fact that Latin *competere*, as they point out, from which English "compete" is derived, means simply "to come together" speaks to the idea of community in the Greco-Roman tradition.

[70] Miner and Longino, pp.35-36.

[71] Harding and Hintikka, eds., *Discovering Reality*, pp.71-95.

[72] Helen Longino, "The Ideology of Competition," pp.250-253, examines the idea of scarcity in social and political thought: Hobbes, Malthus, Darwin, and Herbert Spencer.

[73] Frans de Waal, *Good Natured. The Origins of Right and Wrong in Humans and Other Animals* (Cambridge: Harvard University Press, 1996).

[74] "To break the ideological hold that such divisions [between private and public, personal and political] maintain over our lives, we need to show their historical origins and their changing dynamics ... Unless we can see these divisions in historical terms and not as universal givens outside analysis and change, we will be unable to influence intelligently the future of such divisions," Linda J. Nicholson, "Feminist Theory: The Private and the Public," in *Beyond Domination*, pp.221-230. She also notes that "entanglement of at least

part of this oppression with the very separation of these relationships (personal and familial) from political and economic relationships." The quotations are from p.230.

[75] Both paternal and fraternal bonds are the defining human relationships in Greek and Roman societies and their legacy: paternal are primary in contexts involving the education of the young into patriarchy, both the continuity of generations within the family and the transmission of leadership roles in the public sphere; fraternal are predominant in relations among men of equal rank, brothers within the family and citizens in the body politic. For discussion of male relationships, see, e.g., Gatens, *Feminism and Philosophy*, pp.108f. and 153, n32.

[76] Hannah Arendt, *The Human Condition. A Study of the Central Dilemmas Facing Modern Man* (Chicago: University of Chicago Press, 1958), Chapter 2, "The Public and Private Realm." In what follows, I am summarizing and quoting from Nancy Hartsock's discussion of Arendt in *Money, Sex, and Power*, Chapter 9, "An Alternative Tradition: Women on Power," pp.210-222.

[77] Hartsock, pp.214-218.

[78] Hartsock, p.224. On moral and nonmoral virtue, see also Tong, *Feminine and Feminist Ethics*, pp.28-30, 94-98.

[79] See "Purification and Transcendence in Descartes's Meditations," Chapter 5, pp.75-96, of Bordo's *The Flight to Objectivity*; Jaggar, *Feminist Politics and Human Nature* (Brighton: Harvester, 1983), Chapter 3, "Liberal Feminism and Human Nature," pp.27-50; Jean Grimshaw, *Philosophy and Feminist Thinking* (Minneapolis: University of Minnesota Press, 1985), Chapter 6, "The Critique of Individualism," pp.162-186; Andrea Nye, *Feminist Theory and the Philosophies of Man*, Chapter 1, "Liberte, Fraternite, et Egalite: Nineteenth-century Liberalism and Women's Rights," pp.5-30; Lynn Arnault, "The Radical Future of a Classic Moral Theory," in Alison Jaggar and Susan Bordo, eds., *Gender/Body/Knowledge. Feminist Reconstructions of Being and Knowing* (New Brunswick: Rutgers University Press, 1989), pp.188-206; and Part II, "The Challenge to Liberalism," in Carole Pateman and Elizabeth Gross, eds., *Feminist Challenges. Social and Political Theory* (Sydney: Allen and Unwin, 1986), pp.63-124.

[80] Alison Jaggar, *Feminist Thinking and the Philosophies of Man*.

[81] See, e.g., Eva Feder Kittay, "Taking Dependency Seriously: The Family and Medical Leave Act Considered in Light of the Social Organization of Dependency Work and Gender Equality," in *Hypatia*, Special Issue, "Feminist Ethics and Social Policy, Part I (winter 1995): 8-29.

[82] Feminist critiques of "rights" ethics: Carol C. Gould, "Private Rights and Public Virtues: Women, the Family, and Democracy," Part I, A Proposed Value Framework for Feminism, in Carol C. Gould, ed., *Beyond Domination*, pp.3-20. Also Part 6, "Law, Ethics, and Public Policy," pp.233-310 in this volume. An

ethics of responsibility: Part II, "The Traditional Roots of an Ethics of Responsibility," in Kittay and Meyers, eds., *Women and Moral Theory*, pp.37-86, and Lorraine Code, "Experience, Knowledge, and Responsibility," in Griffiths and Whitford. eds., *Feminist Perspectives in Philosophy*, pp.187-204.

[83] See esp. Catherine MacKinnon and Andrea Dworkin, and, most recently, Alisa L. Carse, "Pornography: An Uncivil Liberty?" in *Hypatia*. Special Issue, "Feminist Ethics and Social Policy, Part I (winter 1995): 154-182 (references, 180-182).

[84] Kathryn Pynn Addelson, *Moral Passages. Toward a Collectivist Moral Theory* (New York: Routledge, 1994). The quotations are from pp.15, 49f, and 38, respectively. For the collectivist perspective, see esp. Chapter 6, pp.137-159.

[85] Catherine Roach, "Love Your Mother: On the Woman-Nature Relation" in *Hypatia* 6.1 (spring 1991): 46-59. The quotation is from p.56. For an overview of what restoring environmental soundness might mean, see Carolyn Merchant, *Radical Ecology. The Search for a Livable World* (New York and London: Routledge, 1992), Chapter 1, "The Global Ecological Crisis," pp.17-40.

[86] Susan Griffin, *Women and Nature. The Roaring inside Her* (New York: Harper and Row, 1978).

[87] Merchant, *The Death of Nature*, Chapter 1, "Nature as Female," pp.1-41. See also Chapters 4 and 5.

[88] Merchant, *Radical Ecology*, p.11 (see chaps. 2 and 3). Instrumentality has created different environmental problems in different parts of the globe: "Environmental problems in the Third World," she notes, "are rooted in poverty and hunger, population pressure on marginal lands, and unbalanced land distribution, while those in the First World stem from industrial pollution, waste, conspicuous consumption, and planned obsolescence," (p.25). Merchant discusses three ethical orientations, ego-, homo-, and ecocentric (pp.60-74). Although she does not discuss the Greco-Roman tradition, it would probably fall within the category of egocentric ethics, whose religious aspect is the Judeo-Christian tradition. Merchant lists five premises of mechanism (Table 3.1, pp.64f.):

1. Matter is composed of atomic parts
2. The whole is equal to the sum of the parts (law of identity)
3. Knowledge is context-independent
4. Change occurs by the rearrangement of parts
5. Dualism of mind and body, matter and spirit.

For the development of the mechanistic worldview, principally in Descartes and Newton, see pp.48-60. This view posits order and predictability by undertaking to break down reality into discrete parts or fragments. Further, it does so by "abstracting the form or structure of reality from the tangled web of its physical, material, and environmental contest" (p.51). See further Sandra Harding, *The Science Question in Feministm* (Ithaca: Cornell University Press, 1986); and Lynn S. Arnault, "The Radical Future of a Classic Moral Theory," in Jaggar and Bordo, eds., *Gender/Body/Knowledge. Feminist Reconstructions of Being and Knowing*, pp.188-206.

See also Merchant's essay in *Reweaving the World*; *Ecological Revolutions: Nature, Gender, and Science in New England* (Chapel Hill: University of North Carolina Press, 1989).

[89] Irene Diamond, *Fertile Ground* (Boston: Beacon Press, 1994).

[90] See, for example, Lynda Birke and Ruth Hubbard, eds., *Reinventing Biology: Respect for Life and the Creation of Knowledge* (Bloomington: Indiana University Press, 1995).

[91] The varied approaches of ecological feminists—liberal, social, socialist, cultural—reflect broader classes of feminist theories. For a survey, see Carolyn Merchant, *Radical Ecology*, pp.183-210. For analogous feminist theories, see Jaggar, *Feminist Politics and Human Nature*; Nye, *Feminist Theory and the Philosophies of Man*; and Grimshaw, *Philosophy and Feminist Thinking*.

For some intersections of ecology and feminism, see Irene Diamond and Gloria Feman Orenstein, eds., *Reweaving the World. The Emergence of Ecofeminism* (San Francisco: Sierra Club, 1990). For women's spirituality, see Judith Plaskow and Carol P. Christ, eds., *Weaving the Visions. New Patterns in Feminist Spirituality* (San Francisco: Harper and Row, 1989); and Charlene Spretnak, ed., *The Politics of Women's Spirituality. Essays on the Rise of Spiritual Power within the Feminist Movement* (Garden City, NY: Anchor/Doubleday, 1982).

[92] Stephanie Lahar, "Ecofeminist Theory and Grassroots Politics," *Hypatia* 6.1 (spring 1990): 28-45. The phrase occurs on p.29.

[93] Ynestra King, "Healing the Wounds: Feminism, Ecology, and Nature/Culture Dualism," in *Gender/Body/Knowledge*, p.130.

[94] King, "Healing the Wounds," pp.133f.

[95] Dorothy Dinnerstein, *The Mermaid and the Minotaur*, pp.95-114. The quotation is from p.95. See also Catherine Roach, "Love Your Mother. On the Woman-Nature Relation," in *Hypatia* 6.1 (spring 1991): 46-59.

[96] Val Plumwood, "Nature, Self, and Gender: Feminism, Environmental Philosophy, and the Critique of Rationalism," in *Hypatia* 6.1 (spring 1991): 3-27, esp.18-22, associates the matrix of issues we have been discussing with male rationalism, Western dualisms, and liberal political theory.

[97] Deane Curtin, "Toward an Ecological Ethic of Care," *Hypatia* 6.1 (spring 1991): 65. The positions which Curtin states so succinctly here are not, of course, due solely to Gilligan's influence. For Gilligan's ethic of care, see also Rosemarie Tong, *Feminine and Feminist Ethics,* chapter 5; Eve Browning Cole

and Susan Coultrap-McQuin, "Toward a Feminist Conception of Moral Life," in Cole and Coultrap-McQuinn, eds., *Explorations in Feminist Ethics, pp.1-14 and* Section I, The Care Debate, pp.15-56; and Virginia Held, *Feminist Morality,* pp.75-80.

[98] Carol Gilligan, *In a Different Voice. Psychological Theory and Women's Development* (Cambridge: Harvard University Press, 1982). She also found that adolescent girls tend to lose or give up independent powers of judgment (and confidence in those powers) in order to fit into the dominant society. See Gilligan et al., eds., *Mapping the Moral Domain: A Contribution of Women's Thinking to Psychological Theory and Education* (Cambridge: Harvard University Press, 1988).

[99] Nel Noddings, *Caring. A Feminine Approach to Ethics and Moral Education* (Berkeley and Los Angeles: University of California Press, 1984).

[100] For discussion and criticism of Noddings, see Tong, *Feminine and Feminist Ethics*, chapter 6. Drucilla Cornell rejects the association of "maternal thinking" and connection as essentialist (*Beyond Accomodation*, pp.21-36). For the complexities and limitations of attempting to define the feminine through the maternal, see Chapter 1, "The Maternal and the Feminine: Social Reality, Fantasy, and Ethical Relation."

[101] Val Plumwood, "Nature, Self, and Gender: Feminism, Environmental Philosophy, and the Critique of Rationalism," in *Hypatia* 6.1 (spring 1991): 3-27.

[102] Karen J. Warren and Jim Cheney, "Ecological Feminism and Ecosystem Ecology," in *Hypatia* 6.1 (spring 1991): 179-197. The quotation is on p.185.

[103] See discussions of Sara Ruddick, Virginia Held, and Carolyn Whitbeck in Tong, *Feminine and Feminist Ethics*, Chapter 7.

[104] Marilyn Friedman, *What Are Friends For?* (Ithaca: Cornell University Press, 1993); Claudia Card, ed., *Feminist Ethics* (Lawrence: University Press of Kansas, 1991), and Tong, *Feminine and Feminist Ethics*, Chapter 9, pp.188-219; and Lawrence Blum, *Friendship, Altruism and Morality* (London: Routledge and Kegan Paul, 1980).

[105] Robin S. Dillon, "Care and Respect," in Eve Browning Cole and Susan Coultrap-McQuin, eds., *Explorations in Feminist Ethics: Theory and Practice* (Bloomington: Indiana University Press, 1992), pp.69-81. The quotation is from p.70.

[106] Dillon suggests, "Our response to the other should be appropriate to the particular person. We should "try to see the world from their point of view," and "help them to pursue their ends and to satisfy their needs and wants." This sounds suspiciously like the selfless and helping role women have long been encouraged to play, unless concern for the other were reciprocal. It is well to keep in mind the extent to which women have been seen only in terms of appearance and male criteria of beauty and attractiveness. It is the outer woman

who counts. On women and the male gaze, see especially Aisenberg, *Ordinary Heroines. Transforming the Male Myth*, Chapter 3, "Woman/Sight."

[107] Virginia Held, *Feminist Morality. Transforming Culture, Society, and Politics* (Chicago: University of Chicago Press, 1993).

[108] Held, p.80.

[109] Held, *Feminist Morality*, chapter 10, "Noncontractual Society: The Postpatriarchal Family as Model," pp.192-214. Carole Pateman, *The Sexual Contract* (Stanford: Stanford University Press, 1988), has pointed out that when philosophers speak of a social contract, they refer to a hypothetical agreement among men, and that women have never been asked whether they wished to participate in such an agreement, or on what terms. Thus, the social contract, as we commonly speak of it, assumes the subordination of women, and social contract theories have always denied women the status of contractors.

[110] Held, p.206.

[111] The quotations are from pp.207 and 214, respectively. For Held's additional critiques of American society, see pp.91-111.

[112] Gould, "Private Rights and Public Virtues: Women, the Family, and Democracy," in *Beyond Domination*, pp.3-18. The quotation is from p.17.

> Conscious human concern is at the heart of human morality.
> Frans de Waal[1]

At the heart of psychoanalytic theory lies an unacknowledged paradox: the creation of difference distorts, rather than fosters, the recognition of the other. Difference turns out to be governed by the code of domination.
Jessica Benjamin[2]

There are good reasons to believe that a society resting on no more than bargains between self-interested or mutually uninterested individuals will not be able to withstand the forces of egoism and disillusion pulling such societies apart.
Virginia Held[3]

Chapter 9

Beyond This Ethical Juncture. Values without Domination

To American Founding Fathers, the Greco-Roman legacy seemed to offer noble social and political ideals and a model of statescraft—the Roman Republic—worth emulating. Its apparent strengths and virtues were fortified by Enlightenment optimism and faith in progress. That legacy, however, is also implicitly at odds with the American spirit, for Greco-Roman attitudes to difference are incompatible with diversity, equality, and inclusiveness. In this sense, America as ideal is a self-contradiction and has been from its inception. The institution of slavery, the Civil War, and twentieth-century struggles for civil rights sounded that ideological dissonance with respect to race; the women's suffrage movement and twentieth-century feminist struggles sounded it with respect to gender. Today, as we race down the Information Highway obsessed with converting New York minutes into hard currency, what Greeks or Romans thought twenty-seven hundred years ago may seem remote at best. Yet only by remembering our classical roots and regarding them differently, as we have done in the preceding pages, do we understand the ways in which those early beginnings of Western culture have made us who we are. By remembering them, we begin to see our way out of some seemingly insoluble contemporary moral and social dilemmas in contemporary America and other Western late-capitalist societies.

Many are now performing what I have playfully imagined as the reconstituted office of Pythian priestess in the New World. They agree that (1) reviewing structures of power is at the heart of intellectual and social change; (2) there can be no reassessment of values without considering them in relation to power; and (3) hierarchies—or declensions—of power have been associated with presumptions about capability. We are taking about the intersection of values, power, and difference.

In classical antiquity, difference was conceived in terms of self-worth, power or lack of it, and separation. Men's narcissistic response to their lack of power in comparison with ultimate power as they imagined it—everlasting life—was to define their lives, their world, and the human condition in terms of power. In order to become like gods, mitigate their awareness that they were destined to lose their own lives, and defend themselves against other losses, they founded and developed human societies based in ideologies and mechanisms of control, especially the quest for transcendence over death through lasting achievement. Even if they are not bought at the price of death, victory and success almost always "inevitably" bring loss and suffering, violence and cruelty. Men created a universe with themselves at its center: From them all light radiates, all things reflect their own image back to them. Existence becomes the milieu in which man must endlessly prove his worth, cultivate his self-esteem and importance in the eyes of others. Woman should reflect him, not herself; she-who-is-lacking is consigned to lack of self-esteem and importance in the eyes of others.[4] Such narcissism characterizes *man*kind in its infancy, so to speak. Defensive, self-absorbed, and obsessed by feelings of powerlessness, men saw themselves as second and subordinate only to the gods, infants longing to become the (seemingly) all-powerful parents who control their lives.[5] Through victory and success, by proving themselves extraordinary mortals, godlike heroes, men overcome the supposed disadvantages of the human condition. Men are forbidden to compete with or vanquish gods, but they acquire a measure of divine power if remembrance of their deeds passes into collective human memory. "Death destroys a man; the idea of death saves him," reflects a character in E.M. Forster's *Howard's End*.

Feelings of powerlessness dominate the worldview of the Homeric warrior. Or rather, a man pits his power against fate, the gods, and death and "proves" his heroic worth in the attempt. This attitude, a blend of defiance and acceptance, makes death The Enemy in a larger-than-life scenario. We try to overcome him, as did the Greeks and Romans, through accumulating knowledge, in particular developing and implementing new technologies. Today, ironically, research in genetics, a foremost area of technology, may be leading toward a new but equally inexorable kind of destiny. The need for control permeates American culture. Even if we relinquish the Greco-Roman heritage of death-centeredness, remembering existential decorum and other human limits is a good antidote to arrogance and megalomania. The question now is, What kinds of control do we need in order to live a good life and create the world we want our descendants to inherit?

But while—originally and thereafter always? heroic—quests for power, control, and immortality are active, feelings of impotence also generate a complementary attitude of passivity. Homeric and tragic heroes challenge mortal limits and limitations through action. Greek epic and tragic heroes were powerless, but Vergil created a hero whose very passivity is a virtue. Aeneas submits himself to a "higher" (divinely given) goal he neither knows nor understands. Men's alleged propensity to action and women's to passivity are deeply rooted cultural stereotypes. Yet male culture is passive in ways neither Vergil nor any other classical male thinkers recognized, for in order to protect its private and public power, it declines to recognize or to take responsibility for many shared aspects of human life or for diverse relationships with a variety of peoples.

The paradigms we have inherited from classical antiquity subordinate ethical claims derived from self in relation to the natural world and to other human beings to the values of the community of achievement. Values arising from self in relationship are at best alternative values, relegated to (at most) second place and often seen as theatening. These alternative values appeared in some works we discussed. Shared qualities in Homer's *Odyssey,* likenesses and likemindedness, emphasize connections and relationships across natural and social boundaries, yet they are nonetheless integrated into a patriarchal social hierarchy. The norms of Phaeacian society and the Epicurean holistic worldview with its advocacy of withdrawal from public life are counterheroic and countercultural. Hesiod, Lucretius, and Seneca urged men to "live in accordance with nature": to develop a sense of timeliness and appropriateness drawn from observation of natural seasons (Hesiod); to strive to integrate one's self into an organic, material universe (Epicurus, Lucretius); to live by the reason and order which nature dictates (the Stoic view, which coopted nature into a male-centered hierarchy of being).

Greek and Roman thinkers defined the human condition in terms of a common destiny, that we all die. Death is one thing we all have in common. But it is also our common destiny that we all live, connected by the necessities of birth, death, and progress through the same stages of the life cycle, and by universal human bonds and needs. At what price has the idea of death saved us? Saved us from what? If it has saved us, perhaps it could save us *better.* What are the ethical implications of "what we all share"? Acknowledgment of universal membership in nature should imply an equality of basic human needs, a radical reversal of the traditional hierarchy of domination and privilege. We might call this value a decorum of need, and regard it as a principle of economic justice. The use of natural and social resources to care for the basic needs of all human beings would constitute an ethic of care in the broadest possible sense, extending well beyond ways of thinking that have been designated feminine or maternal (by feminists as well as by those who have a vested interest in being taken care of). Is this line of thinking hopelessly utopian? Praise of compassion, empathy, and other qualities that acknowledge community (recall, for comparison, the shadowy Greek notion of cooperative *arete*) provide good copy and make people feel virtuous, but in practice Western culture is committed to an achievement/self-interest/profit track, and on this worldview, rightly so, for people are by nature self-centered and selfish. Such rationales keeps us trapped within established dualistic binds. How can we be so certain what "people" are "by nature" when women's—and other alternative—values have been excluded from processes of creating social norms and defining ethical values? There is nothing inherently wrong with virtue, reason, justice, reciprocity—other than that defining and possessing them have been the prerogatives of powerful men. Liberated from long-standing associations with power and the drive to primacy, liberated from demands of the market economy and our contemporary media-driven frenzy for fame, they would become the property of the many.

Yet fear lingers that in challenging traditional values already compromised by social, economic, scientific and technological, and intellectual forces of diffusion, we are striking another blow against the very heart of American culture, or, in the minds of some, civilization itself. Isn't achievement the foundation of civilization? Isn't it "human nature" to desire to do/be more/better, to gain greater knowledge/power/mastery, to keep striving—perhaps for self-aggrandizement, perhaps to improve the human lot? Would anyone achieve anything if s/he were not motivated to compete, to be best (or at least to seem to be, to invoke a very Greek polarity) and therefore first. If men and women were to give up the pursuit of success, victory, and power, or if, alternatively, they no longer strove for achievement under the same circumstances and in the same ways, human progress would be endangered. Thinkers as diverse as Sigmund Freud, Margaret Mead, and Camille Paglia have said as much.[6] It is far from clear, however, what this alleged catastrophe would entail. The costs of traditional mechanisms of "progress" are heavy because they exclude so many aspects of human nature, experience, and need. Contrary to the long-standing assumption that exclusion is the price of civilization, greater inclusiveness would only increase the pool of talent that might enhance civilization. By admitting Others to once exclusive domains of achievement, we open the possibility of more diverse accomplishments that better reflect and serve the scope and complexity of all human experience.

In addition to fear that challenging the ways in which achievement as it has been pursued in the past would endanger civilization, the dominant culture also fears that without order—that is, without the structures we associate with order—"we" would somehow become less than the best that "humans" can be. We would descend perhaps into a kind of Hell for failed or deficient men, men who do not deserve to occupy the apex of the evolutionary pyramid. The opposite of order is, of course, chaos. The idea of chaos reflects men's fear of order which is not theirs or of their making—change, fluidity, unpredictability, multiplicity, complexity, variety, plurality, particularity, specificity. Acknowledgment of difference and diversity are likely to threaten prevailing modes and avenues of control and, paradoxically, to reveal new, unforeseeable possibilities of connection.

Valuations of achievement in the Greco-Roman world, which originated in war and athletic competitions, shaped Western attitudes to sociopolitical, cultural, intellectual, artistic, and scientific endeavors. In the Greek and Latin languages, and therefore in classical thought, however, the drive to primacy was at least constrained by the association of achievement and virtue; in contemporary America, we're having some difficulty maintaining the connection between getting to first place and doing it ethically. In addition, while achievement once applied to the arts, fields of learning, and public service, today it is most prized when won in the realms of business, commerce, industry, and technology. This shift in values has permitted a new dimension of confusion, the conflation of achievement with economic profit and benefit. The dominant contemporary culture is loathe to value anything that doesn't make money. The bottom line, the promise of ongoing unfettered economic growth through expanding global markets and advances in technology—these are the major values American society honors today. As a result, we risk having ambition and expertise without social morality and public discourse which is vague, uninformed, and susceptible to manipulation by the mass media. Ignorance is deplored mainly as a threat to the economy and America's stake in the international marketplace. The constitutional guarantee of freedom of thought was never intended to sanction freedom to not think at all.

The neoconservative defense of Western culture is the current apology of, by and for the dominant, patriarchal tradition, designed to separate men from women, public from private, culture and society from nature and to perpetuate an ethic of domination. Neoconservative critics decry the loss of a sense of community in the modern world, but long before the appearance of modern and postmodern syndromes, the triumph of the value of domination over the value of community derived from nature or a broad spectrum of human bonds radically limited the idea of community and created many varieties of alienation. "Relativism" itself is relative to specific historical contexts, and fluctuations in the way men see their world—in terms of certainty and unpredictability, order and anarchy, the one and the many, faith and reason, religion and science—are a recurrent pattern in history. Our very readings of these vacillations reflect the Western legacy of binary thinking. A unified vision and strong social morality are in part a measure of the authority of the dominant culture. Values can remain stable and unchanging when power is appropriated and conserved by a select group; a historical period may be perceived and censured as "relativistic" when that power is weakened, challenged, or somehow otherwise compromised in the view of the dominant culture. Fear of relativism may mask a fear of deriving values from being in relation to, in a role other than one of dominance.

The multi-voiced and -valued perspective of Others commits us not to moral relativism, but to moral complexity and flexibility tailored to the totality of human experience. We recall Greco-Roman ideas of propriety. The etymological meaning of this old-fashioned word is "proper to" or "appropriate," that is, proper *in relation to* a person or thing, time or place or circumstance. Relativity, relativism, relation and relationship: all these words are derived from the Latin *relatus*, brought back (again) to be seen in association with or as connected to something or someone else. What would it mean to adapt moral judgment and conduct to particular people and circumstances? Even as we observe and evaluate the discreteness and uniqueness of a particular circumstance, we are also comparing it with others we have known. A judgment involving appropriateness is the outcome of such an act of comparison; we recognize recurrent patterns in our experience. No consensus of values, no code of social conduct could exist if we did not acknowledge degrees of similarity. Yet the particularities of women's experiences, their perceptions and interpretations of the particular and the general, have not gone into the making of definitions of appropriateness. An appeal to appropriateness may simply mask the appropriation of the power of one group by another.[7] Connections and relationships are, as we have seen, problematic for a culture oriented to lack, separation, and exclusion. A new and inclusive morality that accommodates everyone must provide multiple and movable locations for alterities.

Suppose that difference could be freed from its associations with narcissism, feelings of powerlessness, and separation and that gender identity were not defined through hierarchies of opposing values. Which kinds of power and control can and should human beings aspire to? What place should difference have in the construction of values? How can we change the ways we make value judgments? How can we approach differences and the relationships among them experientially, as the complex, context-dependent phenomena that they are? How can we modify traditional social constructions of power and the institutions on which they are built in ways that accommodate, as fully as possible, the human potential of all of us?

Notes

[1] Frans de Waal, *Good Natured. The Origins of Right and Wrong in Human*

and Other Animals (Cambridge: Harvard University Press, 1996).

[2] Jessica Benjamin, *The Bonds of Love. Psychoanalysis, Feminism, and the Problem of Domination* (New York: Pantheon, 1988), p. 135.

[3] Virginia Held, *Feminist Morality. Transforming Culture, Society, and Politics* (Chicago: University of Chicago Press, 1993), p. 212.

[4] On the subjectivity of the male gaze, see Luce Irigaray, *Speculum of the Other Woman*, trans. Gillian C. Gill (Ithaca: Cornell University Press, 1985); and Nadya Aisenberg, *Ordinary Heroines. Transforming the Male Myth* (New York: Continuum, 1995). For reflections on social and cultural obstacles to self-esteem, see Gloria Steinem, *The Revolution Within*

[5] Jessica Benjamin, *Like Subjects, Love Objects. Essays on Recognition and Sexual Difference* (New Haven: Yale University Press, 1995).

[6] Margaret Mead, *Blackberry Winter*; Sigmund Freud, *Civilization and Its Discontents*; and Camille Paglia, *Sexual Personae*.

[7] See Helene Cixous's and Catherine Clement's "Sorties: Out and Out: Attacks/Ways Out/Forays," in *The Newly Born Woman*, trans. Betsy Wing (Minneapolis: University of Minnesota Press, 1986), pp.63-132. They trace the appropriation of appropriateness to Greek thought.

Select Bibliography

Adkins, A.W.H. *From the Many to the One: A Study of Personality and Views of Human Nature in the Context of Ancient Greek Society, Values, and Beliefs.* Ithaca: Cornell University Press, 1970.

Addelson, Kathryn Pyne. *Moral Passages: Toward a Collectivist Moral Theory.* New York: Routledge, 1994.

Aisenberg, Nadya. *Ordinary Heroines: Transforming the Male Myth.* New York: Continuum, 1994.

Annas, Julia. *The Morality of Happiness.* New York: Oxford University Press, 1993.
——————. *Hellenistic Philosophy of Mind.* Berkeley: University of California Press, 1992.

Arendt, Hannah. *The Human Condition: A Study of the Central Dilemmas Facing Modern Man.* Chicago: University of Chicago Press, 1958.
——————. *Between Past and Future.* Cleveland: Meridien, 1961.

Bartky, Sandra Lee. *Femininity and Domination: Studies in the Phenomenology of Oppression.* New York: Routledge, 1990.

Becker, Ernest. *The Denial of Death.* New York: Free Press, 1973.

Belenky, Mary Field, et al., eds. *Women's Ways of Knowing: The Development of Self, Voice, and Mind.* New York: Basic Books, 1986.

Bellah, Robert, et al., eds. *Habits of the Heart: Individualism and Commitment in American Life.* Berkeley: University of California Press, 1985.

Benhabib, Seyla, and Drucilla Cornell, eds. *Feminism as Critique: Essays in the Politics of Gender in Late Capitalist Society.* Minneapolis:

University of Minnesota Press, 1987.

Benjamin, Jessica. *The Bonds of Love: Psychoanalysis, Feminism, and the Problem of Domination.* New York: Pantheon, 1988.
———. *Like Subjects, Love Objects: Essays on Recognition and Sexual Difference.* New Haven: Yale Univeristy Press, 1995.

Bennett, William J.,ed. *The Book of Virtues: A Treasury of Great Moral Stories.* New York: Simon and Schuster, 1993.

Benveniste, Emile. *Indo-European Society and Language.* Translated by E. Palmer. London: Routledge and Kegan Paul, 1973.

Bernard, John D., ed. *Vergil at 2000: Commemorative Essays on the Poet and His Influence.* New York: AMS Press, 1986.

Bloom, Allan. *The Closing of the American Mind.* New York: Simon and Schuster, 1987.

Bloom, Harold. *The Western Canon: The Books and School of the Ages.* New York: Harcourt Brace and Co., 1994.
———. *Homer's Iliad* and *Homer's Odyssey.* New York: Chelsea House, 1996.

Blundell, Sue. *The Origins of Civilization in Greek and Roman Thought.* London: Croom Helm, 1986.
———. *Women in Ancient Greece.* Cambridge: Harvard University Press, 1995.

Bordo, Susan. *The Flight to Objectivity: Essays on Cartesianism and Culture.* Albany: State University of New York Press, 1986.

Burkert, Walter. *Ancient Mystery Cults.* Cambridge: Cambridge University Press, 1987.

Brown, Lyn Mikel et al, eds. *Meeting at the Crossroads: Women's Psychology and Girls' Development.* Cambridge: Harvard University Press, 1992.

Cairns, Douglas. *Aidos: The Psychology and Ethics of Honour and*

Shame in Ancient Greek Literature. Oxford: Oxford University Press, 1993.

Cairns, Francis. *Virgil's Augustan Epic.* Cambridge: Cambridge University Press, 1989.

Caldwell, Richard. *The Origins of the Gods: A Psychoanalytic Study of Greek Theogonic Myth* New York: Oxford University Press, 1989.

Cameron, Averil, and Amelie Kuhrt, eds. *Images of Women in Antiquity.* Detroit: Wayne State University Press, 1993 (1983).

Cantarella, Eve. *Pandora's Daughters: The Role and Status of Women in Greek and Roman Antiquity.* Baltimore: Johns Hopkins University Press, 1981.

Card, Claudia, ed. *Feminist Ethics.* Lawrence: University Press of Kansas, 1991.

Casey, John. *Pagan Virtue: An Essay in Ethics.* Oxford: Oxford University Press, 1990.

Chase, Sue-Ellen. *Feminism and Theatre.* New York: Methuen, 1988.

Chodorow, Nancy. *The Reproduction of Mothering: Psychoanalysis and the Sociology of Gender.* Berkeley and Los Angeles: University of California Press, 1978.

———. *Femininities, Masculinities, Sexualities: Freud and Beyond.* Lexington: University of Kentucky Press, 1994.

Cixous, Helene, and Catherine Clement. *The Newly Born Woman.* Translated by Betsy Wang. Theory and History of Literature, vol. 24. Minneapolis: University of Minnesota Press, 1986.

Clay, Diskin. *Lucretius and Epicurus.* Baltimore: Johns Hopkins University Press, 1983.

Code, Lorraine. *What Can She Know? Feminist Theory and the Construction of Knowledge.* Ithaca: Cornell University Press, 1991.

Cohen, Beth, ed. *The Distaff Side: Reflections of the Female in Homer's Odyssey*. New York: Oxford University Press, 1995.

Cole, Eve Browning, and Susan Coultrap-McQuin, eds. *Explorations in Feminist Ethics: Theory and Practice*. Bloomington: Indiana University Press, 1992.

Cooey, Paula M., Sharon A. Farmer, and Mary Ellen Ross, eds. *Embodied Love: Sensuality and Relationship as Feminist Values*. San Francisco: Harper and Row, 1987.

Cornell, Drucilla. *Beyond Accommodation: Ethical Feminism, Deconstruction, and the Law*. New York: Routledge, 1991.

Crotty, Kevin. *Song and Action: The Victory Odes of Pindar.* Baltimore: Johns Hopkins University Press, 1982.

Daly, Mary. *Gyn/Ecology: The Metaethics of Radical Feminism.* Boston: Beacon Press, 1978.

de Beauvoir, Simone. *The Second Sex.* Translated by H.M. Parshley. New York: Vintage Press, 1974.

de Waal, Frans. *Good Natured: The Origins of Right and Wrong in Human and Other Animals*. Cambridge: Harvard University Press, 1996.

Denby, David. *Great Books: My Adventures with Homer, Rousseau, Woolf, and Other Indestructible Writers of the Western World.* New York: Simon and Schuster, 1996.

Diamond, Irene, and Lee Quinby, eds. *Feminism and Foucault*. Boston: University Press of New England, 1988.

Dinnerstein, Dorothy. *The Mermaid and the Minotaur: Sexual Arrangements and Human Malaise*. New York: Harper and Row, 1975.

du Bois, Page. *Centaurs and Amazons: Women and the Pre-History of the Great Chain of Being*. Ann Arbor: University of Michigan Press, 1982.

————————. *Sowing the Body: Psychoanalysis and Ancient Representations of Women.* Chicago: University of Chicago Press, 1988.

Earl, Donald. *The Moral and Political Tradition of Rome.* Ithaca: Cornell University Press, 1967.

Ehrenberg, Victor. *From Solon to Socrates: Greek History and Civilization during the Fifth and Sixth Centuries B.C.* London: Methuen, 1968.
————————. *The Greek State.* New York: W.W. Norton, 1964 (1960).

Elshtain, Jean Bethke. *Women and War.* New York: Basic Books, 1987.
————————. *Public Man, Private Woman: Women in Social and Political Thought.* Princeton: Princeton University Press, 1981.
————————, ed. *The Family in Political Thought.* Amherst: University of Massachusetts Press, 1982.

Euben, J. Peter, ed. *Greek Tragedy and Political Thought.* Berkeley: University of California Press, 1986.

Fantham, Elaine, et al., eds. *Women in the Classical World: Image and Text.* Oxford: Oxford University Press, 1994.

Felson-Rubin, Nancy. *Regarding Penelope.* Princeton: Princeton University Press, 1994.

Flax, Jane. *Thinking Fragments: Psychoanalysis, Feminism, and Postmodernism in the Contemporary West.* Berkeley and Los Angeles: University of California Press, 1990.

Foley, Helene P., ed. *Reflections of Women in Antiquity.* New York: Gordon and Breach Science Publications, 1981.

Foucault, Michel. *History of Sexuality*, Vols.1 and 2. Translated by Robert Hurley. New York: Pantheon, 1980.

Friedman, Marilyn. *What Are Friends For?* Ithaca: Cornell University

Press, 1993.

Gardner, Jane. *Women in Roman Law and Society.* Bloomington: Indiana University Press, 1986.

Garry, Ann, and Marilyn Pearsall, eds. *Women, Knowledge, and Reality: Explorations in Feminist Philosophy.* Boston: Unwin Hyman, 1989.

Gatens, Moira. *Feminism and Philosophy: Perspectives on Difference and Equality.* Bloomington: Indiana University Press, 1991.

Gilligan, Carol, *In a Different Voice: Psychological Theory and Women's Development* Cambridge: Harvard University Press, 1982.
———, et al., eds. *Mapping the Moral Domain: A Contribution of Women's Thinking to Psychological Theory and Education.* Cambridge: Harvard University Press, 1988.

Glenn, Evelyn Nakano, Grace Chang, and Linda Rennie Forcey, eds. *Mothering: Ideology, Experience, and Agency.* New York: Routledge, 1994.

Goldberg, Sander. *Understanding Terence.* Princeton: Princeton University Press, 1986.

Goldhill, Simon. *Language, Sexuality, Narrative: The Oresteia.* Cambridge: Cambridge University Press, 1984.
———. *Reading Greek Tragedy.* Cambridge: Cambridge University Press, 1986.
———. *The Poet's Voice: Essays in Poetics and Greek Literature.* Cambridge: Cambridge University Press, 1991.

Gould, Carol C., ed. *Beyond Domination: New Perspectives On Women and Philosophy.* Totowa, NJ: Rowman and Allanheld, 1983.

Griffin, Jasper. *Homer on Life and Death.* Oxford: Clarendon Press, 1983.
———. *Virgil.* Oxford: Oxford University Press, 1986.

Griffin, Miriam. *Seneca: A Philosopher in Politics.* Oxford: Clarendon Press, 1976.

———, and Jonathan Barnes, eds. *Philosophia Togata.* Oxford: Clarendon Press, 1989.
———, and E.M. Atkins, eds. and trans. *Cicero, De Officiis.* Cambridge: Cambridge University Press, 1991.

Griffin, Susan. *Women and Nature: The Roaring Inside Her.* New York: Harper and Row, 1978.

Griffiths, Morwenna, and Margaret Whitford, eds. *Feminist Perspectives in Philosophy.* Bloomington: Indiana University Press, 1988.

Grimshaw, Jean. *Philosophy and Feminist Thinking.* Minneapolis: University of Minnesota Press, 1986.

Grosz, Elizabeth. *Volatile Bodies: Toward a Corporeal Feminism.* Bloomington: Indiana University Press, 1994.

Hallett, Judith, and Thomas Van Nortwick. *Compromising Traditions: The Personal Voice in Classical Scholarship.* New York: Routledge, 1997.

Hanen, Marsh, and Kai Nielsen, eds. *Science, Morality, and Feminist Theory.* Calgary: University of Calgary Press, 1987.

Hardie, Phillip. *Virgil's Aeneid: Cosmos and Imperium.* Oxford: Oxford University Press, 1989.

Harding, Sandra, and Merrill B. Hintikka, eds. *Discovering Reality: Feminist Perspectives on Epistemology, Metaphysics, Methodology, and Philosophy of Science.* Dordrecht: Reidel, 1983.

Harris, Adrienne, and Ynestra King, eds. *Rocking the Ship of State: Toward a Feminist Peace Politics.* Boulder: Westview Press, 1989.

Harrison, Jane Ellen, *Themis: A Study of the Social Origins of Greek Religion.* Cleveland: Meridian Books, 1912.

Hartsock, Nancy. *Money, Sex, and Power: Toward a Feminist Historical Materialism.* Boston: Northeastern University Press, 1983.

Harvey, Elizabeth D., and Kathleen Okruhlik, eds. *Women and Reason*. Ann Arbor: University of Michigan Press, 1992.

Havelock, Eric. *The Muse Learns to Write: Reflections on Orality and Literacy from Antiquity to the Present*. New Haven: Yale University Press, 1986.

—————————. *The Literate Revolution and Its Cultural Consequences*. Princeton: Princeton University Press, 1982.

Held, Virginia. *Feminist Morality: Transforming Culture, Society, and Politics*. Chicago: University of Chicago Press, 1993.

Hunter, R.L. *The New Comedy of Greece and Rome*. Cambridge: Cambridge University Press, 1985.

Hypatia Reborn: Essays in Feminist Philosophy. Edited by Azizah Y. al-Hibri and Margaret A. Simons. Bloomington: Indiana University Press, 1990.

Jackson, W.T.H. *The Hero and the King*. New York: Columbia University Press, 1982.

Jagger, Alison. *Feminist Politics and Human Nature*. Sussex, Eng.: Rowman and Allanheld, The Harvester Press, 1983.

—————————. *Feminism and Moral Theory* (forthcoming).

—————————, and Susan Bordo, eds. *Gender/Body/Knowledge: Feminist Reconstructions of Being and Knowing*. New Brunswick: Rutgers University Press, 1989.

Jardine, Alice. *Gynesis: Configurations of Women and Modernity*. Ithaca: Cornell University Press, 1988.

Johnson, Paul. *Modern Times: The World from the Twenties to the Nineties*. New York: Harper Collin, 1991 (1983).

Jordan, Judith V., Alexandra G. Kaplan, et., eds. *Women's Growth in Connection*. Studies from the Stone Center. New York and London: The Guilford Press, 1991.

Kaschak, Ellyn. *Engendered Lives: A New Psychology of Women's Experience*. New York: Basic Books, 1993.

Kerferd, G. *The Sophistic Movement*. Cambridge: Cambridge University Press, 1981.

Keuls, Eva. *The Reign of the Phallus: Sexual Politics in Ancient Athens*. New York: Harper and Row, 1985.

Kittay, Eve Feder, and Diana T. Meyers, eds. *Women and Moral Theory*. Totowa, NJ: Rowman and Littlefield, 1987.

Knox, B.M.W. *The Heroic Temper: Studies in Sophoclean Tragedy*. Berkeley and Los Angeles: University of California Press, 1964.
——————. *Oedipus at Thebes*. New Haven: Yale University Press, 1957.
——————. *The Oldest Dead White European Males and Other Reflections on the Classics*. New York: W.W. Norton, 1993.
——————. *Backing into the Future: The Classical Tradition and Its Renewal*. New York: W.W. Norton, 1994.

Konstan, David. *Roman Comedy*. Ithaca: Cornell University Press, 1983.

Kruschwitz, Robert B., and Robert C. Roberts, eds. *The Virtues: Contemporary Essays on Moral Character*. Belmont, CA: Wadsworth, 1987.

Kurke, Leslie. *The Traffic in Praise: Pindar and the Poetics of Social Economy*. Ithaca, NY: Cornell University Press, 1991.

Lears, T.J. Jackson. *No Place of Grace: Antimodernism and the Transformation of American Culture, 1880-1920*. New York: Pantheon, 1981.

Lefkowitz, Mary, *The Victory Ode: An Introduction*. Park Ridge, NJ: Noyes Press, 1976.

Lerner, Gerda. *Women and History*. Vol. 1, *The Creation of Patriarchy*. Oxford: Oxford University Press, 1986.

Levine, Lawrence W. *The Opening of the American Mind.* Boston: Beacon Press, 1996.

Lloyd, Genevieve. *The Man of Reason: "Male" and "Female" in Western Philosophy.* Minneapolis: University of Minnesota Press, 1984.

Lloyd, G.E.R. *Polarity and Analogy: Two Types of Argumentation in Early Greek Thought.* Cambridge: Cambridge University Press, 1966.

Lloyd-Jones, Hugh. *The Justice of Zeus.* Sather Classical Lectures, Vol. 41. Berkeley and Los Angeles: University of California Press, 1983 (1971).

Loraux, Nicole. *The Invention of Athens: The Funeral Oration in the Classical City.* Translated by A. Sheridan. Cambridge: Harvard University Press, 1986.
—————. *The Children of Athens: Athenian Ideas about Citizenship and the Division of the Sexes.* Translated by Caroline Levine. Princeton: Princeton University Press, 1993. (French ed., 1981).
—————. *Tragic Ways of Killing a Woman.* Translated by Anthony Forster. Cambridge: Harvard University Press, 1987.

McAusland, Ian, and Peter Walcot, eds. *Virgil: Greek and Roman Studies.* Oxford: Oxford University Press, 1990.

MacIntyre, Alasdair. *After Virtue.* South Bend, IN: Notre Dame University Press, 1981.
—————. *Whose Justice? Which Rationality?.* South Bend, IN: Notre Dame University Press, 1988.

Marks, Elaine, and Isabelle de Courtivron, eds. *New French Feminisms: An Anthology.* (New York: Schocken Books, 1981.

Merchant, Carolyn. *The Death of Nature: Women, Ecology, and the Scientific Revolution.* New York: Harper and Row, 1982.
—————. *Ecological Revolutions: Nature, Gender, and Science in New England.*
(Chapel Hill: University of North Carolina Press, 1989.

———. *Radical Ecology: The Search for a Liveable World.* New York and London: Routledge, 1992.

Miles, Margaret. *Carnal Knowing: Female Nakedness and Religious Meaning in the Christian West.* Boston: Beacon Press, 1989.
———. *Desire and Delight: A New Reading of Augustine's Confessions.* New York: Crossroad Publishing Co., 1992.

Miner, Valerie, and Helen Longino, eds., *Competition: A Feminist Taboo?*. New York: The Feminist Press, 1987.

Mitchell, Juliet, and Jacqueline Rose, eds. *Lacan: Female Sexuality.* Translated by Jacqueline Rose. New York: W.W. Norton, 1982.

Moi, Toril, ed. *The Kristeva Reader.* Oxford: Blackwell, 1986.

Nagy, Gregory. *The Best of the Achaeans: Concepts of the Hero in Archaic Greek Poetry.* Baltimore: Johns Hopkins University Press, 1979.

Nicholson, Linda J., ed. *Feminism/Postmodernism.* New York: Routledge, 1990.

Noddings, Nel. *Caring: A Feminine Approach to Ethics and Moral Education.* Berkeley and Los Angeles: University of California Press, 1984.
———. *Women and Evil.* Berkeley: University of California Press, 1989.

Nuland, Sherwin. *How We Die.* New York: Knopf, 1994.

Nussbaum, Martha. *The Fragility of Goodness: Luck and Ethics in Greek Tragedy and Philosophy.* Cambridge and New York: Cambridge University Press, 1986.
———. *The Therapy of Desire: Theory and Practice in Hellenistic Ethics.* Princeton: Princeton University Press, 1994.

Nye, Andrea. *Feminist Theory and the Philosophies of Man.* New York: Routledge, 1988.
———, *Words of Power: A Feminist Reading of the History of*

Logic. New York: Routledge, 1990.

O'Brien, Mary. *The Politics of Reproduction.* Boston: Routledge and Kegan Paul, 1981.

Okin, Susan Moller. *Women in Western Political Thought.* Princeton: Princeton University Press, 1979.
——————————— ed. *Justice, Gender, and the Family.* New York: Basic Books, 1989.

Padel, Ruth. *Whom Gods Destroy: Elements of Greek and Tragic Madness.* Princeton: Princeton University Press, 1995.

Pantel, Pauline, ed. *A History of Women in the West.* Vol.1, *From Ancient Goddess to Christian Saints.* Translated by Arthur Goldhammer. Cambridge: Harvard University Press, 1992.

Parker, Robert. *Miasma: Pollution and Purification in Early Greek Religion.* Oxford: Clarendon Press, 1983.

Pateman, Carole. *The Sexual Contract.* Stanford: Stanford University Press, 1988.
———-, and Elizabeth Gross, eds. *Feminist Challenges: Social and Political Theory.* Sydney: Allyn and Unwin, 1986.

Pearsall, Marilyn, ed. *Women and Values.* Belmont, CA: Wadsworth, 1993 (1986).

Peradotto, John, and J.P. Sullivan, eds. *Women in the Ancient World. The Arethusa Papers* Albany: State University of New York Press, 1984.

Pindar's Victory Songs. Translated by Frank J. Nisetich, with a Forward by Hugh Lloyd-Jones. Baltimore: Johns Hopkins University Press, 1980.

Pomeroy, Sarah. *Goddesses, Whores, Wives, and Slaves: Women in Classical Antiquity.* New York: Schocken Books, 1975.

Poole, Ross. *Morality and Modernity.* London and New York:

Routledge, 1991.

Rabinowitz, Nancy Sorkin, and Amy Richlin, eds. *Feminist Theory and the Classics*. New York: Routledge, 1993.

Rahe, Paul A. *Republics Ancient and Modern*. Vol.1, *The Ancien Regime in Cla*ssical Greece.
Vol.2, *New Modes and Orders in Early Modern Political Thought*.
Vol.3, *Inventions of Prudence: Constructing the American Regime*.
Chapel Hill and London: University of North Carolina Press, 1994.

Rawson, Elizabeth. *Cicero: A Portrait*. London: Lane, 1975.

Raymond, Janice G. *A Passion for Friends: Toward a Philosophy of Female Affection*. Boston: Beacon Press, 1986.

Redfield, James, *Nature and Culture in the Iliad: The Tragedy of Hector*. Durham: Duke University Press, 1994 (Chicago: University of Chicago Press, 1975).

Reinhold, Meyer. *Classica Americana*. Detroit: Wayne State University Press, 1984.

Rosaldo, Michelle, and Louise Lamphere, eds. *Women, Culture, and Society*. Stanford: Stanford University Press, 1974.

Ruddick, Sara. *Maternal Thinking: Toward a Politics of Peace*. Boston: Beacon Press, 1989.

Saxonhouse, Arlene. *Fear of Diversity: The Birth of Political Science in Ancient Greek Thought* Chicago: University of Chicago Press, 1992.
————. *Women in the History of Political Thought: Ancient Greeks to Machiavelli*. New York: Praeger, 1985.

Scarry, Elaine, *The Body in Pain: The Making and Unmaking of the World*. New York: Oxford University Press, 1985.

Schein, Seth. *The Mortal Hero: An Introduction to Homer's Iliad*. Berkeley and Los Angeles: University of California Press, 1984.
————. *Reading the Odyssey*. Princeton: Princeton University

Press, 1996.

Schott, Robin May. *Cognition and Eros: A Critique of the Kantian Paradigm*. Boston: Beacon Press, 1988.

Seaford, Richard. *Reciprocity and Ritual: Homer and Tragedy in the Developing City-State*. Oxford University Press, 1994.

Segal, Charles. *Tragedy and Civilization: An Interpretation of Sophocles*. Cambridge: Harvard University Press, 1981.
——————. *Dionysiac Poetics and Euripides' Bacchae*. Princeton: Princeton University Press, 1982.

Segal, Eric. *Roman Laughter. The Comedies of Plautus*. New York: Oxford University Press, 2d ed.,1987.
——, ed. *Oxford Readings in Greek Tragedy*. Oxford: Oxford University Press, 1983.

Shay, Jonathan. *Achilles in Vietnam: Combat Trauma and the Undoing of Character*. Atheneum: Maxwell Macmillan, 1994.
Skinner, Marilyn. *Rescuing Creusa: New Methodological Approaches to Women in Antiquity*.
Helios ns 13.2. Lubbock: Texas Tech University, 1987.

Slater, Philip. *The Glory of Hera*. Boston: Beacon Press, 1968.

Snyder, Jane. *The Woman and the Lyre: Woman Writers in Classical Greece and Rome*. Carbondale: Southern Illinois Press, 1989.

Sourvinou-Inwood, Christiane. *"Reading" Greek Death to the End of the Classical Period*. Oxford: Clarendon Press, 1995.

Spariosu, Mihae. *Dionysus Reborn*. Ithaca: Cornell University Press, 1989.

Spelman, Elizabeth. *Inessential Woman: Problems of Exclusion in Feminist Thought*. Boston: Beacon Press, 1988.

Thompson, Dorothy, ed. *Women against the Bomb*. London: Virago, 1983.

Threadgold, Terry, and Anne Cranny-Francis, eds. *Feminine, Masculine, and Representation*. Sydney: Allyn and Unwin, 1990.

Tong, Rosemarie. *Feminine and Feminist Ethics*. Belmont, CA: Wadsworth, 1993.

Treblicot, Joyce, ed. *Mothering: Essays in Feminist Theory.* Totowa, NJ: Rowman and Allanheld, 1983.

Young-Bruehl, Elisabeth. *The Anatomy of Prejudices.* Cambridge: Harvard University Press, 1996.

Vermeule, Emily. *Aspects of Death in Early Greek Art and Poetry*. Berkeley: University of Calfiornia Press, 1979.

Vernant, Jean-Pierre. *Myth and Thought among the Greeks.* Boston: Routledge, 1983.
——————————— and Pierre Vidal-Naquet. *Myth and Tragedy in Ancient Greece.* Translated by Janet Lloyd. Atlantic Highlands, NJ: Humanities Press, 1981.

Versenyi, Laszo. *Man's Measure: A Study of the Greek Image of Man from Homer to Sophocles.* Albany: State University of New York Press, 1974.
Vickers, Brian. *Tragedy Drama, Myth, Society.* Comparative Tragedy. Vol. 1, *Towards Greek Tragedy*. London: Longman, 1973).

Wartenburg, Thomas E., ed. *Rethinking Power.* Albany: State University of New York Press, 1992.

Weil, Simone. "The Iliad: The Poem of Force." In Siaan Miles, ed. *Simone Weil. An Anthology.* New York: Weidenfeld and Nicolson, 1986.
Wilhelm, Robert M., and Howard Jones, eds. *The Two Worlds of the Poet: New Perspectives in Virgil.* Detroit: Wayne State University Press, 1992.

Williams, Bernard. *Shame and Necessity.* Berkeley: University of California Press, 1993.

Wiltshire, Susan Ford. *Greece, Rome, and the Bill of Rights.* Oklahoma Series in Classical Culture. Norman and London: University of Oklahoma Press, 1992.
———————————. *Public and Private in Vergil's Aeneid.* Amherst: University of Massachusetts Press, 1989.

Winkler, John. *The Constraints of Desire: Sex and Gender in Ancient Greece.* New York: Routledge, 1990.
——————— and Froma Zeitlin, eds. *Nothing to Do with Dionysus?.* Princeton: Princeton University Press, 1990.

Winnington-Ingram, R.P. *Sophocles: An Interpretation.* Cambridge: Cambridge University Press, 1980.

Wise, Stanley and Sue. *Breaking Out Again: Feminist Ontology and Epistemology.* New York: Routledge, 1993.

Wright, John, ed. *Essays on the Iliad: Selected Modern Criticism.* Bloomington: Indiana University Press, 1978.

Young, Iris Marion. *Throwing Like a Girl and Other Essays in Feminist Philosophy and Social Theory.* Bloomington: Indiana University Press, 1990.

Zeitlin, Froma, ed. *Mortals and Immortals.* Collected Essays in honor of Jean-Pierre Vernant. Princeton: Princeton University Press, 1991.

Index

Achievement, ethic of: *arete*, competition, transcendence over death, 47ff., 65-6; replaces heroic ethic, 47ff.; Pindar, 52-9; Athens 59, 60-1; Roman Republic (Cicero), 163-71; community of, v. community of nature, 75-7, 89, 92-3, 94, 103, 112-3, 120-1, 122-4, 125,, 214-7; classical legacy and U.S., 6, 48, 64-9, 207-11, 239-43; exclusion of women from, 6-7, 47-8, 51-2, 63-4, 64-8, 75-9, 94, 103, 120-1, 125, 133-4, 181-2, 197-8, 199-200, 202-11, 212-8

Active/passive: 47-9; *ponos*: 26-8 (Heracles), 37-8 (Philoctetes); 175,181-2 (Aeneas); *ataraxia*, 116ff.; alleged passivity of women, 34, 239; passivity of men in male culture, 38-9, 175, 181-2, 239. See also Separation/connection.

Addelson, Kathryn Pyne, 214

Analogy and polarity, 14

Appropriateness: to mortals, 15-6; *hora, metron* (Hesiod), 104-5; New Comedy 143-51; *decorum* (Cicero) 169; as appropriation, 179-80 (Pindar), 149-50 (Terence); reconsidered 313. See also *Chre.*

Arendt, Hannah, 195, 211-2

Arete (conflation of excellence, capability, and moral virtue): 45-50, 77-8, 79, 79, 89, 205, and *passim*; Homer, 50; Pindar, 52, 55, 103-4; post-Homeric, 59, 60-1; Pericles-Thucydides, 60-4; Aristotle, 140-3; female, 59, 63-4. See also V*irtus*.

Aristotle, *Nicomachean Ethics*, 140-3

Arthur, Marilyn, 80, 86

Augustine of Hippo, 182-3

Authochthony, 81-2

Autonomy: Antigone, 32 female (Hesiod), 108; Aeneas, 181-2; and separation v. connection, 79, 198-201, 212, 216-7. See also Separation v. connection.

Balance and antithesis (Cicero), 162

Benjamin, Jessica, 199

Bordo, Susan, 195

Capitalism, late-twentieth-century, 201-2, 297-8

Care v. justice ethic, 218-9

Chaos: and *chaos*, 80; fear of (associated with female), 94
Chodorow, Nancy, 199
Chre, it is necessary, proper, fitting (Homer), 134-40
Cicero, *De Re Publica*, 164-7; *De Legibus*, 167; *De Officiis*, 167-70
Civilitas, 163
Civility, 143-4, 153-5
Civitas: ideal Roman State, 163-71 (Cicero); 123-4 (Seneca); associated with cosmic order (Vergil), 171, 174, 181-2; 182-3 (Augustine)
Cixous, Helene, and Catherine Clement, 205
Competition: hallmark of Greek culture 49-52, 59-63; warrior-hero in single combat, 16-22; Hesiod, 50-1, Heraclitus, 51-2; panhellenic contests, 52-3, 58-9; v, cooperation, 6,   66-7, 170, 208-10; as cultural value in U.S., 6, 48-9, 196-7, 207-10, 239-40; feminist analyses of, 204-7, 207-10. See also *Arete*, Achievement, ethic of.
Community: in Greco-Roman political thought, 140-3 (Aristotle), 163-71 (Cicero); in U.S., 1-2, 237-8; redefining, 193-4, 205-6, 214-5. See also Achievement, ethic of, Nature/culture.
Countercultural attitudes: Phaeacians, 110-4; in Greek and Latin poetry, 112-4; Sappho, 114-5; Lucretius, 115-22; Horace, 122-4

Daly, Mary, 202-3
De Beauvoir, Simone, 206-7
Demeter-Persephone, 107, 109-10
Democracy: U.S., 1-3, 6, 9-10, 193-5; "family values" in, 7, 153-5; virtues in the *polis* (Aristotle), 140-3; virtues of ideal Roman republic, 164-7; male virtues in Roman republic, 168-9
Difference: gender, 3-4, 8-9, 33, 80-7, 193-4, 197ff.; mortals and immortals, 16ff.; as differentiation in cosmos (Hesiod), 80-7; and diversity (U.S.), 193-5. See also Otherness, Gender.
Dike (justice): associated with Zeus and male authority, 82-3, 85-7; and *themis*, 82-3. See also Reciprocity.
Dionysus, and tragic drama, 23-4; dissolver of boundaries (Otherness), 106-8. 110
Dissolution of opposites: See Dionysus, Horace.
Dualisms: and gender difference, 3-4; binary thinking, 14. See Nature/culture, Mind/body, Reason/passion, Public/private.
Du Bois, Page, 78-9

Education: and competition, 6; purpose of, 9; and the classics, 7-8, 161-2

Embodiment: and vulnerability, 15-6, 16-22, 75-9, 86-9, 91-2, 106-10, 125, 203-4, 206-7; associated with earth, body, and woman, 86-90, 215-7. 220-1; associated with pleasure and pain, corruption of reason, 86-90, 110-4, 123-5, 167, 205; acceptance of, 115-22 (Lucretius)

Epicureanism, 115-6, 120-1

Epistemology: and mortal deficiency, 15-6, 24-5, 28-30, 32-3, 38-9, 79-80 (Muses), 175; knowledge and power, 33; 90-4 (Stoic view); 115-6, 118-20, 120-1 (Epicurean view); feminist analyses of, 195-6. See also *Logos, Ratio*, Reason/passion duality.

Eros: male, female, dangers of, 87-9, 107, 144-5, 174, 175-6; cooptation of, Plato, *Symposium* 78, Pindar 88, Vergil 88-9; and *philia*, 45; in ideal American society (Addelson), 214

Essentialism (feminist theory), 196-7

Ethics: 1-10,, 24-5, 37-9, 47-9, 60-1, 64-8, 90-4, 103, 119-22, 133-4, 143-5, 151-3, 153-5, 162-3, 163-71, 171-2, 181, 193-4, 202, 214, 219-20, 220-1, 237-43. See also Heroic ethic, Achievement ethic, Care v. justice ethic.

Euripides, *Bacchae*, 108-9

Eurocentrism, v. multiculturalism, 7-8

Experience as basis for ethics: 140-1, 196-7, 219-20

Family: values, 137-9 (*Odyssey*), 141-2 (Aristotle), 144-5, 145-6 (Menander), 146-8 (Plautus), 148-51 (Terence), 169 (Cicero), in U.S., 7, 153-5, 214, 216-7; subordinate to the *polis*, 110; in tragic drama, 23-5, 25-34; microcosm of and subordinate to society, 26, 110, 134, 169, 210-1, 218; and psychoanalysis, 197-201; locus of care ethic, 204, 218-9. See also Relationships, Private/public duality.

Flax, Jane, 196, 198

Foucault, Michel, 87, 196

Freud, Sigmund, 79, 88, 198, 200, 295, 241

Gatens, Moira, 194

Gender: fundamental to Greco-Roman concept of difference, 3-4, 8, 75-7, 77-9, 83-4, 125, 133-4, 193-5; New Comedy as reflection of gender roles in Greek society, 143-5; male-good/female-evil duality, 172-7 (Vergil); ideal male life pattern, 181-2 (Aeneas); and male values, 197-8, 238-9; psychology of gender roles, 198-201; gender roles and social conditioning, 206-7, 213-4, 216-7; and feminist morality, 216-20, 220-1, 238, 242-3

Gilligan, Carol, 181-2, 217-8

Gimbutas, Marija, 76-7
Goldhill, Simon, 135
Gould, Carol, 220

Harrison, Jane Ellen, 82-3
Hartsock, Nancy, 196, 205, 211-2
Held, Virginia, 196, 219-20
Hesiod, 94, 104-5; *Works and Days*, 50-2, 83-6, 104-5; *Theogony* 79-84
Homer, *Iliad*, 16-22, 176-9; *Odyssey*, 105-6, 110-1, 137-9
Horace, 122-4
Human condition: defined in the classical legacy as mortality and powerlessness, 51-2, 68-9, 79-80; redefining, 203, 197, 240
Humanitas: Terence, 149-50, 154-5

Individuality: and liberal thought, 2, 9-10, 194, 212-4
Jardine, Alice, 3
Justice: See *Dike*, Reciprocity.
Kaplan, Louise, 200-1
King, Ynestra, 216-7
Knowledge, power, and technology: 29-30. 32-3, 196, 208-11, 215-6, 239. See also Epistemology.
Knox, Bernard, 8, 26

Lacan, Jacques, 198-9
Logos: as order, male defined, and speech and reason, male prerogative, 79, 81, 86-7, 89, 92, 94, 196-9. See also *Ratio*.
Lucretius, 115-22

MacIntyre, Alasdair, 58-9, 194
Merchant, Carolyn, 215
Miles, Margaret, 138
Mind/body duality: 3, 48, 76-9, 86-7, 91-3, 107-8, 112, 118-20, 182-3, 182-3, 202-3, 206-7. 215-7
Moral authority: linked to superior power of gods and fate, 14-6, 23-4, 33, 34, 82-3, 85-7, 135, 171-2, 307; of poet, 32-3; linked to power and achievement, 47-9, 65, 67-9, 164-71, 181-2; conflicts among men, 35-7; and nature, 104-5, 120-1; and derived from reason and philosophy, 90-4, 140-3, 164-71; and social norms, 134-5, 135-9, 143-4; and women, alleged lack of, 195; feminist analyses of, 195-8, 214, 216-7, 219-20; in U.S., 2, 9-10, 37-8, 164-5, 237-43

Mortality: *Iliad*, 16-22; tragic drama, 26-8, 30-3; death-centeredness of Greco-Roman legacy, 4-5, 13-6, 202-4; transcendence over death, 47-9, 53, 64, 65, 68-9, 77-8, 94, 147-8, 166-7, 210-2, 238-40. See also Human condition.

Narcissism: 8, 175, 257-9, 238-40; and values, 197; Narcissus, 198; and autonomy, 199-201
Nature/culture duality: in relation to gender, 77-9; in relation to mortality/transcendence, 13-4, 16-22 (Homer); Dionysus, 23-4; integration of 103ff.; communities of, 75-7; Epicurean views of, 115-22; feminist critiques of, 215-7
New Comedy: 143-5; Menander, *Dyskolos*, 145-6; Plautus, 146-8; Terence, 148-51
Noddings, Nel, 218
Nussbaum, Martha, 77-8, 90

Others and Otherness: informs Greco-Roman tradition, 3-4, 7-9, 195. 196. 197-8. 201-2. 202-4, 242-3; existence in nature, 75ff., 94, 122, 125; in the *polis*, 25-6, 103; and patriarchal values, 195

Pandora, 83-4 (Hesiod); embodiment of evil, 83-4, 203; syndrome, 195
Paradigms: male: Homeric warrior-heroes, 18-22; tragic hero, 25-6, Heracles, 26-8; Oedipus, 28-30; Creon, 30-3; panhellenic victor, 52-9; Athenian male citizen, 60-4; Aeneas, 181-2; female: Penelope, 59-60; Pandora, 83-4; Antigone, 32; Dido, 175-6; Lucretia, 152. New Comedy, 143-4, 150-1; in contemporary U.S., 8, 48-9, 195, 210ff., 216-7, 219-20, 238-40
Parker, Robert, 77
Parthenogenesis, 81-2
Patriarchal rule: State and society, 23-4, 26, 28-9, 35-8, 82-3, 85-7, 133-4, 140-3, 162-71, 171-82, 182-3; family, 23-4, 26, 28-9, 34, 143-51; male subversion of, 26, 27-9, 30, 35-7, 83-4, 140-3, 143-51, 151-3; female subversion of, 26-8 (*Women of Trachis*), 171-82 (*Aeneid*); feminist critiques of, 251-90; and values of Greco-Roman legacy in the U.S., 1-2, 7, 153-5, 237-43
Philia: See Reciprocity.
Pietas: male (Aeneas) 172-6; female (Dido), 175-6
Pindar, victory songs: 52-3; *Nem.*3, 53-9; *Nem.*8.40, 77-8, 88
Poole, Ross, 6
Postmodernism: U.S., 6, 134, 220-1,

Power: and difference: 3, 242-3, mortals and immortals, 8, 14-6, 22, 24, 26, 30-3, 38-9, 53, 80-7, 171ff., male and female, 3-4, 47-50, 62-5, 75-7, 83-4, 90-4, 94, 124-5, 171-6, 176-7; control of family, 143-51; power to v. power over, 49, 6-67, 211-2; and language (Athens), 24-5; political, 140-3, 151-3, 162-71, 181; 238-9; as control gained through philosophical understanding, 90-4, 115-20, esp. 119-20, 162-71, 182-3; feminist analyses of, 196-7, 204, 214-5, 220-1, 237-43

Powerlessness: defines "human" condition, 38-9, 68-9, 175, 197-8, 203-4; feminist views of, 196-7

Primacy, drive for: U.S., 6, 47-8, 201-2, 297-8; and competition, 49-52, 204; Hesiod, 50-1; Pindar, 52-9

Public/private duality: 3-4, 6-7, 23-4, 26,47-8, 94, 119-21, 122-4, 143-4, 151-3, 163, 170-1, 172-81 (*Aeneid*), 201-2, 210-5

Race of woman: 83-4, 86-7, 195

Ratio (reason): 121-5. See also Reason/passion duality.

Reason/passion, irrationality duality: 3-4, 24, 87-9, 91-3, 108-9, 112-4, 166, 168-9, 172-5, 180-1, 182-3, 202, 214-5

Reciprocity: due honor and respect (*time, honor*) among men, 35-7 (Ajax, Philoctetes), 47-8, 50-1, 68-9, 85-6, 140, 140-3 (Aristotle), 167-9 (Cicero), 177-80 (Vergil); *philia*, 135 Homer), 175-6 (Antigone), 183-6; between male individual and male community, 52-9 (panhellenic victor), 91 and 93 (Stoic wise man), 120-1 (Epicureans), 140-3 (Aristotle), 156-71 (Roman Republic); exclusion of women from, 63-4, 68-9, 205, 212, 219-20; contemporary feminist thought, 219-20

Recognition: through competition among men, 168 (see also T*ime*); psychology of, 199

Redfield, James, 17-8

Relationships: among warrior-heroes, 18, 35-7, 136-7; paternal, 23-4, 28, 80-3, 106, 137-8, 144-5, 148-9, 149-50, 151, 233-7; fraternal, 23-4, 30, 148-9, 224-5; among male citizens, 23-4, 140-3, 163, 164ff.; among members of the community of achievement, 47-53, 63-4, 64-5, 170, 175; rethinking, 197-201, 217-8

Relativism, moral: 24-5, 242-3

Ruddick, Sara, 203-4, 206-7

Ruth, Sheila, 203

Sappho, 114-5

Saxonhouse, Arlene, 26, 33-4, 61

Scarry, Elaine, 48, 203-4
Schein, Seth, 17
Seaford, Richard, 110
Self identity: 8-9, 198-201
Separation and connection: 86-7, 94, 103; 104-5 (Hesiod), 105-6 (Homer); and gender difference, 198-201; feminist critiques of, 214-8
Social norms: as patriarchal values, 133-4, 153-5; Homeric, 135-40; New Comedy, 143-51; nudity, 152 (Candaules); rape, 147-8, 150-1, 152-3 (Lucretia); decorum, 169 (Cicero)
Sophocles: *Women of Trachis*, 26-8; *Oedipus the King*, 28-30; *Antigone* 30-34; *Electra*, 34-5; *Ajax*, 35-6; *Philoctetes* 36-7
Stoicism: 92-6 (Seneca)
Time (honor): and *kleos* (fame), as heroic-warrior values, 16, 22, 35-7, 47-9; 52, 58-9 (panhellenic victor); in ideology of *polis*, 61-1, 64-5, 140-3 (Aristotle); Stoic view of, 92-3; Epicurean view of, 120-2. See also Reciprocity, Achievement, ethic of,
Tradition: 22-3, 24-5, 48. 183, 193-4, 199-200, 220-1, 237-43
Tragic drama: Dionysus, 23-4; patriarchy and the *polis*, 24-6

van Gennep, Arnold, 77
Vergil, *Aeneid*, 171-81
Virtus: Roman concept of, 89-90, 92, 165-6; Cicero, 168-9; Seneca, 92-3; Horace, 122-4. See also *Arete*.

War and violence: 5-6, 16-22, 47, 49-51, 60-4, 85-6, 88-9, 112-4, 144-5, 115-7, 122-3, 166, 172-3, 174, 177-81, 182; and male culture, 201, 202-5
Winkler, John, 49
Women: "all of a kind," 83-4, 86, 157, 195; identified: with nature, earth, and body, 75-9, 84, 109-10; identified with sexuality, generation, and death, 6 (Fates), 78, 83-7, 173, 174-5, 175-7, 206-7, 221-1, 212-4, 215-7; subversiveness of, 80-2, 83-7, 203-4; and evil, 86-7, 210-1; "nonequals," 140-2. See also Others and Otherness, Gender, Embodiment.
Work: and gender roles, 6-7, 64-8, 205-11, 212-3; Hesiod, 51-2, 85-6; attitudes to in U.S., 64-9, 205-11, 212-3. See also Achievement, ethic of.